MW00461861

PRAISE FOR *SPIES ON THE SIDELINES*

"The first systematic and detailed examination of espionage tactics, techniques, and procedures continuously used by NFL teams to gain the game-day competitive advantage against their opponents. Kevin Bryant provides the only comprehensive review of the extreme measures NFL teams' owners, coaches, players, and managers take to collect information, steal play signals, and to disrupt opposing NFL teams to "win at all costs." This original work gives us insights into what our favorite NFL teams will do to win on game day, with dirty tricks, cheating, bribery, deception, lies, coercion, and betrayal that would rival the most thrilling James Bond movie. This thorough and lucid book is indispensable for NFL fans."**—David P. Garey, former deputy director of counterintelligence and human intelligence for headquarters, U.S. Army, European Theatre of Operations**

"Kevin Bryant has drawn on his experience as a former special agent and his years of experience collecting and protecting information for the Department of Defense to research this fascinating look into the cutthroat world of NFL 'espionage.' Very detailed and vivid and one hell of a read."**—John Willis, retired intelligence officer**

"*Spies on the Sidelines* is a well-researched examination of the measures taken by professional sports organizations, in this case some teams in the NFL, to achieve success commercially and on the field. In doing so, Kevin Bryant has opened possibilities and interest of similar work relating to high-value sports, an underresearched area."**—M.Hanif Majothi, assistant professor of intelligence studies, University of North Georgia**

"In *Spies on the Sidelines*, Kevin Bryant takes a deep dive into the murky waters that pro football's millions of fans never see—the effort by teams to gain an advantage by any means. SpyGate and DeflateGate are just the most notorious examples of the sign stealing, clandestine information gathering, and other nefariousness that goes on behind closed doors. Bryant's guided tour is a total page-turner."**—John Eisenberg, author of *The League: How Five Rivals Created the NFL and Launched a Sports Empire***

"Kevin Bryant's *Spies on the Sidelines* is the single most revealing book about espionage in professional sports."**—Brian Hooper, former associate director for WMD Terrorism Threats, U.S. Department of State**

"A great book! I learned during my career that great teams that cheat aren't unbeatable, but they sure are more difficult to beat, especially in the postseason."**—Cam Cameron, former Dolphins head coach and Chargers and Ravens offensive coordinator**

"Sports story or true crime story? Kevin Bryant nails it. It's both. Professional football is actually just a big business. Profits rise on wins and fall on losses. As in any business, spying for competitive advantage is—in the end—about stealing money. With incidences compiled and documented in a fascinating read, the true scope of espionage materializes. Football is definitely not 'only a game.'"**—Kevin D. Murray, corporate counterespionage specialist and technical surveillance countermeasures consultant for NFL teams**

SPIES ON THE SIDELINES

The High-Stakes World of NFL Espionage

Kevin Bryant

ROWMAN & LITTLEFIELD
Lanham • Boulder • New York • London

Published by Rowman & Littlefield
An imprint of The Rowman & Littlefield Publishing Group, Inc.
4501 Forbes Boulevard, Suite 200, Lanham, Maryland 20706
www.rowman.com

86-90 Paul Street, London EC2A 4NE, United Kingdom

British Library Cataloguing in Publication Information Available

Library of Congress Cataloging-in-Publication Data

Name: Bryant, Kevin, 1975–, author.
Title: Spies on the sidelines : the high-stakes world of NFL espionage / Kevin Bryant.
Description: Lanham, Maryland : Rowman & Littlefield, [2022] | Includes bibliographical references and index. | Summary: "The first book to fully explore the arsenal of methods NFL teams use to spy on their opponents and the countermeasures used to deter them, Spies on the Sidelines includes incredible stories of covert surveillance, encryption, radio frequency jamming, stolen documents, and more"—Provided by publisher.
Identifiers: LCCN 2021052815 (print) | LCCN 2021052816 (ebook) | ISBN 9781538166376 (cloth) | ISBN 9781538166383 (epub)
Subjects: LCSH: National Football League—Corrupt practices. | Football—Corrupt practices—United States.
Classification: LCC GV955.5.N35 B78 2022 (print) | LCC GV955.5.N35 (ebook) | DDC 796.3326406—dc23/eng/20220104
LC record available at https://lccn.loc.gov/2021052815
LC ebook record available at https://lccn.loc.gov/2021052816

To my dad—for your help with this book
and for being a great father.

CONTENTS

ACKNOWLEDGMENTS

I am grateful to a great many people who helped make my dream of publishing this book a reality. I would not have crossed the finish line without their generous support. Literary agent Jacques de Spoelberch was kind enough to provide his valuable advice for an early draft of the manuscript that was not yet ready for prime time. His suggestions resulted in ditching three chapters, stripping out tens of pages of older anecdotes, reading 15 more books for research, adding about 50 pages of newer material, and including the "whatever it takes" theme. I may have used his name as a curse word for about a year because of how long all this took, but his advice was unquestionably spot on, and I likely would have never been published without it. Thanks, Jacques!

I also want to thank my agent, Steve Schwartz, and acquisitions editor, Christen Karniski, who were willing to take a chance on a debut author with no preexisting social media sites or followers. Additionally, I owe a big thanks to the wonderful team at Rowman & Littlefield. Christen and her assistant, Erinn Slanina, held my hand through the publishing process and patiently answered the endless stream of emails I sent, and Kellie Hagan and team did a fantastic job correcting all my mistakes while editing the book.

Additionally, I wish to thank everyone who took the time to read the book in various versions of draft form and offer their constructive criticism. I am also grateful to Jennifer Mayes, who let me bounce a ton of marketing ideas past her on a regular basis and took my photo for this book (yes, I know I need a better iPhone and that I'm cheap).

My parents, Mike and Linda Bryant, are wonderful enough to have always supported my dreams. I will never be able to thank them enough. My dad spent endless hours helping me with this book as a consultant, assistant writer, editor, project manager, and cheerleader (the pom-poms were weird). What an awesome father-son project this turned out to be!

Last, thanks to my wife and daughter, Amy and Addison, for your patience and love. Writing, and the research that comes along with it, takes a lot of time and energy. I appreciate your allowing me to pursue this incredibly time-consuming hobby. Additionally, I owe a special thanks to my wife (who likes to keep a tidy house and is a minimalist by nature) for allowing me to store a library's worth of research books in our bedroom closet. I probably broke my promise not to continue growing the library about 10 times, and I'm sure I'll break it at least 10 times more before the shelf eventually breaks under the weight of all those books.

PREFACE

Winning isn't everything. It's the only thing.[1]—Vince Lombardi

Like many National Football League (NFL) fans, I really enjoy watching the draft. Every year as the draft approaches, I think about taking time off from work and ignoring my family for four days to binge watch the festivities (although I never quite manage to make this a reality). Seeing college players enter the professional ranks and have a lifelong dream fulfilled is exciting to watch. Add to that the thrill of hoping the prospect you like will miraculously fall to your team, the trades, the speculation, the hype, and all the crazy, football-obsessed fans in attendance, and the draft is a lot of fun to watch. So, when I heard the NFL draft would be virtual in 2020, I was pretty bummed. Just like it had ruined everything else that year, COVID-19 had also messed up the draft. I wanted to assemble my friends and boo COVID-19 just like NFL fans do when league commissioner Roger Goodell makes his first appearance onstage to kick off the annual draft. "Boo! You suck, COVID-19! I'd throw vegetables at you, but I'm still too worried about food shortages."

To my pleasant surprise, the virtual draft was actually pretty cool. Fans had the opportunity to see the homes of coaches and be entertained by their goofy kids. Additionally, we learned the secret of the Patriots' drafting success when the cameras caught coach Bill Belichick's Alaskan Klee Kai dog, Nike, standing on the seat of a dining room chair analyzing the remaining prospects on two laptops. The draft was sweet and endearing and made the whole NFL feel a little warmer and fuzzier, less "look at me, look at me" and more family game night in your pajamas.

Because of this the NFL's first virtual draft was deemed a success, but this outcome was far from assured and presented new and unique challenges in the lead-up to the big event. For instance, once the change in draft format was announced, football pundits and draftniks alike began to analyze the various ways the draft might be impacted by being held virtually. One of the main concerns was the possibility of hackers gaining access to encrypted Zoom and Microsoft Teams draft-related meetings. After all, the NFL had mandated that all team coaches and executives attend the NFL draft from their homes, and while this might pose less of a problem for today's tech-savvy generation, whose five-year-olds understand the capabilities of the iPhone much better than I ever will, this created a lot of anxiety for a great number of NFL coaches and staffs. Team secrets were suddenly being protected by home Wi-Fi passwords like "Password123," "YouWontGuessThis," "NewPassword," "CleoCatra," and "GoGiants." The NFL handed out its list of best practices to encourage enhanced security measures, but would all the teams implement them, and would users be tech savvy and security conscious enough to follow them? Undoubtedly, there would be weak links, and this raised concerns. Could hackers potentially interrupt connectivity at critical points and disrupt a team's draft? And could a rival possibly listen in on a team's draft conversations and gain an advantage in this manner?

Ravens coach John Harbaugh openly shared his concerns with the media and noted that he barraged the Baltimore information technology (IT) staff with articles about security issues related to Zoom. When his IT staff tried to assure him that all would be well, he replied, "That's what Wells Fargo and all those other places said about our private information." Experts lent credence to Harbaugh's worries and confirmed it was theoretically possible for the NFL draft and team rooms to be hacked, not that expert opinions were truly needed. Zoom meetings all across the world were being hacked around this time, and this activity became so commonplace that the term "Zoombombing" was coined. Meanwhile, the league downplayed the risk of conducting the draft virtually, assuring everyone that the draft would be secure. For instance, Troy Vincent, the NFL executive vice president of football operations, replied to Harbaugh's concerns by saying, "Coach Harbaugh, no one is going to hack into your system, stop it."[2]

While Mr. Vincent was rather blunt, he was only saying what the vast majority of NFL fans already believed. Harbaugh was acting paranoid. The ensuing draft only seemed to confirm this viewpoint. No one spied, right?

Well, are you sure? How would you know? How would the NFL know? How would a team being spied upon know? There really is no way of being completely sure—not now, not ever. Many cases of espionage—whether international or sports related—are never discovered. Those that are found out are often learned of years or even decades after the fact.

What I am sure of is that Harbaugh's concerns, as far-fetched as they might seem, were completely founded. Because, as this book will demonstrate, spying in the NFL is not just a common occurrence; it is a daily occurrence.

While the phrase "three-letter agency" is a euphemism for American spook organizations such as the CIA (Central Intelligence Agency) and the NSA (National Security Agency), the NFL is a three-letter agency in its own right. Behind the game day action of the NFL is a world much like the cloak-and-dagger realm of American intelligence agencies. The NFL has its own history filled with espionage-related stories that sound like something right out of the Cold War: spies disguised as reporters, military officers, and priests and even a dwarf playing the role of a baby being pushed in a stroller; covert surveillance of targets' movements; hiding draft prospects by shuffling them in and out of hotels in aliases; tapped telephones, signals interception, decoy signals, encryption, code breaking, and radio frequency jamming; false flag operations; monitoring air traffic and airline passengers; spies scaling rooftops and telephone poles and clandestine photography undertaken from high-rise hotels with long-lensed cameras; peepholes, secret listening devices, surveillance photos relayed by zip line and whispered conversations masked by running water; stolen documents and trash cans sifted for secrets; subversion of individuals mired in debt; and a hilltop secured by Navy SEALs.

These stories and more are contained herein and highlight the extraordinary measures NFL teams are willing to undertake to gain an advantage over their adversaries. In fact, the phrase "whatever it takes" runs throughout this book and expresses the NFL's win-at-all-costs mentality perfectly. I encountered this saying repeatedly while conducting research for this book. It gained popularity in NFL circles from its use by Steelers coach Chuck Noll and Raiders coach-owner–general manager Al Davis, who both worked on Sid Gillman's Chargers staff from 1960 to 1962. Undoubtedly, one of these two football greats poached the expression from the other. While both coaches used the expression throughout their careers, their interpretations differed substantially. Noll perceived the expression to mean sacrifice at the individual and team level. Davis interpreted it more ruthlessly and literally, as in "The end justifies the means." Regardless of their interpretations of the expression, Davis and Noll both used the strength of their wills to inject the essence of these words into the souls of their players and respective organizations, contributing to seven Super Bowl wins between the pair.

While it may never be clear who coined the phrase "whatever it takes," it is clear that this mentality pervades the NFL and is in fact the mainspring behind the seemingly bizarre and often illicit use of intelligence operations and intelligence collection.

Although these types of activities may seem better suited to hostile nations than football teams, consider the other extremes players and coaches go to in order to break into the NFL, keep their jobs, and help their teams win. They work hours that are inconceivable to all but deployed military members and accountants in the midst of tax season. Players also endure incredible amounts of pain. If you think your Insanity or P90X workouts are tough, NFL workouts make those look like Richard Simmons's *Sweatin' to the Oldies*. The pain NFL players endure often comes from injuries as well. They play injured all the time, often with devastating long-term consequences, and players demonstrate a pain tolerance well beyond what the average Joe is willing to endure. For instance, while I can barely get out of bed to work a desk job when I am suffering from what my wife calls a "man cold" (men's colds are surely more severe than women's), Browns offensive lineman John Morrow once finished a drive with a broken fibula protruding from his calf. (As a quick side note: nobody likes an overachiever that makes the rest of us look bad, Morrow!) Even superstitious rituals are turned to on the off chance they might bring a bit of luck. And of course cheating, such as Saints defense players deliberately trying to injure key opponents during the Bountygate scandal, is an unfortunate mainstay of the game. Like intelligence collection, these methods are used by players and coaches in an attempt to survive and carve a name out for themselves in the NFL.

While such measures might seem drastic, anyone who has ever truly loved playing a sport can relate to the nearly overwhelming urge to do "whatever it takes" to play and win. During college I played on a pulled hamstring for several soccer games, not wanting to let my team down. Twenty-some years later, the injury still bothers me when taking shots with my right leg. I try to shoot with my left now, but in the heat of a game, knowing I will regret it the next day, I still occasionally shoot with my right. If I miss, I remind myself never to do that again, but if I score I convince myself—although not my wife—that the pain was worth the glory.

Sports are addictive. There is something magical about the combination of competition, exertion, a crowd, a well-tended playing surface, and the camaraderie of a team. Whether playing professionally, competitively, or recreationally, the end of a sports career—whether because of age, injury, or other factors—can be devastating. NFL players and coaches are obsessed with the sport they love too, and anything that stands in the way of their love affair with football is seen as an obstacle that threatens to take away their very way of life. Compounding this problem, NFL players and coaches also have their jobs, sources of income, and possibly their entire network of friends stripped away from them when their time in the league comes to an end. Such losses can be traumatic, and this is why players and coaches do everything within their power to remain a part of the game for as long as possible.

This feverish dedication is not unique to the NFL, but extends throughout the ranks of professional sports. Athletes in all sports engage in extreme measures such as cheating and playing through injuries. What sets football apart, though, is the extent of spying that teams conduct trying to gain an advantage over their opponents. This is not because football players and coaches want to win more than their counterparts in other sports but is rather a by-product of the rules of the game. Football is unique by virtue of being a sport with many brief pauses. These short breaks between plays allow coaches to strategize, to call rehearsed plays, and to provide instructions to the players on the field. Such control over players is impossible in more free-flowing sports such as soccer and basketball due to the longer stretches of uninterrupted action inherent in these games. Rehearsed plays in football, and their selection and dissemination by coaches, create an endless supply of intelligence-collection opportunities for opponents. Because of these factors and the win-at-all-costs attitude that permeates the league, the NFL is rife with teams trying to gain the upper hand by collecting on opponents.

Spying in the NFL occurs on a daily basis, and almost everything is a topic of interest. Teams are, of course, interested in information about opponents' game plans and strategies but collect intelligence on a broader range of topics as well, anything really that might grant them an advantage. For instance, prior to the 2013 Super Bowl, the Saints gathered information on the 49ers' weight-training methods while San Francisco worked out at the Saints' facility in New Orleans.

Because of the intense pressure to win in the NFL, teams engage in espionage on a routine basis; however, most of the spying activity goes undetected, or at least unreported, due to the secretive nature of this activity. For this reason, outside of Spygate, very few examples of espionage in the NFL are well known. Additionally, the lack of literature on the subject as well as the NFL's attempts to downplay scandals have kept the extent of collection efforts from becoming common knowledge. Incredibly, never before has a book been written about the topic of league-wide collection.

To shed light on this arcane but fascinating subject, I wrote this book in an effort to provide the first detailed description of the types of collection taking place in the NFL and the countermeasures teams employ to discourage, counteract, and exploit the collection attempts of adversaries. Part 1 focuses on less common and often less reputable methods—what I have labeled trick plays. Part 2 of the book concentrates on the most common collection techniques—the core of the playbook, so to speak. Part 3 examines how teams collect information on draft prospects and free agents, and concludes with the NFL's battle with the American Football League (AFL) for college prospects and players, and ultimately for its very survival. The last section, part 4, is a case study of Bill Belichick's New England Patriots and offers the best documented, and certainly the most recent, example of a team that employs most, if not all, of the espionage techniques mentioned in this book. This section covers Spygate, Deflategate, the suspected and known collection techniques New England employs, the advantages the Patriots garner from these, and the NFL's unsuccessful attempts to control an incorrigible team willing to trade draft picks and fines for championships. If you thought the Patriots were villains before, just wait!

While this book contains numerous anecdotes about espionage, attempts that have taken place throughout the history of the NFL—and a few tales from AFL and All-America Football Conference (AAFC) teams that would later join the NFL—it is not a complete compilation of NFL spy stories. The main reason for this is most NFL espionage activities are never recorded. Coaches and staffs still working in the league typically conceal their collection efforts, as revealing these could potentially compromise future opportunities and even risk league punishment. Even personnel long removed from the game are often reluctant to share spook stories out of fear of having wins, seasons, and even legacies tainted.

Those tales that are recorded are sprinkled about in old and dusty football books that typically contain a story or two among hundreds of fascinating but otherwise irrelevant pages. I read too many of these, and then I read some more. But no matter how much I read, I could not read all the books I would have wished, and thus I am sure I left undiscovered many fine tales relevant to the subject at hand. And last, some stories sadly had to be left out in order to avoid burying you, the reader, under an avalanche of anecdotes. In spite of this, I think you will find plenty of amusing tales to enjoy.

Part One

TRICK PLAYS

1

COLLECTION DURING PRACTICES

Teams do spy on each other. There's so much more film exchange that there's less reason to do it. Back in the days Halas was doing whatever he was doing you didn't have the availability of all the data and video, and you had much smaller staffs. I think it's been going on forever and it's part of the game and you deal with it and do whatever you can to counter it.[1]—Jack Vainisi

DESPERATE TIMES CALL FOR DESPERATE MEASURES

The year was 1958, and Bob Shaw was once again a pawn on a chessboard being moved around by powerful men. More than a decade before he had served in World War II with the 104th Infantry Division, along battlefronts where life-and-death orders were routinely issued and expected to be carried out with expediency. Commands in that environment had been absolute, and saying no had not been an option; but those were the rules of war, thousands of miles from where he stood and more than a decade past. So, why then did his current situation seem so analogous, and why did his control over life seem as evasive as it had been along the front lines?

All he could do was wait and hope for the best. Everything was on the line for him—his job as an assistant coach, his career in the NFL, and even his reputation. If the wrong person spotted him now, Giants security would snatch him up before he had a prayer of escaping. They would likely retrace the steps he had taken to arrive—entering through the lobby of the building, ascending by way of the elevator to the top floor, and then climbing the stairs up to the roof. After that, everything about his life would change, and not for the better.

The league could very easily ban Shaw for what he was doing today. The ramifications of that were almost unthinkable. Sure, Baltimore Colts owner Carroll Rosenbloom had promised him another job if he was caught, but would he follow through? If not, perhaps with a little luck he might be able to go back to coaching high school football. Either way, his reputation would be in tatters. He would be labeled a cheat, and his story would serve as a cautionary tale for decades to come. He had never wanted this, but what option did he have?

After the Colts had secured a spot in the championship game, coach Weeb Ewbank and later Rosenbloom had requested Shaw avail himself to spy on a Giants practice in the days leading up to the match, and he had grudgingly conceded. After all, Rosenbloom wasn't a man to be crossed. Those who did found themselves with a one-way ticket out of town.

Furthermore, both Ewbank and Rosenbloom were hell-bent on winning the game against the Giants. Both wanted to give the people of Baltimore their first NFL championship. Coach Ewbank had even guaranteed the team would win one within five years after being awarded the job as the head coach of Baltimore. Well, this was now year five and Ewbank's last chance to make good on his promise. Additionally, Ewbank wanted to show the world that his plebeian Colts were superior to the elitist Giants, whose players basked in the spotlight of New York, mingled with stars and politicians, and earned fame and fortune with advertising gigs. As the son of a grocer, Ewbank liked the idea of the little guy prevailing over the powerful, of the meek inheriting the earth, of David toppling Goliath.

These were the factors playing into the owner's and coach's willingness to stretch the bounds of propriety, not that they were taking the risk, of course. Both were too important and recognizable for skullduggery. As a mere assistant coach, however, Shaw was neither of those things and therefore expendable. He was once again a soldier in a general's game.

Using a set of binoculars, Shaw studied the field below from his rooftop perch, watching to see if the Giants were implementing anything new for the upcoming game. Thus far, he had only spotted a single gadget play, a double halfback reverse. This tidbit was hardly worth the risk he was taking. Nonetheless, just knowing that the Giants were not implementing any major changes would be useful and probably prevent Coach Ewbank from wasting time planning strategies to counter scenarios the team would never face. Preparation time between opponents was a precious resource, especially against a team as capable as the Giants.

New York under coach Jim Lee Howell was a formidable threat. The Giants had been the only opponent to beat the Colts during the regular season, at least when the games had still counted—before Baltimore had claimed the western conference title and all but given away the last two games. Additionally, the Giants had one heck of a roster. Not only were their players gifted, stacked with much of the same expensive talent the team had won the championship with in 1956, but so were their coaches, particularly offensive and defensive coordinators Vince Lombardi and Tom Landry, respectively.

The championship game would inevitably be a tremendous battle. Who would prevail between the Giants' top-ranked defense and the Colts' top-ranked offense was a hotly debated topic among pundits and fans. The two teams were incredibly evenly matched, as the last game had illustrated. The narrow 24–21 defeat at Yankee Stadium had been a bitter pill to swallow and had left a bad taste in the mouth of everyone in the Colts' organization. The Giants' home-field advantage had seemed the difference, and unfortunately, the Colts would have to play there again for the championship game. The 70,000-plus fans seemed to hold back opponents by their sheer determination at times, and their animalistic cries made communication on offense all but impossible. The Colts could certainly use an advantage in an environment like that, but the question for Shaw was, would the life he loved be smashed under the foot of Giants security while trying to gain that advantage?

THE RATIONALE BEHIND SKUNKING

While the type of sordid collection undertaken by the Colts prior to the 1958 championship game, a game Baltimore narrowly won in overtime, might seem like an anomaly, spying on opponents' practices is actually a fairly common occurrence and is commonly referred to as "skunking" in NFL circles. Skunking is of course extremely controversial, but some teams employ the practice, nonetheless, as the pressure to win in the NFL is intense.

Others eschew the practice on principle and due to the risks involved and the availability of information via permissible means. Advance scouting—watching opponents' games live or on film—is deemed so useful some coaches believe there is no need to utilize clandestine methodologies to collect on opponents (a phrase used in the intelligence world to describe gathering information about adversaries). Rams coach George Allen made this claim once, saying, "There would be no reason for it in the first place. You win games with personnel and execution. They have our films, we have their films. We have played each other and know all we need to know about each other."

Take this proffered opinion with a grain of salt as Allen made this statement after Dallas caught a member of his team spying on a Cowboys practice. Nonetheless, Allen was correct that film review has radically altered how teams prepare to face one another; however, he purposefully exaggerated its value. Teams add new wrinkles before almost every game, and these simply cannot be learned by watching past films. Skunking is one of the only ways to obtain advance knowledge of changing tactics, plays, and personnel and can provide a considerable advantage to teams willing to dabble in the dark art.

New York Giants coach Alex Webster belabored this point after he mistook a columnist by the name of Merchant for a Los Angeles Rams spy sometime between 1969 and 1973 when the writer climbed up on a roof and shaped his hands as if using binoculars to pretend to spy on a practice. "You change maybe fifteen per cent for a game. That guy could see everything: what holes we plan to hit, how we changed our blocking. And there's not a damn thing we can do about it now. It's a shame, but some guys just have to have an edge."[2]

MEANS AND METHODS

During the early days of the NFL, teams held practices open to the public, and skunking was relatively easy. Today all teams close off the majority of their practices to the outside world, although many teams still hold open practices during portions of the preseason. For example, the 2019

Denver Broncos closed just three training camp sessions and allowed the public to watch 19 of them. These open practices are not only fantastic for generating extra revenue from merchandise, food, and beverage sales, but also wonderful skunking opportunities. Slipping spies into a crowd that can exceed 20,000 people is a relatively simple endeavor. However, effectively collecting information and not being caught is another matter entirely.

Spies must retain what they see and hear to be of use, and few have memories good enough to rely on them alone. Thus, they typically record the information they acquire by either writing it down or taking notes using a voice recorder. Needless to say, these methods increase the risk of discovery, as the next anecdote illustrates. In 1962, Sid Gillman, the legendary coach of the Chargers, caught a Broncos spy taking notes on a paper Dixie cup he had pretended to use for drinking Coke at an open practice before an opening-day Broncos-Chargers game.

Even with the risks of being caught, many teams are still willing to assume the dangers of skunking for the potential advantage it can provide. The possible rewards are simply too alluring for some to ignore. For instance, quarterback Rob Johnson related that Titans defensive coordinator Gregg Williams in 2000 sent an unnamed coach to spy upon the Bills during training camp. This led to the Titans learning the Bills' blocking system and most of the Bills' offensive plays. As a result, during their regular-season Week 1 matchup, the Titans threw a slew of blitzes at Johnson, sacked him five times, knocked him out of the game, and pounded him so mercilessly that the quarterback was still sore weeks later.

Results like these are why teams engage in skunking, even after practices are closed to the public and the difficulty of collection increases exponentially. While the option always exists to conduct collection activities from afar in order to reduce the chances of being spotted, skunking is most effective when carried out from up close. Being near the practice field is beneficial not only to see the action more clearly, but also to hear the coaches' instructions.

Upon occasion teams share the same field for practices. This is most common for walkthrough sessions the day before games and warm-ups the day of games. The problem with sharing a field is that it can be very easy to lose track of a spy left behind when one team departs and the other arrives. In 1960, Denver coach Frank Filchock learned this firsthand after the Broncos had concluded a practice at Braves Field in Boston. Heading out of the locker room, Filchock noted the Patriots had started their practice as planned and had kindly left the gate leading to the field wide open. Denver's coach thus slunk inside, stood in the back, and watched Lou Saban's team practice every single offensive and defensive play the Patriots planned on using the following day. As a result, the underdog Broncos defeated the heavily favored Patriots 13–10.

Because teams do not usually practice on the same field, skunking from up close is typically more difficult and often involves hiding a spy inside of a facility. This is precisely what Bears scout Fido Murphy coordinated in 1955. He dispatched a spy to attend a Rams practice to collect information on their upcoming opponent's defense as

> they were all zone, but I wanted to make sure . . . so I had this kid watch their practice—he was kind of a hero worshiper. I told him just what to watch for. The Rams were practicing at the old Hollywood Park. This kid hid under the scoreboard, see—he didn't know what time the Rams started practice so he got there early—took his lunch and a thermos of coffee. Turns out he had to stay all day because they didn't start till late afternoon. . . . He was so close to the players and coaches that he could hear 'em talkin'. He confirmed that they were still all zone by watching for what I told him. When I was sure they were still all zone, I got together with the offensive coach, Luke Johnsos, and told Luke how he could beat the zone— Force 'em out of the zone by going to a double-wing set, which would necessitate man-on-man coverage. We killed 'em with it. . . . Every third-and-long situation we just killed 'em . . . and it was all from the information I gave 'em by [usin'] the spy.[3]

Of course, this type of up-close collection has its drawbacks. Naturally, the closer spies slink to the action the more likely they are to be caught. For instance, in 1969 Wayne Robinson, an assistant coach with the Packers, caught two men sneaking through a gate carrying cameras with high-powered lenses. A police officer dealt with the trespassers and confirmed the two were from Chicago, although they promised, "We're not Bears fans."[4]

To reduce the chances of being caught close to the practice field, spies often employ various ruses to ensure they appear innocuous. In 1963, coach Hank Stram of the Chiefs sent Marine Colonel Frank Barnes to spy on Sid Gillman's Chargers practices leading up to games between Kansas City and San Diego. Barnes attended the practices dressed in military uniform, surely as a means to convey that he was both a local—San Diego has a huge Marine presence—and trustworthy by virtue of his official position.

Gillman likely caught on to this tactic, because he mimicked it for the AFL championship game later that year versus the Patriots. In the lead-up to the game, Gillman telephoned his Patriots counterpart Mike Holovak to say, "I've got it all set up for you. You're going to train at a Navy base. They're going to have everybody ready to help you." Holovak naively accepted the kind offer. Little did he know that two of Gillman's assistants disguised in naval uniforms watched the Patriots' practice.[5] The Chargers' defense stymied the Patriots' offense as a result, and San Diego won in crushing fashion, scoring 51 points and racking up 610 yards. Patriots fullback Larry Garron said this about the game: "The Chargers' people knew everything that we were doing. The only way we were able to score was that Babe Parilli came back to the huddle and designed a play that they didn't know."[6]

Even better, in 1967 the Los Angeles Rams under coach George Allen are alleged to have engaged in collection on the Colts during a Hollywood practice using a mother pushing her baby in a stroller. Supposedly a dwarf inside the baby stroller filmed the Colts' formations as he and his "mommy" went past the field. After all, what could be more innocent than a mother and her newborn?

Perhaps the clergy? Well, yes, even they have been suspected of spying. The Steelers once had misgivings about a priest watching a team practice, and the Bills once made a nun hurry along after she was spotted watching a training camp practice at the Catholic Niagara University. On both occasions the clergy members were suspected of cooperating with the Raiders' Al Davis.

While spies can sometimes manage to acquire a front-row seat for the action during the regular season, more often than not they need a place to hide a little farther back while observing opponents' practices. One of their favorite locations is sitting inside of a parked car as these blend in rather nicely when parked on a street and can provide a degree of concealment.

Under coach George Allen the Rams used vehicle-based collection as part of an aggressive spying program the coach started in 1966. On a Thursday before the Rams and Cowboys faced off against each other, the Cowboys were practicing in an open area when a Dallas custodian noticed a nearby car that had been parked on an adjacent street for two days in a row. A member of the Cowboys' staff wrote down the vehicle's license plate number and went to talk with the driver. Before he reached it, though, the car zoomed away. The Cowboys conducted a brief investigation, tracked the car back to a rental company, and discovered the last person to have rented the vehicle was Rams player personnel director Johnny Sanders. The Cowboys then sniffed around and learned Sanders was staying in town with Rams scout Norm Pollom in a nearby motel.

Cowboys president and general manager Tex Schramm was livid when he learned about this and filed a complaint with the NFL commissioner. George Allen returned fire with a ridiculous accusation of his own, stating that the Rams' staff had spotted a man who looked like the Cowboys' head scout, Frank Kilroy, lurking in a tree and using binoculars to spy on a Rams practice. Allen claimed the man ran off before the Rams were able to detain him. The Rams' staff had a good chuckle at this since Kilroy, a.k.a. Bucko, weighed around 300 pounds and was in no shape to climb a tree or outrun anyone. This classic counterintelligence defense of deny, deny, and make counteraccusations cast enough doubt on the situation that Allen and the Rams avoided league punishment, although it did land Allen in hot water with Rams owner Dan Reeves.

As bold as spying in your own vehicle is, Al Davis's Raiders took vehicle-based collection to a whole new level by spying from an opponent's vehicle. In 1965, Jets' head coach Weeb Ewbank caught Raiders scout Maury Schleicher on the Jets' bus returning to the hotel after a pregame practice in Oakland. An irate Coach Ewbank ordered the bus to a halt on Route 17 and had Schleicher promptly removed. Schleicher had not only observed the preceding practice but might also have picked up some useful tidbits by listening to conversations on the return trip.

When security or other countermeasures prevent spies from approaching practice facilities, they resort to higher vantage points from which to observe. High-rise buildings are frequently utilized, particularly hotels because of their public access and the privacy they afford. From their hotel rooms spies can monitor practices in comfort using high-powered binoculars or even telescopes. A Rams scout working for George Allen used this tactic in the lead-up to a game versus the Cowboys. He checked into a room at a hotel overlooking the Cowboys' training facility and watched Dallas practice a week before the teams played. As recently as November of 2019, there was consternation when *Dallas Morning News* writer Calvin Watkins tweeted a photograph of a person he spotted on a roof overlooking the Cowboys' practice a few days before their matchup with the Patriots.

When buildings are not around, teams can always find a creative perch to assist their spying efforts. In 1997, the Tennessee Oilers' coaching staff had two employees use binoculars to keep watch on several people driving around in a bucket truck and changing lights in a mall parking lot located next to the field where the Oilers were practicing. The Oilers had an upcoming game against the Raiders, and the Tennessee coaching staff suspected the bucket truck operators were Raiders spies sent by Al Davis. This might seem a bit overly suspicious on the part of the Oilers, but Raiders owner Wayne Valley hired Al Davis precisely because he was willing to go to this type of extreme to get the job done. He said, "We needed somebody who wanted to win so badly, he would do anything. Everywhere I went, people told me what a son of a bitch Al Davis was, so I figured he must be doing something right."[7]

SKUNKING AND THE MODERN GAME

If many of these examples of teams spying on practices seem antiquated, rest assured, skunking still occurs in the modern game. During Mike Martz's stint with the Saint Louis Rams, he caught a couple of National Football Conference (NFC) teams spying on their practice facility in Earth City, Missouri. Martz stated, "I caught two guys filming us. You could see the cameras from the field. They were outside the practice field and thought they were covered up. One guy had a home camera kind of deal. He might have been a fan trying to help his team. We just told him to pack his stuff and get out. The other guy was in a building adjacent to the practice field. He took off by the time security got there."[8]

Likewise, former Titans coach Jeff Fisher confirmed that vehicle-based collection is still common in the modern game, that teams are still sending security personnel out to handle the problem, and that teams are still running license plates to see who is behind the collection. He had to deal with this issue at least a couple of times while coaching the Titans.

Yet, even though skunking is still taking place in today's NFL, truth be told, it is less prevalent than in the past due to countermeasures teams have implemented.

COUNTERMEASURES

The oddest countermeasure teams use to deter skunking is allowing fans to attend training camp practices for free. Strangely, the NFL has a rule that prohibits teams from scouting another team's practices during training camp so long as admission is free to the public. For this reason, and of course to foster excitement for the upcoming season, teams do not charge fans to watch preseason practices.

In 2010, Redskins owner Daniel Snyder decided to buck this trend and charged fans $10 in order to generate extra revenue. As Snyder predicted, fans still showed up in droves; however, he did not account for the abundance of opposing scouts who showed up as well. Needless to say, Snyder promptly reversed course.

A more conventional method teams utilize to safeguard practices is to secure facilities with fencing, as teams without this protective barrier are very vulnerable to skunking. For example, in 1963 Chiefs scout Don Klosterman convinced coach Hank Stram to build a fence around the team's practice field by informing him the Chargers under Sid Gillman were watching every Chiefs practice leading up to games between the two teams. Klosterman would know, as Kansas City had just hired him away from the Chargers.

Unfortunately for some of the early NFL coaches, fences around team practice facilities were not always well maintained. For instance, Gene Ronzani, who coached the Packers from 1950 to 1953, ran into a problem with holes in his screening fence at Joannes Stadium where Green Bay practiced. To prevent any potential spies from gaining the upper hand by peeking through the fence, Ronzani would have injured players stand in front of holes and openings along the wooden fence the week before games versus the Bears in order to block the view of anyone attempting to peer inside. This had to be done for the entire length of each practice. When there were not enough injured players to do the job to his liking, Ronzani helped out as well.

As NFL team budgets expanded, problems with fence upkeep disappeared. Today, most practice facilities are screened with 6-to-10-foot-tall, hole-free, tarpaulin-wrapped fences. Some are even shielded by larger monstrosities. For example, the Saint Louis Rams have a wall of green tarp attached to 30-foot steel poles erected on a hill to block the view of the practice field from a nearby hotel.

While screening at home facilities is rarely an issue for contemporary NFL teams, screening at practices away from home is still often problematic. One method they use to deal with this problem is to erect makeshift screening. In 2012, upon the recommendation of a 49ers security member, the San Francisco staff screened off a walkthrough practice held in a parking lot before a game versus the Jets by strategically parking four team buses around the perimeter of the practice area.

While having a fence is great, having a security element is equally essential in keeping unwanted spectators from spying on practices. Without guards, fans, curious onlookers, and spies would inevitably find ways to watch team activities all practice long. During the early years of the NFL, teams lacked security specialists due to budget restrictions and thus utilized various staff members to help safeguard practice grounds. Paul Brown, the head coach of the Cleveland Browns from 1946 to 1962, used equipment manager Morrie Kono to act as the Browns' security specialist, cook, babysitter, and handyman. Leery of a potential spy, Brown once had Kono investigate a man standing on the roof of a school near the field where the Browns were practicing. He ended up being a janitor sharpening tools, but Kono still asked him to get down.

At another practice coach Brown noticed a car parked just past the field and told Kono, "Morrie, check it out. It must be a spy." Kono hustled over to see a man sleeping in the car and knocked on the vehicle's window. The groggy man in the car explained, "I'm a salesman from Chicago, and I arrived early for a ten o'clock appointment and thought I'd get some shut-eye." Kono politely asked him to move along nonetheless. On another occasion the team was practicing at Hiram College when Coach Brown spotted a guy on an electrical pole and again said, "Morrie, go check it out; it's probably a spy." So, Morrie hurried over, saw the man was an electrician working on a power line, and just to be safe told him not to take any pictures.[9] Perhaps Coach Brown's paranoia stemmed from his own doings. Rumor has it he sent a Cleveland scout to a course to learn the art of telephone pole climbing before sending the scout on missions to spy on opposing teams' practices.

Eventually, as budgets expanded, teams began employing professionals to secure their practice facilities. Probably because he knew how far his team was willing to go to collect information and figured others were doing the same, George Allen was the first coach to hire a full-time security guard, a former Long Beach police officer named Ed Boynton, who was lovingly nicknamed "Double-O" (as in 007).

Allen would often send Boynton off on counterespionage missions whenever his Spidey senses tingled and he suspected something was amiss. While with the Rams, Boynton once pursued a man suspected of spying on the Rams' practice field from a chemistry lab on the second floor of Wilson High School. After accompanying Allen to Washington, Boynton's main concern was a warehouse overlooking the remote practice field at Dullesville. The rooftop of the warehouse had a great view of the practice field below. Once he found a welder eating lunch there. Another time he discovered a power company employee trying to supply electricity to the Redskins' own facility. Sometimes fans would sneak up there to watch practice and snap a few pictures. Boynton was devout in checking up on these folks, as anyone involved in skunking would likely attempt to blend in as a Washington fan. Double-O even exposed film when required. While Boynton found nothing of concern on most occasions, he pointed out the logic of such checks. "People don't usually go to such lengths as climbing warehouses to watch a football team, and when they do, you wonder what motivates them. It takes a little effort to go to the lengths of finding a ladder and climbing up, and if there's sufficient reason to motivate people that much maybe there's something behind it. As innocuous as it may seem, you have to play it safe."[10] Boynton would know; one day he found an actual spy watching practice behind a fence just before a game versus the Vikings.

Eventually every NFL team followed George Allen's example and hired their own guard force to help secure practice facilities. While the number of guards vary from team to team and facility to facility, most teams ramp up their security prior to big games. Such was the case when George Halas's Bears and Vince Lombardi's Packers, one of the NFL's great rivalries, prepared to face one another. Ed O'Bradovich, who played for the Bears during the 1960s, recounts, "During Packers week, and just that week, we'd come to Wrigley Field for the first practice. And there would be guards. They were up on the scoreboard. We saw them peeking their heads out of the scoreboard. They were in the balcony, two of them, maybe three. And they were on the side door where we got in. [Halas] shut everything down for the Packers. It was tight as a drum. It was like we were hiding the A-bomb formula."[11]

Of course, no practices are more heavily guarded than those leading up to the championship game. For the 1998 Super Bowl between the Broncos and Packers, Denver coach Mike Shanahan hired 18 Navy SEALs to secure the large hill overlooking Denver's practice facility in San Diego to ensure no spy could collect on the Broncos' practices. Broncos owner Pat Bowlen said that when a news helicopter flew over a practice one day "Mike went crazy. I think he expected one of these guys to shoot a SAM missile at it and knock it out of the air."[12]

Fencing off practice facilities and adding guards made it possible for coaches to effectively close off practices to the public, a practice that dates all the way back to 1925. Packers coach Curly Lambeau was the first to do this while preparing for George Halas's Bears. Today, an open practice during the regular season is practically unheard of, and even during the preseason many teams host only a few training camp practices that are accessible to the public.

While closing practice to the public, screening, and guards can prevent spies from doing their job, these methods are wasted if the wrong people are invited right inside to watch. For this reason, ever since it became known that coach Paul Brown had team employees attend opponents' practices under the guise of reporters, coaches have typically restricted out-of-town journalists from attending practices. Many teams even restrict local journalists as well. Green Bay coach Vince Lombardi, for one, removed all reporters. Like most coaches, he was suspicious of anyone not belonging to the team but added a personalized exception for the clergy. Seeing them outside the facility, he would yell, "Those are my agents, let them in."[13] Being Catholic, Lombardi should have known the Vatican has one of the most robust spying networks in the world. Hopefully the Pope wasn't a Bears fan back then.

Sometimes media members are even restricted from practice because of their past affiliation. Forrest Gregg, who coached the Packers from 1984 to 1987, refused to let television broadcaster Johnny Morris view any Green Bay practices, as Morris had played wide receiver for the Bears.

While some media access is necessary to inflame fan interest, limiting access is important to ensure that sensitive information does not make its way into enemy hands. Therefore, many teams today limit the duration of the media's access to practices and avoid going over anything sensitive during their time in attendance. As of 2012, the 49ers only allowed media personnel to view 20 minutes of warm-ups. Even teams and coaches that allow more generous access tend to be more restrictive before big games. For example, before a playoff game versus the Giants in 1984, the 49ers under Bill Walsh did not allow the media access to the team's practice facilities for two weeks.

If all the aforementioned countermeasures are being effectively employed, the most probable venue for skunking is a high vantage point outside the facility. Tall buildings are a likely spot as they provide the necessary height to see over fences. They also offer concealment and even provide protection from inclement weather. To counter spies watching from nearby buildings, some teams utilize security personnel equipped with powerful binoculars to scan these structures for onlookers.

While spying from privately owned buildings is possible, most such buildings are not accessible to the public and therefore not likely to be accessible by those engaged in skunking activities. Although rooftops can work in a pinch, the obvious issue of encountering other people can prove problematic. After all, there are not many good reasons to be hanging out on a rooftop unless you are Spider-Man.

For this reason, hotels are a favorite hot spot for skunkers as they are accessible to anyone willing to pay. Many coaches thus take special precautions with hotels surrounding their training facilities. Sometimes a security team works with the hotel staff and management, usually composed of people supportive of their local team, to ensure that the hotel is not being utilized as a spying platform. This typically entails coordinating to allow team personnel to question anyone suspected of skunking from the hotel premises. Some teams even go a step further. When Jeff

Fisher coached the Tennessee Titans, his team coordinated to have hotel management contact team officials if anyone came in and specifically requested a room overlooking the practice field. The Titans would then run background checks on such individuals to ferret out anyone known to be an employee of an opponent.

Even more extreme, from approximately 1969 and continuing on into the early 1970s, the Cowboys purchased all the rooms in a nearby motel with a view of the team's practice field at their facility on Forest Lane prior to matchups with Los Angeles. Coach Landry started this practice after the Cowboys discovered George Allen's Rams were defeating the fence that blocked a ground-level view of the field by spying on Dallas from an upper level of the motel.

Because tall buildings and urban environments make it incredibly difficult to shield practices from observers, another countermeasure teams use is to build practice facilities in remote locations. George Allen of the Redskins had a massive complex, known as Dullesville, built in a secluded pastoral setting for just this reason. The setting was ideal for security. Just finding the complex was a huge challenge, and anyone lingering around the isolated area easily stood out.

While remote settings reduce or eliminate the chances of being spied upon from a high-rise building, coaches still worry about who might be watching from above as aerial vehicles have long been suspected of serving as monitoring platforms. Some coaches even stop practices when these pass over team facilities. Bears owner-coach George Halas once halted a practice at Wrigley Field prior to a Packers game because of a plane flying so far overhead the players could barely even see it. "They're spying on us," Halas said. The Bears' players grew used to Halas's paranoia prior to playing Green Bay and called the days leading up to the game "Packer Panic" week.[14]

Some coaches go beyond just stopping practices: 49ers, and later Panthers, head coach George Seifert attempted to ban helicopters from being allowed to fly over practice areas. Chargers coach Sid Gillman, who was convinced that the Raiders under the direction of Al Davis were spying on his team, even ordered personnel to attempt to identify the registration identifier of planes flying over the field so that he could call the Federal Aviation Administration (FAA) to check up on who owned them.

If anything, the paranoia associated with aerial vehicles has only increased over time with the emergence of drones. These unmanned aerial vehicles are relatively easy to fly, are inexpensive, can go almost anywhere, frequently come standard with video recording devices, and make for ideal spying platforms. The FAA granted the NFL the right to use drones in 2015, as long as teams do not fly them over stadiums filled with spectators. Quite a few teams, including the Cowboys, Redskins, Patriots, and Giants, are already using drones to help film their own teams' practices, and the idea of using them to spy on opponents' practices has certainly been considered if not attempted. The Falcons worried this is what was happening in the days leading up to the 2017 Super Bowl versus the Patriots when a drone flew over an Atlanta practice. Security officers at Rice University downed the drone (surface-to-air missile Shanahan-style?) and determined it belonged to a local.

Due to concerns over drones spying on practices, the Steelers had a tarp constructed over their practice field in 2018. Coach Mike Tomlin stated, "You know how it is, man. This is interesting times, drones and so forth, you know? We do what we got to do to prepare and be ready to play on a level, fair, competitive playing field."[15]

When all else fails, indoor practice fields serve as the "Star Wars" shields of countermeasures. They prevent onlookers, even those in tall buildings and aerial vehicles, from seeing what is going on inside. While some teams transitioned to indoor practice facilities primarily due to inclement weather issues, others made the switch due to the enhanced security that indoor facilities provide. For instance, people watching Giants' practices from atop a nearby Sheraton Hotel in the 1990s convinced the Giants to make the transition.

Other teams have since followed suit. As of 2010, 14 NFL teams had indoor practice facilities with regulation fields, seven teams used practice bubbles (essentially huge tents covering the entire football field and extending close to 100 feet into the air), two teams used their dome stadiums to hold practice, and four teams rented a location to practice indoors. Inevitably, the number has only grown since, and even teams that continue to use outdoor practice facilities often move indoors before installing new plays. The costs of such structures can be astronomical, but as football teams are essentially the toys of billionaires, many owners are willing to shell out huge sums of money to give their team a small advantage. For example, in 2016 the Cowboys unveiled a new practice and training facility, with a Texas-sized indoor stadium, that cost around $1.5 billion. Say what you want about eccentric Cowboys owner Jerry Jones, but he is certainly willing to spend "whatever it takes" to win.

Yet no matter how good a team's practice facility security measures are, coaches know a persistent opponent will find a way to spy on practices given enough time. So, some coaches have been known to hold secret practices in order to trick opponents that are tracking routine practice schedules. Late in George Halas's career he held a secret practice for the Bears at Wrigley Field. Ray Sons of the *Chicago Daily News* published an article about it after the fact, much to the dismay of Papa Bear. Halas confronted Ray the next day and said, "Wrigley Field is our home. What you did when you printed that story was walk in our house and shit on the living room carpet."[16] Halas apparently took his secret practices quite seriously.

While secret practices at home facilities can be advantageous, they are even more beneficial for practices held at away facilities where security measures such as screening and security guards are often lacking. Sometime around the 2013 season, Peyton Manning strong-armed the Broncos' staff into holding a walkthrough practice in a forest before a road game in New England. Manning was paranoid that the Patriots would spy on the Broncos if the practice was held at the facility. The rest of the players were unaware of the change of venue, so they were a bit confused when the bus halted in the middle of nowhere and they were led on a trek through the surrounding forest. After about five minutes they reached their destination, a clearing where the Broncos would hold practice with no one but the birds and squirrels watching. To Manning, this enhanced security was well worth the effort. Offensive tackle Orlando Franklin, who played with Manning at the time, explained, "When Peyton was here, he was a stickler on that. [He] didn't want anybody to see any plays, so everything that we did was really top secret."[17]

The longer a team is away from its home facility, the more important secret practices like this become, and while airline travel has reduced time spent away from home, teams still spend as much as a week on the road at times. This happened twice to the Eagles during the 2017 season alone, as they spent a week in Los Angeles after playing Seattle before a game with the Rams and spent a week in Minneapolis before the Super Bowl. A secret practice or two in these situations is not a bad idea.

Despite all these countermeasures, and sometimes because of them, teams occasionally identify people who are engaged in worrisome activity. Most of these people end up just being curious fans excited to see professional football players in action and are typically asked a couple of questions and then told to move along. When some of the spectators inevitably take pictures or record footage, teams attempt to quickly stop this because of the difficulty in telling a spy from a fan. For instance, in 2011 Chiefs security noticed a person parked near their practice field taking photographs from a cell phone while practice was ongoing and sent a security guard over to the vehicle to ensure that the photographs were deleted "voluntarily."

When suspicion exists that onlookers are more than just casual observers, teams attempt to identify them in order to determine if they are employees of another team. Yet disguises, appearance changes, and fake forms of identification can render these efforts ineffective.

Even when known or potential spies are identified, team security is not always able to reach them or force them to relocate. Coaches have thus developed a number of sneaky strategies in high-threat situations to render collection efforts ineffectual. Having players switch their jerseys with one another is one such tactic. Coach Vince Lombardi of the Packers was one of the first to use this method. Before a game with George Halas's Bears, he had his players change jerseys during an open practice so anyone watching would not be able to associate names and numbers.

Another method that coaches use to confuse spies is to add extra players when running plays. This prevents spies from knowing exact formations, personnel, and routes. Walt Michaels used this stratagem with the Jets when traveling to California to play the 49ers, Raiders, or Rams. He would simply add an extra receiver in practices, as a 12th man, just to confuse any potential onlookers.

For practices in San Diego prior to the 1988 Super Bowl, Redskins coach Joe Gibbs used a combination of these two tactics. He had his players switch jerseys and also ran plays with up to 13 players on one side of the ball. Gibbs explained his rationale for this: "It was my idea to change the jerseys. We do that every now and then when we are practicing someplace other than home. We do that just from a security standpoint. . . . We use 12 and sometimes 13 guys on offense for the same reason that we change the numbers. We run our regular offense with another guy or two in there, just in case somebody is watching somewhere."[18]

Coaches also occasionally use fake plays in practice to deceive any potential or suspected spies. Al Davis did just this in 1964 after his equipment manager, Dick Romanski, discovered a man viewing a Raiders practice with binoculars from a nearby apartment building. Unable to get anyone inside the building to question the man, Davis had the team run fake plays from strange formations.

While these methods can be effective at confusing anyone skunking around a practice field, they can be equally confusing to the team practicing and can additionally waste valuable practice time. They are therefore used sparingly.

Sometimes the paranoia is so great that coaches refuse to even practice plays and formations they think might catch an opponent off guard or that have big-play potential. Former Eagles coach Doug Pederson noted that, in the days prior to the 2018 Super Bowl against Bill Belichick's Patriots, he was unwilling to practice a gadget play called the Philly Special because he feared a New England spy might be watching the team's practice. Pederson merely reviewed the play a few times on film and during walkthroughs with the team. The secrecy paid off as the play caught the Patriots off guard, and Eagles tight end Trey Burton tossed a one-yard touchdown pass to quarterback Nick Foles, contributing to Philadelphia's 41–33 win.

Another ploy that teams use when they know or suspect opponents are skunking around a practice is to try to trick the other side. This is precisely what occurred in 1954 when Cleveland personnel spotted a Green Bay scout in the stands during a practice. After weighing his options, coach Paul Brown decided to let the spy stay and to exploit his presence there. The Browns had recently offered to trade two newly drafted first-round picks, guard Jonny Bauer and quarterback Bobby Garrett, in exchange for Packers quarterback Babe Parilli. Coach Brown realized the Packers had secretly sent the scout to take a look at Bauer in order to assess the proposed trade. Coach Brown badly wanted Parilli and thus orchestrated a show for the Packers' scout. Browns offensive line coach Ed Ulinski set up a signal with defensive tackle John Kissell. In whatever direction Ulinski turned his cap, Kissell let Bauer block him that same direction and angled himself to give Bauer the best chance of success. Bauer, of course, looked incredible because of this, and the Packers consummated the trade shortly thereafter. Kissell, however, was not too pleased with being repeatedly beaten by the rookie guard who had not even managed to make the Browns' team. The charade abruptly terminated when Kissell groused, "To hell with this," signaling an end to his participation in the sham.[19] Apparently Kissell had reached his "whatever it takes" limit for the day.

2

LOCKER-ROOM COLLECTION AND SEARCHING FOR PAPERWORK

People that are successful in this league have a little larceny in their hearts.[1]—Tex Schramm

THE PLACE MAT THAT HELPED WIN A CHAMPIONSHIP

Chiefs coach Hank Stram and his friend Monsignor Mackey, the team's unofficial clergyman, were hanging out in Stram's suite in the days leading up to the AFL's championship game in California when Stram received an unusual phone call. The man on the other end claimed to be a Kansas City fan who had been having dinner with his wife at a restaurant while sitting near two Raiders players, one of whom was quarterback Daryle Lamonica. The caller stated the two Raiders had been discussing football and diagrammed some plays on a place mat, and after the two players had departed the table, the caller had quickly retrieved the place mat and now wished to surrender it to Stram.

Stram's initial impression was the caller was part of an elaborate ruse orchestrated by the Raiders' Al Davis, perhaps attempting to get the Chiefs in trouble with the league or to feed Kansas City false information. Of course, Davis might not be involved at all. The caller might have just fabricated the tale in an attempt to acquire some tickets to scalp for the sold-out game, but there was always the remote possibility the story was legitimate. After all, scribbling plays was an occupational obsession, particularly among coaches and quarterbacks. Stram himself constantly sketched plays on whatever paperwork was within arm's reach at the time—newspapers, napkins, and even receipts. In fact, Stram was even persona non grata at a few nice restaurants after having drawn plays on their fancy cloth napkins. He was so obsessed he even kept a notepad by his bed just in case a new play came to him in the middle of the night.

While the odds of the tale being real and the place mat being valuable were unlikely, Stram encouraged the caller to stop by the hotel where the Chiefs were staying nonetheless. The Chiefs could use any help they could get, and the place mat story needed to be explored. The Raiders had already beaten Kansas City twice during the regular season and were only getting better. Oakland had won its last game in the divisional playoffs against the Houston Oilers 56–7.

The Chiefs' medicine man, Monsignor Mackey, had been listening to the conversation and said Stram should avoid personally taking the place mat from the caller due to the risks involved. After all, a chieftain must be careful with how far he sticks his neck out. Stram agreed and tapped Mackey for the job, not at all what his friend had in mind. "Come on, all you have to do is open the door, take whatever he gives you, and give him the tickets. That's it," Stram said.

"Oh my God. What if it's for real?" the monsignor asked.

"Exactly," Stram replied. "Blow this and I'll put you on waivers."

When the caller arrived at Stram's hotel room, the exchange was made without incident. Once the caller departed, Monsignor Mackey handed the place mat over to Stram and the coach saw well-drawn diagrams of plays that were the work of a professional. Stram then called a powwow, assembling his defensive coaches in his suite, and together they concluded the diagrams appeared to be never-before-used plays that put Warren Wells, the Raiders' primary wide receiver threat, in the slot. The Raiders had not positioned Wells there previously in the season, but there was the very real possibility that the Raiders' coaches had counted on that to catch the Chiefs off guard. Before disbanding, Stram had his defensive coaches take a vow of silence over the matter of the place mat and requested they prep the defense to be ready to defend against the plays on it.[2]

LOCKER-ROOM COLLECTION

The Chiefs would go on to beat the Raiders 17–7 in the AFL championship game on January 4, 1970, and while acquiring the sketches did not play a critical role in the outcome, the drawings did help prepare the Chiefs' defense for Wells lining up in the slot during the third quarter of the game. Having information such as this seemingly fall from the sky is always a welcome boon and does happen upon occasion, but acquiring paperwork regarding the upcoming plans of an opponent is rarely so easy. Typically, teams have to go out in search of such documents, and locker rooms, particularly visitor's locker rooms, are one of the most common targets of this type of collection.

George Halas, the original and long-standing head coach of the Bears, was suspected of employing the visiting team's locker-room towel boys as spies to watch, listen, and report back to him. While having a spy planted inside of an opponent's locker room is a great way to learn what is being said in there, other methods are available as well. Even without technical support such as listening devices, peepholes and vents can provide ample opportunities. While this next example is not necessarily tied to espionage, it does show the ease of penetrating a visiting team's locker room via such means.

In 1982, reports surfaced that visiting players spied for years on the locker room of Philadelphia cheerleaders inside the Eagles' Veterans Stadium through gaps around doors, holes and cracks in walls, and scratched-off portions of windows that had been painted over for privacy. In one instance, a departing Eagles cheerleader pushed the locker-room door into the head of a player attempting to peer through a crack. The injured player missed a significant portion of the game as a result. Imagine explaining that to the coach! If cheerleaders can be spied upon in this manner, how difficult would it be to listen in on an opponent's halftime adjustments using similar tactics, such as listening through door cracks, vents, or even good old-fashioned tin can telephones?

Another way that opponents collect on visiting teams is to search the locker room after the visitors have departed, as sometimes players and coaches are kind enough to leave behind paperwork with information of value, usually in the trash. Kevin Murray, the president of Murray Associates, a firm specializing in counterespionage that has been hired repeatedly by NFL teams, confirmed that rummaging through an opposing team's trash is one of the most common collection methods in the NFL. These searches can uncover a wealth of information. Just think how much someone could learn about you by going through your trash.

HOTEL COLLECTION

The search for paperwork does not end in the locker room. Trash cans and dumpsters at team facilities are also common targets as they can contain lots of paperwork and searching them poses way less risk than trying to sneak inside an opponent's building. Hotels are even easier locations to exploit. Home teams inevitably recruit hotel staff members—likely fans of the local team—to snoop through visiting teams' rooms or provide keys so that the home team can do this. Even without inside help, penetrating another team's hotel room is a fairly simple matter.

Undoubtedly you have experienced firsthand the lax nature of hotel security. Ever forgotten your keycard and left all forms of identification inside your room when you went to use the hotel gym or pool? So have a million other people. No worries, right? The staff member at the front desk likely asked for your name and room number, and you had another keycard within minutes. Well, that is all the information football teams need to obtain the keycards of their opponents' rooms as well. Additionally, there is always the possibility that teams are utilizing radio frequency identification (RFID) electronics to sneak inside without keycards. No matter how entry is obtained, as long as a spotter is left in the lobby, there is little risk of being caught. All of this may sound a bit extreme, but these are the lengths teams are willing to go to in order to gain an advantage.

Tight end Ben Watson noted just how careful players must be with team documents during away-game visits. "You also can't leave them in the hotel. People in the hotel are fans of their teams, so we can't leave things in the meeting room, in your hotel room or in the cafeteria. You have to carry those things with you at all times, especially on the road because you are in enemy territory."[3] Ben Watson would know, being a Patriots player during the Spygate era. Former coaches with New England allege the Patriots had the hotel rooms of visiting teams searched.

COLLECTING PLAYBOOKS

The most lucrative items of intelligence value are perhaps opponents' playbooks. These display plays, the names associated with them, and responsibilities by position. Because they contain such detailed information, playbooks are frequently targeted. Lee Grosscup, an oft-shuffled NFL quarterback from 1959 to 1964, noted one AFL coach had acquired notebooks with playbook information from at least half of the NFL's teams. Such collection can provide a tremendous advantage. Sometime between 1989 and 1991, while Tony Dungy was on the Kansas City staff as a defensive backs coach, Chiefs defenders memorized the 49ers' offensive playbook. Armed with this information, the Chiefs' players voiced the 49ers' upcoming plays before every snap.

Even when opponents' playbooks prove difficult to acquire, much of the information contained inside them can be found elsewhere with a little hunting. In 2016, a Redskins fan known only as Josh found a bag in a dumpster belonging to recently cut linebacker Ejiro Ederaine. The bag contained a Washington defensive workbook. Josh said, "It's the entire defensive playbook with audibles, descriptions of what the guy's supposed to do, the whole nine yards." When the *Washington Post* called to inquire about the matter, a Redskins spokesman said the workbook did not contain proprietary information and was not a playbook. Indeed, the material was not a playbook, but, as Josh pointed out, it nonetheless contained a lot of sensitive information. "It has what you do in a hot route, what his assignment would have been, what the guy next to him's assignment would have been. It has breakdowns and handwritten things of the new calls, like the defense changed the call or whatever. He scratched it out and put in the new verbiage for it. I mean, it's got everything." In spite of this sensitive information just lying about, Redskins security showed no real urgency to retrieve the information, illustrating how opponents have opportunities to collect playbook-like material and that team security is not always as vigilant as it should be.[4]

COUNTERMEASURES

While Redskins security was rather lackadaisical in the above example, typically teams are very diligent in protecting team materials and secrets. One way they do this is by safeguarding their locker rooms, particularly during away games, to ensure that no one can see or hear what they are doing inside. Cleveland coach Paul Brown achieved this by having team equipment manager Morrie Kono cover every crack, hole, and seam that might allow sound to travel outside or a peeping eye to peer inside.

Another way that teams protect their locker rooms is by placing security outside. After the infamous Spygate scandal broke, this became an extremely common practice, and only personnel with the proper badge or escort were allowed to enter. Many teams stationed a guard in front of the locker room the entire day of the game at Gillette Stadium, home of the Patriots. One team distrusted New England so much that the staff piled trunks against the back door of the visitor's locker room so that no one could sneak inside. Another team put padlocks on the visiting locker-room doors at Gillette Stadium.

Because the home team routinely searches the visiting locker room for paperwork once the visiting team has departed, it is incumbent upon visiting team members not to toss sensitive paperwork in trash receptacles. The Jets go so far as to shred any unwanted paperwork before departing an opponent's locker room. They are far from the only team to do this. Additionally, visiting teams typically make a visual sweep of the locker room before departing just to be sure nothing of importance is left behind.

Even with this precaution, individual pieces of paper can be easy to miss. Many teams address this problem by binding papers together. For instance, some coaches like to review the game plan before the team takes the field, but instead of distributing a stack of loose papers, teams hand out bound products. Then when the players have finished referencing the game plans, a member of the staff, typically a security official, collects the game plans before the team departs the locker room.

An additional method teams use to thwart locker-room snoops is to deliberately leave behind paperwork with misleading information. Sid Gillman, who coached the Chargers from 1960 to 1971, used this approach and intentionally left fake reports behind in visiting locker rooms. Many teams later used this same method after Spygate to counter the Patriots' alleged theft of play sheets from visiting locker rooms. Teams employing this tactic hope opponents waste valuable time trying to decipher and implement the information and might even attempt to set up big plays by suckering opponents into a false sense of security.

As for playbooks, coaches employ a variety of methods to keep them from falling into enemy hands. First, coaches emphasize the importance of safeguarding these and stress how much damage they can cause in the wrong hands. Coaches reiterate this point repeatedly so that the value of playbooks is firmly entrenched in the players' minds and exhort players to take playbook security as seriously as wide receiver Derrick Mason: "You have to guard that thing with your life. It's like gold."[5]

Teams place so much emphasis on playbook security that it can create a fair amount of stress on players, particularly those who lose or temporarily misplace a playbook. In 2012, Giants rookie wide receiver Julian Talley slept with his playbook tucked underneath his pillow to ensure its safekeeping.[6] As an undrafted free agent, and a long shot to make the team, he knew he could not afford to make a mistake. This may seem extreme, but the loss of a playbook can be quite traumatic to a player. Former Colts linebacker Gary Brackett stated: "I don't think there is a worse feeling in the world than to be a young player and to walk into a meeting without your playbook. Everyone just looks at you, like, 'So, these are our secrets, and you don't think it's important enough to keep track of, huh?'"[7]

Players not understanding the impact of failing to secure playbooks and the information therein are often quickly released. In 2012, Broncos linebacker D. J. Williams posted a page of his playbook on Twitter showing one formation with six different plays run out of it. His defense was that he was "old school" and preferred paper to electronic playbooks.[8] The Broncos did not seem to appreciate the justification. The talented linebacker finished out the season with the Broncos and was then cut with a year left on his contract.

Coaches also fine players for losing playbooks as a means to encourage players to safeguard them. Cleveland coach Paul Brown brought the idea of playbooks with him from his coaching days at Ohio State. He was also the first NFL coach to issue fines for lost playbooks. This practice was soon emulated throughout the league and continues to the present day. While the fine varies by coach and organization, it is always substantial so that players take protecting them seriously. As of 2017 a lost Cowboys playbook cost $12,655.

Coaches also rely on players to help police one another. Since the introduction of playbooks into the NFL, teammates have been attempting to steal them from each other as a means to reinforce the importance of securing them and a bit of raillery. While losing a playbook temporarily to a teammate is nothing more than a peccadillo, it is a stressful ordeal nonetheless. Additionally, teammates sometimes go to great lengths to prank those who lose a playbook. For example, when Redskins tight end Chris Cooley found an unguarded playbook, he would switch out the material inside with papers from the last year's playbook. Just imagine the confusion that would cause.

When playbooks go missing for real, teams sometimes request assistance in locating them from local police and NFL security officials. NFL security assisted the Broncos when a playbook was offered in a Denver ad, and the Philadelphia police helped Eagles linebacker Shawn Barber locate a playbook stolen from his car.

The threat of lost or stolen playbooks has driven some coaches to implement rather crazy security measures. Gene Ronzani, the Packers' coach from 1950 to 1953, was so afraid the unscrupulous George Halas would steal a Green Bay playbook that he refused to issue them to his players at all. A more pragmatic measure teams resorted to was to create, package, and bind their own playbooks, refusing for security reasons to let this be done by an outside source.

Starting in 2011, many NFL teams began transferring their playbooks over to iPads. Besides being much easier to carry than the dictionary-sized playbooks, iPads have some added security features as well. Pass codes are required to access them and are unique for each player. Playbooks on iPads are also encrypted so that even if these devices are stolen, the perpetrator will be unable to view the content. Furthermore, the contents of a stolen or lost iPad can be deleted remotely. Any opponent stealing an iPad with a playbook would have to work quickly to break a code, decrypt the playbook, and transfer the contents elsewhere prior to the team learning of the problem and wiping the iPad clean. Clearly, the chances of success are low. Still, coaches want these iPads protected every bit as zealously as printed playbooks. Former Eagles coach Doug Pederson threatened to fine players as much as $13,285 for losing an iPad but added that he typically only fines players for the cost of a new one.

Despite the added security advantages iPads provide, some teams still have not converted their playbooks into this format and instead issue them in bound paper form. Other teams have a half-and-half situation where the offensive playbooks are on iPads and the defensive playbooks are paperbound, or vice versa. Former Colts coach Tony Dungy explained the reluctance many coaches feel toward issuing electronic playbooks. "Most of us coaches are too old school and too afraid of the electronic age. If we do it on paper and hand out 35 copies, then we can collect them and count them all back in. But if we put them out electronically, I could see coaches worrying about the wrong people getting access or someone pushing the wrong button and—wooosh—it's out there and 2 million people have all their biggest secrets."[9]

To minimize the damage of playbooks that make their way into enemy hands, some teams leave off familiar or well-known plays. The Jets under head coach Rex Ryan left some plays out of their playbooks. Ryan called these unwritten plays "lemon juice," as this acidic liquid has long been used by spies as an invisible ink that can only be read by holding it up to a light source.

Perhaps the most interesting countermeasure a team has ever taken to protect the information in its playbook occurred in the lead-up to a Pro Bowl. Coaches have always struggled with how to prepare for this game featuring the league's best players. Given only a short amount of time to prepare, coaches of this prestigious event have to figure out a way to install offensive and defensive systems for players from around the league without giving away too much of their own team's secrets. Frequently coaches install a limited and rather bland selection of their own team's offensive and defensive plays, as the limited preparation time leaves few alternatives. However, for the 1964 Pro Bowl, George Halas of the Bears found an effective solution to this problem. Packers offensive guard Jerry Kramer arrived and began looking over the playbook, to quickly discover it was full of nothing but Green Bay plays. Seeing the shocked look on Kramer's face, Halas said, "Jerry, we didn't want you Green Bay boys to get behind, so we put in your offense." Not only did this prevent the Packers' players from learning Chicago's system, but it gave half the league a heads-up on how the Packers operated.[10] Surely Packers coach Vince Lombardi was eagerly awaiting a report from his players on the Bears' system. Boy, was he in for a surprise!

Shenanigans like this were commonplace in the Halas-Lombardi rivalry and undoubtedly just reinforced Lombardi's belief that Halas would go to any lengths imaginable to give his team an edge, just as his counterpart believed the same. Such paranoia is far from atypical, and more than one coach has cursed the underhanded tactics of an opponent, only to respond with skullduggery of his own.

3

LISTENING DEVICES

We didn't have a lot of strategy discussions inside the locker room there.[1]—Tony Dungy, discussing the visitor's locker room at Gillette Stadium

THE WALLS HAVE EARS

While people were relocating their lives, homes, and families away from the recently ravaged city of New Orleans in the wake of Hurricane Katrina, Drew and Brittany Brees were trying to decide if the ironically nicknamed Big Easy might be a place they wanted to call home. To facilitate this conversation, Brittany dragged her husband Drew into their bathroom at the Loews Hotel, and with the sound of running water from the shower to mask their conversation against the threat of listening devices, they discussed their options in free agency.

Incredibly, given his past success, few teams were interested in Drew's services. Just two years ago he had led the Chargers to a 12–4 season and had been the NFL's Comeback Player of the Year. A torn labrum on his right shoulder during the last game of the 2005 season had seemingly uprooted all of those accomplishments. He was now a has-been, or at best a huge question mark, depending on which team you asked.

Not even Drew's quick recovery had been able to sway the opinions of most of the league, in spite of being well ahead of the recovery timetable Dr. Andrews had provided. His team over the last five seasons, the Chargers, had been one of the few willing to take a chance on him. They had submitted a $50 million offer during the offseason. On the surface the proposal was an answered prayer, but the details floating just beneath were less than ideal. Drew's 2006 base salary would have only been around $2 million, and most of the $50 million would have to be earned through performance incentives.

Additionally, quarterback Phillip Rivers had blown into San Diego two years ago and was waiting his chance to wreak havoc on the NFL. He was a promising young player, had been the fourth player selected overall in the 2004 NFL draft, and had already spent two seasons as an understudy. How long would San Diego let him ride the pine? The Chargers had a lot invested in Rivers, including a $40.5 million contract.

Drew had thus been reluctant to sign a long-term deal with the Chargers and ultimately refused their offer. With a great deal of faith that everything would work out, he decided to test his luck in free agency instead. Unfortunately, due to his injury, only the Dolphins and Saints decided to vie for his services. Drew had already met briefly with Dolphins coach Nick Saban in Birmingham, Alabama, and would soon travel to Miami for a lengthier chat after his visit to New Orleans had concluded. Both of these teams were determined to know as much as possible about Drew's injury and recovery. The Dolphins would subject him to six hours of medical tests and prod and poke him to the point that Drew would worry Miami's medical staff would reinjure his shoulder all over again.

Once the teams finished their medical assessments and decided if they wanted to sign him, and Drew chose where he wanted to play—if there was a choice—there would be what is known as a "rapid intensification" in hurricane parlance. Whichever team did not acquire Drew's services would be contacting free agent quarterback Daunte Culpepper as soon as possible, or they might both be reaching out to Culpepper if neither found Drew's shoulder situation acceptable. Neither team wanted to be the loser of the quarterback version of musical chairs and left without a quality starter when the music of the offseason stopped. While Culpepper was available now, it was only a matter of time until some team snatched him up, and minutes were oftentimes critical in free agency situations like this. The eye of the storm was near, and everyone knew it.

Both the Dolphins and Saints were on edge because of their current uncertainty at the quarterback position, and clearly Brittany had picked up on their anxiety during her meetings with both teams. Perhaps she sensed their hesitancy to sign Drew to a big contract with the lingering doubts over the future of her husband's shoulder. Perhaps the paranoia simply stemmed from watching too many spy movies. She and Drew had been watching a lot of those lately. But no matter what the reason, Brittany believed at least one NFL team was possibly desperate enough to plant a listening device in the couple's hotel room.

THE PERCEIVED THREAT

While precautions such as the Brees family undertook to guard against a potential listening device might seem excessive, the use of listening devices to gain an advantage over the competition is a commonly feared tactic, and it should be. Kevin Murray, of Murray Associates, a company that specializes in identifying electronic surveillance and has worked for NFL teams on numerous occasions, stated, "Some people sound on the paranoid side, but they're really just normal people, following their instincts. And usually, they're correct. Coaches would be silly not to be checking."[2]

Fears regarding listening devices date all the way back to George Halas—one of the cofounders of the league—and continue up to the present day. Many a coach has wondered about their possible use, and some have been all but certain team conversations were monitored by the opposition.

Whether or not listening devices have been used to collect on opponents in the NFL, the threat certainly exists. Technological advances over the years have only made listening devices smaller and easier to conceal. Although apparently installed by team officials, Jets players just discovered in 2020 that video cameras had been hidden in their locker-room smoke detectors for over a decade.

HIGH-THREAT LOCATIONS

Teams are most commonly worried about listening devices being planted at opponents' facilities. The visiting locker room is an obvious area of concern, as key information is typically addressed here before the game and at halftime, and the space is large enough to make finding a device difficult. Therefore, quite a few coaches have suspected listening devices in their locker rooms, and some have been quite certain their teams were spied upon in this manner. Harland Svare was one of the latter. The head coach of the Chargers from 1971 to 1973 once yelled at the Oakland locker-room lighting, "Damn you, Al Davis! Damn you! I know you are up there."

Davis loved keeping coaches around the league guessing, and so when he heard of the allegations he teased, "The thing wasn't in the light fixture. I'll tell you that much."[3] Most likely there was no listening device in the Raiders' visiting locker room, but Oakland general manager Scotty Stirling explained the benefit of keeping the opponent in doubt: "I tell you, we used to do a lot of stories just to keep people off balance, because it kept them focusing on stuff that didn't mean anything. Like that we had listening devices in the locker room . . ."[4]

Another accusation of a listening device in a visitor's locker room occurred in 2012 when an anonymous source claimed Saints general manager Mickey Loomis had an electronic device reconfigured to enable him to listen in to conversations of visiting coaches from 2002 to 2004. The device was allegedly installed in 2000 to give Loomis the ability to listen to pregame conversations of the Saints and rewired in 2002 to allow the monitoring of the opposing team. The league investigated the matter without finding any proof of wrongdoing.[5]

While the coaching booth is much smaller than a locker room, it is also an area of concern for teams as sensitive information—including play calls—is often relayed from there. Therefore, teams are very wary of anything unusual they notice in this area. For instance, sometime between 1944 and 1955, Fido Murphy, a game scout for the Bears, was conversing on a phone in the coaches' booth with a member of the Bears' staff down on the field about how the Rams were trapping defensive end Ed Sprinkle. During the course of the conversation, Murphy heard a tapping sound that led him to believe his conversation was being monitored. No longer trusting the phone was secure, Murphy ran about a half mile to get down on the field to relay the information to coach George Halas. Unfortunately, the delay in passing along the information allowed the Rams to trap Sprinkle five more times and score before the Bears could make an adjustment in a game that ended in a close loss for Chicago.

Team headquarters—particularly coaches' offices, conference rooms, and draft rooms—are also considered high-value targets. Even hotel rooms where coaches and players might discuss and plan for an upcoming game are areas of concern.

The fear of listening devices extends onto the field as well. Some teams suspect that during the Spygate era Bill Belichick's Patriots placed a concealed microphone on Patriots defensive linemen to overhear opposing offenses' audibles. Another rumor stemming from scouts with knowledge of the Spygate scandal alleged a video camera used by the Patriots to record signals was equipped with a high-powered microphone to listen in on the conversations of defenses in the huddle. Whether or not the Patriots acquired opponents' audibles via microphones, New England collected these one way or another. Linebacker Ted Johnson, who played for the Patriots from 1995 to 2004, revealed that he would mysteriously receive a list of opponents' offensive audibles in his locker roughly an hour before game time.

MUCH ADO ABOUT NOTHING?

Another factor that flames the fear of listening devices being used in the NFL is their known use in college football. An anonymous former collegiate coach, who was coaching in the NFL by 2009, admitted to using this collection method against Bobby Bowden's Florida State University. After having spied on numerous Florida State practices earlier, the anonymous coach confessed:

> We put microphones in the visitor's locker room of our stadium. We heard just about everything before the game and at halftime [that] Florida State was planning. At halftime we listened in to what Bobby told the team. We knew some of the plays they were going to run. Bobby and his assistants were talking about some defensive stuff too. We stole a bunch of stuff.

> I would guess we knew probably 30 or 40 percent of what they were going to do based on cheating like that. It might have been more. But you know we still lost. We wired Bobby's locker room and still lost. . . . We wired his locker room like we were the damn CIA. We did all that and he still beat us.[6]

With this activity going on in college football, it is easy to jump to the conclusion that it is likely taking place at the professional level as well; but whether or not listening devices are being used in the NFL, teams will continue to implement countermeasures as if they are. This is simply part of teams ensuring they have done everything possible to help them win while knowing their opponents are doing the same.

COUNTERMEASURES

The most common strategy teams use to deal with the threat of listening devices is to simply avoid discussing sensitive information in the locker room. For instance, Colts quarterback Peyton Manning suspected the Patriots under head coach Bill Belichick of planting a listening device in the visitor's locker room in New England. For that reason, Manning often refused to discuss game-related matters there at halftime and waited to speak with his offensive coordinator, Tom Moore, until after they had left the locker room.

Waiting to leave the locker room to communicate is not always an option, especially for coaches who need to relay information to an entire team. Therefore, coaches find creative ways to communicate with players in locker rooms that are suspected of being bugged. One such way is to merely mouth instructions and hope the players can lip-read them. Weeb Ewbank used this method prior to the NFL's championship game in 1958. He was so paranoid that the Giants would reciprocate for the Colts spying on the Giants that he started his locker-room speech by pointing at the ceiling overhead and peering under the benches to convey his belief to the players that the locker room was bugged. After this he silently mouthed the first offensive play call to the team. It involved an imbalanced line that he hoped would catch the Giants' defense by surprise.

Whispering instructions is another way coaches deal with the threat of listening devices in the locker room. Cleveland coach Paul Brown did this on a rather routine basis; however, not even this was enough when the Browns played at Wrigley Field, home of the Bears. Here Coach Brown would resort to gestures at times to communicate his instructions. Mike McCormick, an offensive tackle who played under Brown, said someone walking into the locker room would have believed Brown "was coaching the State School for the Deaf."[7]

Like Brittany Brees in this chapter's introductory anecdote, coaches have also used running water to mask the sound of their voices. Brown would occasionally drag his quarterbacks into the shower room at Wrigley Field when he needed to pass some vital piece of information their way. Quarterback Peyton Manning also used this strategy for away games versus the Patriots. He said, "Every time I played against New England I used to go and talk to my receivers in the shower in the far corner. I'm like, 'Don't talk about a play next to my locker because I know it's bugged. I know it's got a hot mic in there.' We were in the shower. Very strange to see seven guys hanging out back there in the shower, but take all precautions."[8] Of course, a fan or white noise would work equally well to mask a conversation, and both are undoubtedly utilized as well.

Although the aforementioned countermeasures would be effective at defeating or minimizing the effectiveness of listening devices, they also make it very difficult for coaches to efficiently communicate with their players. Because of this, coaches today predominately rely on professionally trained personnel with specialized equipment to check locker rooms and other key areas for listening devices. This gives coaches the peace of mind they need in order to speak to their teams freely and to ensure that critical information is passed securely.

Mike Shanahan, the head coach of the Broncos from 1995 to 2008, was one such coach who regularly had facilities checked for listening devices. Shanahan said, "I did it with a lot of different teams. You know, we'd have a look in the locker rooms and we'd have people sweep the locker rooms [for listening devices] and just make sure that there weren't any type of devices or anything along those lines. It wasn't with New England, but it was with a number of teams in the National Football League just to make sure that they didn't get an advantage, same thing on the sideline."[9]

While denying opponents information is important, deceiving opponents by feeding them false intelligence is even better. This deception can potentially trick opponents into taking actions that are against their best interests. Bears owner-coach George Halas used this method. He issued fake instructions inside the locker room for the benefit of the Packers and then issued the real instructions to the Bears' players once outside, as he was certain that the locker room at Lambeau Field had been bugged.

LEAGUE INTERVENTION

If the fear of listening devices seems like "much ado about nothing," consider that even the league takes steps to deal with the threat of listening devices. Firstly, the NFL has several rules regarding their use. Article 9 of the NFL's Constitution & Bylaws restricts teams from using recording and listening devices during games and applies to monitoring locker rooms. Furthermore, the NFL's Game Operations Manual states: "Any device that is capable of recording or replaying video is prohibited in the coaches' booths, on the sidelines, in the locker room (after kickoff), or in any other club-controlled area on game day beginning ninety (90) minutes prior to kickoff and continuing through the end of the game, including halftime."[10] While it does not take a lawyer to find wiggle room in these policies, the intent is clear. Teams are prohibited from using listening devices, and teams attempting to circumvent the intent of these policies will certainly face punishment from the commissioner.

Secondly, the league conducts periodic sweeps of facilities to discourage teams from attempting to plant listening devices. Such a sweep seems to have taken place in 2015 when the Jets and Patriots played a game in Foxboro, Massachusetts. Broadcaster Boomer Esiason announced that the Jets had requested their locker room be swept for listening devices. The NFL denied the Jets had made the request, and a league spokesman stated, "We have conducted for years routine and random checks around the league. We do not get into the details of specific games."[11]

Thirdly, if the need arises, the NFL even investigates allegations of the use of listening devices, such as occurred in 2012 with the accusation against the Saints and general manager Mickey Loomis. Whether or not these league- and team-implemented countermeasures are needed is anyone's guess, but in a league filled with personnel who are willing to do "whatever it takes" to achieve a competitive advantage, the threat of listening devices will ensure continued use of the countermeasures.

4

MISCELLANEOUS GAME-TIME COLLECTION

Let me just say this, young man. Anything good in this life is worth cheating for.[1]—Al Davis

NOT ALL INTERCEPTIONS INVOLVE PASSES

NFL commissioner Bert Bell had a decision to make, one that could drastically change the way football was played, one pushed on him by Cleveland coach Paul Brown. Coach Brown was the NFL's version of Thomas Edison. He was an innovator, an inventor of sorts; some of his critics might even say he was a mad scientist. He never stopped brainstorming and experimenting. He was a trailblazer who had already brought game plans, playbooks, and film scouting to professional football and was now tinkering with play calling, again.

The NFL and its coaches were still trying to acclimate to the changes brought about by Coach Brown's last experiment in this field. In 1946, after accepting the head coaching job in Cleveland, he had taken many of the play-calling responsibilities out of the hands of his quarterbacks by shuttling offensive guards into the huddle with instructions from him. This tactic had been used in collegiate football for quite some time but had been made possible in the NFL only recently with the introduction of unlimited substitutions in 1943.

Initially, only Brown took advantage of the rule change to shuttle in plays to his offense. Most of the league's other coaches felt quarterbacks should call the offense's plays since they were the ones immersed in the action. Even when the Browns won four straight AAFC championships, NFL coaches still had their doubts. It was not until the Browns joined the NFL in 1950 and won the championship in their very first year that other NFL coaches started paying attention to what was going on inside Cleveland's football laboratory and attempted to reproduce coach Brown's sideline-to-huddle-communication experiment with their own teams.

Since then the Browns had appeared in every NFL championship game and won three titles between 1950 and 1955. While many teams continued to allow their quarterbacks to call the shots, no one questioned Brown's method of shuttling plays in to the offense any longer.

Now Brown was once again trying to change how plays were sent in to the offense by passing them in through the quarterback's helmet. This strategy was made possible when two local inventors had approached him with a novel idea prior to the 1956 season. They handed over a radio receiver and suggested Brown plant it inside the quarterback's helmet to allow the coach to speak directly to the quarterback via shortwave radio transmissions.

Brown liked the idea and began field-testing it. The direct coach-to-quarterback communication was clearly advantageous, but a preseason game versus Detroit showed its limitations. The Lions picked up on the Browns not shuttling play calls in through players and became suspicious that Cleveland was utilizing an alternative method of communication. When Detroit spotted a transmitter on the Browns' sideline and noticed Cleveland quarterback George Ratterman appearing to listen to a voice in his helmet, the Lions pounced. Ratterman quickly became a target, and at one point a Lions player was overheard saying, "Kick him in the head." The Lions proceeded to do everything they could to break the communications device. That in itself was a problem, but the main issue for the Browns was that Ratterman's head shared the helmet with the radio receiver. When the speaker inside Ratterman's helmet finally quit working, the quarterback made a point of throwing his helmet onto the ground just so the Lions could see that the speaker no longer functioned.[2]

In spite of this, Brown stuck with the new method of communication heading into the regular season, and with good results, until the Browns played the New York Giants in Week 3. The Giants showed Brown they, too, could think outside the box and used a radio receiver to intercept play calls issued by Cleveland's coach. Halfback Gene Filipski, who had recently been acquired from the Browns, then translated the play calls for Giants defensive coordinator Tom Landry, and this knowledge of the Browns' upcoming plays helped the Giants secure a 21–9 victory.

Commissioner Bert Bell now had to resolve what to do about the complaints made by Browns owner Ray Walsh over the incident and determine whether to continue to allow the new form of communication between coaches and quarterbacks. If Bell allowed the communication to the quarterback's helmet, the commissioner would also need to address what if anything to do about protecting quarterbacks from the brutality Ratterman had endured at the paws of the Lions and determine what to do about opponents listening in on coach-to-quarterback conversations. Brown was undoubtedly a talented progressive, but was the NFL ready for his latest innovation?

HEADSET TAMPERING

Ultimately, NFL commissioner Bell decided to forbid headset communications in order to resolve the controversy between the Browns and Giants in 1956. After that, a great deal of time passed before the league came back around to the idea of using headsets. Improvements in technology that made communications more secure ultimately led the NFL to reexamine its stance, and in 1977 the NFL reintroduced the use of wireless headset communication, although only between coaches and coordinators at the time. Then in 1994, the NFL instituted wireless communication between coaches and quarterbacks in order to speed up the pace of the game. Still, 14 additional years would pass before the NFL allowed defenses to communicate with the sidelines in the same manner, leaving defensive play calls more vulnerable than offensive play calls in the interim and ultimately leading to one of the most complex and lengthiest collection efforts of all time—Spygate.

Since the commencement of league-sponsored use, the NFL has assured teams that wireless headset devices are a secure means of communication. In spite of these assurances and league prohibitions in Article 9 of the NFL's Constitution & Bylaws that restrict opponents from monitoring opponents' headsets, coaches have remained skeptical. One of the main reasons behind this is that on several occasions, teams' encrypted channels have been jointly utilized by other commercial entities. During a game in Oakland, the Vikings picked up a Madonna rehearsal. During another game, 49ers offensive coordinator Greg Roman overheard a Southwest Airlines pilot's conversation. Most disturbing of all, in 2002 Broncos quarterback Brian Griese was linked in to the San Francisco stadium communication system through his headset and could hear security guards and vendors conversing. Such instances led teams to wonder, "If we can overhear outside conversations, could others—particularly our opponents—overhear what we are saying?" Some teams and coaches felt quite strongly that there were instances where their headset communications had been hacked by the opponent. Both the Eagles' and the Vikings' organizations suspected the Giants had monitored their headset conversations during the 2000 season playoffs.

To alleviate such concerns and suspicions, in 2012 the NFL switched from analog to digital protection of frequencies, essentially transitioning from a walkie-talkie system to a phone system. This not only provided teams with heightened security, but also solved the problem with outside interference or dual channel utilization—at least in theory—and reduced fears of opponents being able to listen in to headset communications.

While teams today are less worried about their headset communications being hacked, coaches are very concerned that opponents might block signals to render headsets ineffective. The reason for this is headset malfunctions occur frequently and all too often at extremely inopportune times. These malfunctions can be tremendously problematic. For instance, in a 2011 game the Cowboys were penalized twice with delay-of-game calls resulting from headset issues. More than one team has blamed a loss on malfunctioning headsets, and probably rightfully so.

The Patriots' home field at Gillette Stadium is infamous for the visiting team experiencing headset problems when games get close, but this problem is not endemic to just New England. While there is no irrefutable proof that intentional headset jamming does occur, there is some anecdotal evidence indicating this is likely. The tendency for malfunctions to take place on the road, at crucial times, and late in games is certainly indicative of a problem. For instance, in 2012 Tampa Bay quarterback Josh Freeman experienced an abrupt headset malfunction on a third down with 2:32 remaining during the Buccaneers' final drive of a close game in Dallas.

While blaming communication issues on sabotage may seem a bit extreme, consider that an anonymous former Patriots assistant coach stated that tampering with communications is practiced throughout the league by numerous teams.

On the other hand, blocking opponents' headset communications would not be an easy feat. Many, including experts, believe teams would have to use jammers to accomplish this. Jammers can disrupt almost all wireless communications, and while they are illegal in the United States, they can be easily purchased abroad. They can be as small as a cell phone and even designed to appear like one. To guard against any such tampering, the NFL monitors the radio spectrum at games. "They have special equipment set up to locate almost any interference problem," says communications frequency expert David Viglione. "If there was an overriding signal, they may be able to see it and record it."[3] An additional problem with the jamming theory is that the use of a jammer would block all signals within an area, both the defensive and offensive headsets, which is not occurring. Furthermore, Control Dynamics Corporation, the company in charge of the headset technology for the NFL, conducts routine random checks at games to deter any monkeying with headsets.

While many controls are in place, Viglione explains how only one team's headset could be jammed: "The radio signal from the coach does not go directly to the helmet. The radio signal goes to another transmitter higher up in the stadium, and then that radio signal is sent to the helmet on the field. If there are two repeaters, one for the home team and one for the visiting team, and if they are located in different locations in the stadium, then I can see where only one would be affected. The jammer could position himself close to one of the repeaters and cause a problem to only the home team or the away team."[4]

To counter the threat of jammers being utilized to disrupt coach-to-player communication, teams often practice headset malfunctions.

Redskins quarterback Robert Griffin III talked about this, saying, "In practice, every week we always practice me calling the plays in two-minute acting as if the headset goes out."[5]

LIPREADING

Even though modern headset communication technology is übersecure, the information being passed on these devices is still vulnerable to collection through the ancient and arcane art of lipreading. A lip-reader does not need to overhear a conversation to know what someone is saying but can simply watch a person's mouth move to decipher the words that are being spoken. Thus a lip-reader can potentially intercept conversations between players and coaches on the field or sideline or, even more frightening yet, intercept plays being relayed in from the offensive and defensive coordinators via headsets.

The Baltimore Colts proved this was possible in 1977. After losing three straight games, coach Ted Marchibroda procured the services of Bob Colbert, a coach from the Gallaudet School for the Deaf and a professional lip-reader. Under instructions from the Colts' staff, Colbert used binoculars to zoom in on the Patriots' defensive coordinator and passed along the Patriots' play calls to Colts quarterback Bert Jones. This tactic proved very effective. Prior to one play, Colbert saw the New England defensive coordinator mouth "double safety blitz" and quickly informed Jones of this. Knowing the cornerbacks were without help, Jones then threw a long pass that went for 78 yards and a touchdown. The Colts won the game and clenched the AFC East division championship as a result.[6]

Just how much lipreading is used in the NFL remains a bit of a mystery, but some coaches clearly rely on this collection method quite heavily. Former Broncos coach Mike Shanahan was one of these. He said this about lipreading: "Our guy keeps a pair of binoculars on their signal-callers every game. With any luck, we have their defensive signals figured out by halftime. Sometimes, by the end of the first quarter."[7]

For lipreading to be its most effective, teams have to do a lot of homework on their opponents. First, teams have to learn the names of play calls their opponents are using. One way they do this is by scouting opponents' games with powerful binoculars and attempting to read the lips of coordinators as they call out plays into their headset microphones. Second, scouts watch televised playbacks and read the coaches' lips during close-ups. Third, videographers can record footage of a coordinator standing on the sideline or sitting in a coaching booth. The first two methods are permissible under NFL rules and bylaws; the third likely violates the Ray Anderson memo of September 6, 2006. In it the NFL executive stated, "Videotaping of any type . . . is prohibited on the sidelines, in the coaches' booth, in the locker room, or at any other locations accessible to club staff members during the game."[8]

Intercepting play calls through lipreading is so feared today that almost all coaches cover their mouths when issuing them, to prevent lip-readers from being able to see what they are saying. Additionally, some coaches have made play calls lengthy and confusing, just in case anyone is trying to decipher what they are saying by watching their lips move. Defensive play calls are typically easier to decipher than offensive play calls simply because they are shorter and less complicated, but this is not always the case. Bears defensive coordinator Clark Shaughnessy utilized plays with names like "the hossy-gee-shuffleback mini-blast."[9] Try saying that 10 times fast.

At least one player was even careful about having his lips read in the locker room. Colts quarterback Peyton Manning suspected the away locker room in New England might have a spy camera in it, as well as a listening device, and thus he spoke to his teammates in a whisper while in there and made a point of covering his mouth so that his lips could not be read.

PHOTOGRAPHY

Another more reputable game-time collection method teams employ is photography. Packers coach Vince Lombardi was one of the first, if not the first, NFL coach to capture game-time photography of defenses. He learned the art during his time as an assistant coach with Army under Colonel Earl "Red" Blaik and brought this practice to the New York Giants, where he served as the offensive coordinator from 1954 to 1958. Lombardi had photos sent down to the benches so his quarterbacks could study how opposing defenses lined up to defend against the Giants' offense in various formations. He believed viewing the photos provided "a different view and a good idea of how the defense is reacting" and argued, "Visual education is much better than telling the quarterback the defenses." Giants defensive coordinator Tom Landry quickly saw the benefit of Lombardi's innovation and began having photos of opponents' offensive formations sent down for his defense to study as well.[10] Giants president Wellington Mara loved this practice so much that he often relayed the pictures down himself. A thin line ran from a deck overlooking the field to the Giants' sideline, and Mara would stuff developed photos in a sock attached to the line and send them on their way. Can you imagine today's billionaire owners sending sock mail? Mara, though, was just happy to help out the team any way he could and was literally willing to get his hands dirty to do this.

Over the years, technology changed, the number of photos taken per play continued to expand, and the process was refined, but the essence of the collection remained the same until 2014. That year the NFL transitioned to Microsoft tablets, and instead of using team-acquired, black-and-white photographs, the league began providing teams with nearly instantaneous, color, high-resolution pictures sent directly to these tablets. Thus equipped, coaches are now able to zoom in for close-ups of the action and can doodle over the top of photographs to provide direction to players.

COACHING-BOOTH COLLECTION

While most photography of opponents' formations has historically taken place from coaching booths, this is far from the only type of collection to have taken place there. In the early days of the NFL, when budgets were tighter and space in stadiums was more limited, coaches and assistants sitting in booths above the stadium often had to share this location with others. Inevitably this led to some spying opportunities.

In 1954, the week before the Bears played the Packers, Green Bay assistant coaches moved to a booth to watch the game and relay information down by telephone. When they arrived at their seats, the head scout of the Bears and the brother of the Bears' owner were seated right next to the Packers' assistants. The Bears' staff refused to move when asked and thus received an inside look at how the Packers operated.

At least the Packers' assistants knew they were compromised; not all coaches have had that advantage. For the 1960 AFL championship game between the Los Angeles Chargers and Houston Oilers, Al Davis served as the Raiders' advisor from on high, feeding coach Sid Gillman input from a bird's-eye view high up in Houston's Jeppesen Stadium. Little did Davis know that the three gentlemen sharing a box with him, per assigned seating from the Houston staff, were coaches from high schools around the Houston area and were reporting back to the Oilers. These gentlemen glanced at the Chargers' play charts every chance they could get and listened to Davis provide input to Gillman over the phone. In addition to their roles as spies, they served as a distraction by constantly asking Davis questions and talking to him during the game. This effort just might have made the difference, as Houston narrowly defeated Los Angeles 24–16.

WRISTBANDS

One of the more interesting and potentially painful game-time collection methods is attempting to steal opposing quarterbacks' wristbands. The use of wristbands came into practice in 1965 when Colts running back Tom Matte became the team's starting quarterback after injuries were sustained by Johnny Unitas and Gary Cuozzo. To help Matte with his newfound responsibilities, his wife created the NFL's first wristband to serve as a memory aid—as play calls can be complex and difficult to remember. Ever since, quarterbacks have used wristbands, and opponents have attempted to swipe these.

Wristbands contain small, laminated sheets of paper with the names of plays and numbers associated with the plays right next to them. An offensive coordinator tells his quarterback the play he wants run by issuing the play number. The quarterback then looks down at his wristband, sees the name of the play that corresponds with that number, and distributes the play call to the remainder of the offense, typically in the huddle. As wristbands list the names of plays, opponents sometimes attempt to acquire these in an effort to link plays run with the names of plays.

The bottom of a pile is a frequent location for these attempted muggings. Raiders quarterback Derek Carr recalled one such incident:

"When I was in Houston, we had a fumbled snap and I dived on it in the pile. And guys weren't grabbing for the ball, they were going for my wristband and trying to get it off. They'll use any trick they can."[11]

As captured wristbands are problematic, ideally quarterbacks become familiar enough with their teams' play calls not to need them. Giants quarterback coach Mike Sullivan noted how happy he was when quarterback Eli Manning stopped using a wristband in 2009, as he previously feared a defensive player would manage to rip it off Manning's wrist and stuff it in his pants for temporary storage until it could be delivered to a coach on the sideline. As strange and gross as this might seem, these are the lengths teams are willing to go to in order to get a leg up on their opponents.

SIDELINE SPYING

Another devious collection method some teams attempt in order to gain a game day advantage is to have someone affiliated with their team wander over to an opponent's bench and see what they can learn. Lee Grosscup revealed that an unnamed coach he played for, sometime between 1959 and 1964, routinely ordered him to pay a visit to the opposing team's sideline to collect information on injuries or plays run frequently in warm-ups. He is far from the only one to have done this.

Former Houston general manager Don Klosterman alleged the Chiefs used a photographer from a Kansas City television station to help them spy against the Oilers during a game in 1966. He said, "Oh yeah, Kansas City spies, we caught 'em last year when we played them in their Municipal Stadium. See, the benches are on the same side of the field and they had this guy who was supposedly a roving photographer, but he was really a spy. . . . He was snooping by our bench. Every time one of our coaches would say something important to one of our players, this guy would run over and relay the information to the Kansas City bench. I'm not makin' this up. . . . We've got pictures of it." Houston protested the matter with the league, and according to Klosterman Kansas City received a fine. That same season the Dolphins claimed the photographer was gathering information on upcoming Miami plays by standing next to the Dolphins' bench and then hustling over to the Chiefs' bench to share what he had learned. Miami noticed this occurrence on five different occasions, and four of those led to Chiefs interceptions.[12]

The Browns under current Patriots coach Bill Belichick were even bolder. Former Patriots videographer Matt Walsh claimed Ernie Adams—the man running the Patriots' collection efforts—told him the following when the pair worked together in New England. Adams had Browns personnel dress up as league employees, tape sideline conversations on game strategy, and film grease boards (whiteboards) from behind opponents' benches.

Such activity is common enough that teams use security personnel to safeguard their sidelines. For example, to prevent and identify sideline collection attempts, Ed Boynton carefully watched the Rams' bench for coach George Allen. During games Boynton would stand guard and scrutinize everyone in the vicinity to ensure that no potential spies were lurking. He took his job so seriously that he would even review tapes looking for any signs of suspicious activity he might have missed during the game. One day while looking at film, he noticed a suspicious-looking fellow. "Who's that codger? How did I miss him?" Boynton asked himself, only to realize moments later it was Boynton himself on the screen.[13] If you think watching game film repeatedly would be tedious, imagine scrutinizing sideline footage. Yet this is just considered part of the job in the sleepless world of the NFL, where "whatever it takes" almost always means "even when it is no fun at all."

5

ELICITATION

I don't think anybody would stop short of anything that gives them a chance to win.[1]—Sam Wyche

WHEN THE MASTER WAS STILL THE APPRENTICE

Under the guiding hand of Al Davis, the Raiders were the stuff of legend during the 1970s and early 1980s. They won the 1977, 1981, and 1984 Super Bowls and failed to make the playoffs only four times in the 18-year stretch between 1967 and 1985. Unfortunately, by the mid-80s the Raiders' fortunes had declined dramatically. From 1986 to 1997 the Raiders made the playoffs just three times, twice as a lowly wild-card team, and reached the AFC championship game only once, an embarrassing 51–3 loss to the Bills in 1990.

As a result, the Raiders had churned through head coaches during that last decade. Tom Flores, Mike Shanahan, Art Shell, and Mike White had already walked the plank, and Joe Bugel currently had a cutlass at his back. The Raiders finished the 1997 season with a disappointing 4–12 record, and Davis was recruiting a new captain for the job, interviewing talented assistant coaches around the league and searching for someone who could deliver the most elusive treasure of all, the Lombardi Trophy.

One of the men Davis conferred with was none other than current Patriots head coach Bill Belichick, who at the time was the Jets' defensive coordinator. The interview between the two men was anything but typical. Where most coaching interviews lasted a matter of hours, this one stretched on for a full two days and delved much deeper into tactics than was the norm. This put Belichick in the uncomfortable position of fighting for the new job while shielding the Jets' secrets at the same time. Reflecting on the interview, Belichick recalled, "He was asking a lot of questions about what we did defensively. . . . You kind of don't want to give too much information because, you know, he's running the defense. . . . He's a great mind. It was unlike any other interview I've ever had with an owner because he was so in-depth. His interview was so in-depth, really, about football, about Xs and Os and strategy and use of personnel and acquisition, all the things really that a coach would talk about, that's really what he talked about. That made it pretty unique."[2]

While Belichick was highly flattered to be interviewed (after all, he had long idolized Davis), by the end of day two he knew something was amiss and curtly asked the Raiders' owner, "Why are you trying to hire me? You only hire offensive coaches, because you're the one who wants to run the defense. You've never hired a defensive head coach."[3]

While this was not entirely correct, Belichick's comment was apt nonetheless. Six of the seven men Davis had hired to be Raiders head coaches came from offensive backgrounds—the venerated John Madden had been the sole exception. Why indeed had Davis brought Belichick into the heart of his Raiders' hideout?

COLLECTION EFFORTS

Clearly Davis interviewed Belichick in order to learn information about the Jets and rummage through the mind of one of the best assistants in the game, using the guise of a job interview to conduct elicitation on the Jets' defensive coordinator. Elicitation, another collection technique that teams use to fill in intelligence gaps about their opponents, is nothing more than engaging in a conversation with someone for the purpose of attempting to acquire specific information, ideally without the other person knowing the purpose of the exchange. To make this happen, the conversation needs to feel natural. We have all engaged in elicitation at one time or another—whether you knew the term for it at the time or not. Perhaps you wanted to know what your spouse did all afternoon when you came home to a cluttered house. If you are still married, you knew better than to start the conversation with, "What the H-E double hockey sticks happened here?" Instead, you likely eased into the subject by asking, "How was your day?" You then learned over the course of the ensuing conversation that YOUR dog tore the head off YOUR daughter's favorite doll—thus the stuffing all over the living room floor—and your spouse (definitely not capitalized today) spent the last two hours searching store to store for a replacement. This is elicitation, and it can help preserve your marriage just as easily as it helps NFL coaches learn about their opponents.

While elicitation is certainly a sneaky practice, it does not violate any league rules or bylaws, and teams are free to exercise this tactic with impunity. The wizard of this stratagem was undoubtedly Al Davis—the spy master of his generation. The man who quite possibly coined the phrase "whatever it takes" truly lived by these words. He bluffed, deceived, and worked his fingers to the bone to conquer the NFL. Using an opening on his coaching staff to interview an abundance of assistant coaches from around the league was a common tactic he utilized. Many of Davis's peers strongly suspected the main reason he did this was for the opportunity to listen to bright, young football minds and to collect information on his opponents. Belichick clearly had reason to be wary of the cunning Davis, and his question about why Davis was interviewing a defensive coach seems almost prescient in retrospect, particularly since Davis selected the offensive-minded Jon Gruden to replace Joe Bugel as head coach.

While this tactic of using job interviews to solicit information might seem particularly dastardly, Davis is far from the only coach to employ it. In 1987, during a job interview for the Cowboys' defensive coordinator position, Wade Phillips was duped by the holier-than-thou Tom Landry into revealing a lot of information about the 46 defense that he had learned from Buddy Ryan while serving as the defensive coordinator on the Eagles' staff. Phillips diagrammed and explained the defense at length in order to explain how it worked and what he would implement in Dallas. Unfortunately for Phillips, he had been conned. Landry kept his defensive coordinator from the previous year, and the two of them attempted to implement the 46 defense in Dallas with the knowledge that Phillips had shared. Phillips got the last laugh, though, because he had held back some key details. This contributed to the

Cowboys struggling through a miserable 3–13 season that cost Landry his job.

Using elicitation during job interviews, such as in the aforementioned anecdotes, is a brilliant ploy, as the interviewee will undoubtedly feel pressure to answer any and all questions in the hopes of landing the desired job; however, elicitation can be just as effective in less formal settings as well. Oftentimes a relaxed environment helps put a target at ease. Jets quarterback Joe Namath was almost caught in one of Al Davis's snares in this manner. Namath wrote, "I sat down with Mr. Davis for the first time at the Monmouth racetrack in New Jersey prior to the 1966 season. We talked about football, and very casually he said, 'Well, Joe, when you get the ball in your hands and you're going back, who are you looking at? Are you looking at a linebacker, or are you looking at a safety?' I said, 'Well, you know, it depends on the play, but I usually look at . . .' And then I stopped cold. I just looked at him, and he just looked at me. And a big smile broke out on his face and mine, and we ended the football conversation right then. Of course he was trying to figure out what players I was reading. When I visited with him over the years, sometimes we touched on that and chuckled."[4]

Naturally, there is also the cliché method of using alcohol to help loosen the tongue as well. This method has been used throughout history, as attested to by the Latin phrase "In vino veritas," translating roughly to "In wine there is truth." Spies engaging in international espionage have used this stratagem for millennia, and likewise NFL spies have long made use of this tried-and-true ploy. Colts and later Broncos quarterback Peyton Manning employed this ruse during his Pro Bowl visits, according to Patriots cornerback Ty Law. Manning used the workcation as a weeklong spying mission and would invite fellow Pro Bowlers from other NFL teams to drink mai tais with him in their free time, providing players a steady stream of alcohol on his dime. Inevitably, the talk would eventually turn to football, and Manning would seize the chance to start asking his drinking buddies questions about why they did certain things on the field or what they saw on certain plays. Of course, alcohol does not always ensure success. When Manning tried this tactic out on Ty Law, a player with a history of routinely intercepting him, Law replied, "Peyton, I ain't falling for that shit."[5]

A particularly effective elicitation technique, which has inevitably been used before in the NFL, is having an attractive female chat up a player while at a club, restaurant, or bar. A woman could even potentially establish a long-term relationship with a player for the purpose of collecting information from him. While I could find no evidence of this in NFL accounts, I did uncover relevant findings in the annals of National Collegiate Athletic Association (NCAA) football, clearly indicating its likely presence in the professional game as well.

In January 1988, one of coach Barry Switzer's players at the University of Oklahoma came to him and told the coach a pretty amazing tale. Near the start of the 1987 season, the player, who Switzer gave the alias of "Big Red," was walking to the chow hall when a young woman honked her car horn and waved him over to chat. She claimed to be Janeeo Dior, heiress to the Dior fortune, and invited Big Red back to her apartment. Their relationship quickly blossomed. Big Red began cohabitating in her off-campus apartment, and the pair lived together the remainder of the season. All seemed well, but when Big Red returned home from the Orange Bowl—the last game of the season—Janeeo was gone from the apartment along with all her stuff, never to be seen or heard from again. With a tip-off from the housekeeper and a bit of research, Big Red and the University of Oklahoma staff soon learned that Janeeo had been the undercover informant of a journalist from the *Dallas Times Herald*. They also uncovered that she had been recording conversations with Big Red and his other teammates.

The woman claiming to be Janeeo Dior had utilized elicitation throughout her relationship with Big Red in an attempt to gain incriminating evidence for an investigative journalism piece on illegal drug use within the University of Oklahoma football program. As the Red River Rivalry between the University of Texas and the University of Oklahoma is one of the most heated battles in college football, and Dallas is firmly in University of Texas football territory, it was pretty clear to the victims that they had been the targets of a conspiracy to undermine the University of Oklahoma football program. While it appears Janeeo and the *Dallas Herald Times* were not out to uncover tactical football secrets, this anecdote just goes to show how easily an attractive female spy could penetrate a football team and gain access to this type of information.

As in the preceding examples, most of the time elicitation takes place between two individuals who know each other, but this is not always the case. Sometimes NFL personnel get away with rather daring elicitation attempts simply by pretending that they belong behind enemy lines.

Between 1959 and 1964, an unnamed coach instructed quarterback Lee Grosscup, who played on three teams during this time period, to walk over to the other team's bench in the midst of a game to learn how badly an opposing cornerback had been injured. So, Grosscup walked past a security guard just like he belonged there and stood beside the injured player. He asked the attending doctor, "How's the kid, Doc?"

"He won't play anymore today," the doctor answered. Just like that Grosscup had his information, wandered back to his side of the field, and informed the coach. As a result, the coach changed the game plan to target the other team's backup cornerback.[6]

Teams have even resorted to the faking or disguising of identities to finagle information from their opponents. After a game versus the Chargers, sometime between 1960 and 1962, Broncos safety Goose Gonsoulin was approached in the locker room by a man he thought to be a sports reporter holding a notepad. The man congratulated Gonsoulin on his fine performance and said, "Tell you what, what's the hardest play for you to cover?"

The man then handed Gonsoulin a piece of chalk, and the safety diagrammed a play on the blackboard. "It's this option play right here because this happens, this happens."

The man wrote all of this down in his notepad, and then Dean Griffing, the Broncos' general manager, walked over and said, "Al, get your ass out of the room."[7]

Gonsoulin had been swindled by Al Davis, the Chargers' assistant, and he was far from the only one. This same ploy worked against the Bills, as well, and who knows how many other teams. Of course, this trick could not be used on people who recognized Davis, but there was always the phone for those instances. In 1983, Walt Michaels, the coach of the Jets, received a phone call from someone impersonating Jets owner Leon Hess during halftime of a game against the Raiders. Michaels suspected the brazen Al Davis was behind the phone call, because who else had the panache to attempt a con job like that?

COUNTERMEASURES

The threat of team personnel divulging secrets is constantly on the minds of head coaches. After all, people love to talk about their jobs and share secrets, and a slipup to the wrong person can have devastating results. There is a reason the navy promulgates the adage "Loose lips sink ships." Likewise, to keep opponents from acquiring team information via elicitation, NFL coaches routinely preach operational security to their teams. Packers legendary coach Earl Lambeau went so far as to hang a sign on a wall of the Green Bay locker room as a reminder to his players and coaches. It read:

> What You See Here
> What You Say Here
> What You Hear Here
> Let It Stay Here
> When You Leave Here[8]

Lambeau likely stole this bit of wisdom from a sign in Oak Ridge, Tennessee, located outside of a Manhattan Project building. The sign was photographed and made famous by *Life* magazine photographer Ed Clark. As nuclear secrets are among the most tightly controlled in all the world, Lambeau knew where to turn to for advice on protecting information.

Because elicitation can be such an easy trap to fall into, many coaches and players who converse routinely with members of rival ballclubs refuse to talk to their peers the week before their teams play one another. These individuals simply do not trust themselves not to let something slip. For instance, brothers and opposing head coaches Jim and John Harbaugh did not even exchange phone calls prior to the 2013 Super Bowl between the Ravens and 49ers—affectionately coined the "Harbowl" or "Superbaugh." When asked about this, Jim Harbaugh of the 49ers stated, "It doesn't matter who the coach is, what relationship you have with the person on the other side."[9] Not even family ties were stronger than the brothers' desires to win a Super Bowl.

The Harbaugh brothers were wise not to call one another before the game because they knew any conversation they had could potentially lead to valuable information being divulged. Human nature is to share information. Former Packers guard Buckets Goldenberg is an excellent example of a player's desire to talk overruling his better judgment. In 1942, just prior to the second Packers-Bears game of the season, Goldenberg met up with a former teammate, Connie Mack Berry, to catch up on old times. During the course of the conversation, Goldenberg revealed the Packers had noticed that Bears quarterback Sid Luckman bent his knees when calling pass plays. When Berry informed Luckman of this, the wily quarterback exploited the information by bending his knees when calling runs and standing tall when issuing passes. This ploy by Luckman resulted in numerous big plays for the Bears and helped Chicago to a dominant 38–7 victory.

While players inevitably form friendships and talk with players from different teams, coaches are rightfully leery of such relationships and the threats they pose. Therefore, Bears coach George Halas did not want his players talking to Packers players at all, as the two teams shared one of the great rivalries in football history at the time. Before a game in 1940 or 1941, Bears quarterback Bob Snyder greeted Packers wide receiver Carl Mulleneaux with, "Jesus, Carl, how the hell are you?"

Snyder immediately felt a kick in the butt and turned around to see coach Halas, who said, "Come on Snyd. This is Green Bay."[10]

The paranoia was mutual. Packers coach Lambeau went so far as to tell his team not to talk to strangers before they played the Bears, out of fear that his nemesis, Chicago owner-coach Halas, had spies in hotels, bars, and everywhere else players were likely to go. This even included when the Packers played the Bears in Green Bay. Halas issued similar instructions when the Bears played in Wisconsin. The Bears' all-time leading receiver of touchdowns, Ken Kavanaugh, recalled a typical Halas lecture. "You don't talk to the elevator operator, anybody. That Lambeau would do anything to beat you. So don't tell anybody anything about what we're going to do or how we're going to do it."[11] While this level of paranoia may seem extreme, elicitation is an easy trap to fall into, and coaches have to figuratively, and sometimes literally, kick their players in the butt to remind them that opponents will go to any lengths to find a way to win.

6

INSIDER INFORMATION

During World War II, if the Navy had made him and Paul Brown spies instead of football coaches, we'd own Russia now.[1]—Artie Donovan referring to Weeb Ewbank

THE DOUBLE CROSS

Cleveland coach Paul Brown knew he had made a mistake. He had been hoodwinked. Round by round his draft targets were slipping through his fingers. The Baltimore Colts, who were routinely positioned ahead of the Browns in the 1954 draft, were selecting Cleveland's draft targets round after round, and each time this occurred, Coach Brown felt the knife in his back twist a little deeper. Losing his prized targets hurt, but the betrayal he felt made the pain so much worse, especially since he and Wilbur "Weeb" Ewbank shared such a lengthy past.

They had served in the navy together during World War II. Ewbank had been an assistant under Brown for a service team at the Great Lakes Naval Station near Chicago and then later joined Brown again in Cleveland as the tackles coach. Together they had won an AAFC championship and an NFL championship and had made it to the NFL championship game every year since the team's entrance into the league. They were thick as thieves, but just like happens with thieves, cracks in their partnership eventually formed over matters of power and money.

This started when the Colts offered Ewbank the head coaching position in Baltimore. Brown had been less than enthusiastic about the opportunity for his assistant coach. Not because Ewbank was undeserving of the position and not because finding a replacement of Ewbank's quality would be nearly impossible, but simply because of the situation in Baltimore. The Colts were a brand-new franchise, had only won three games during their debut season, and were lacking the talent to compete with the elite teams of the NFL. Brown had simply felt Ewbank should hold out for a better head coaching offer and told him he would fail if he took the Colts job. Anyone would! Ewbank, though, had felt otherwise and had accepted the offer presented to him by Colts general manager Don Kellett. This meant Brown would be losing his top two assistants at the same time, as Blanton Collier was leaving for the head coaching job at the University of Kentucky. The situation was certainly not ideal, and the timing of Ewbank's departure was particularly disconcerting for Brown.

Ewbank had been in charge of preparing Cleveland for the upcoming draft and knew all about the Browns' draft day targets. As Cleveland routinely drafted better than the rest of the teams in the league, Brown was certain the Colts would want to made good use of Ewbank's knowledge regarding Cleveland's draft targets. To prevent his team from being swindled, Brown thus asked NFL commissioner Bert Bell to require Ewbank to continue working for Cleveland through the end of the NFL draft. Bell had granted the request, and the issue had thus been resolved, or so Brown had thought. Then the Colts had begun picking off his draft targets one by one. This happened too frequently to simply be a coincidence. By the time the Colts selected end (the name for a wide receiver back in the day) Ray Berry in the 20th round, Brown was nearly positive the Colts were somehow obtaining insider information from his staff. After all, Berry's collegiate career at Southern Methodist University had been rather unassuming, and while Brown liked the way he ran sideline routes, he had been quite certain no other team would select Berry this early in the draft.

Brown was all but certain Ewbank was the leak. After all, he not only possessed knowledge of Cleveland's draft targets but also had the motivation to share this information with the Baltimore staff. The only real question was, how was Ewbank passing the information to the Colts?

The man was sitting right next to him. So, Brown watched and waited. Time passed, and there was no obvious contact between Ewbank and members of the Colts staff. Perhaps he had been wrong. Then, just like that, Ewbank slyly passed a note to Baltimore sportswriter John Steadman, and the mystery unraveled. Brown realized why he had been unable to spot Ewbank with the Colts staff. They were not meeting with him. Instead, they were using Steadman as an intermediary.

Confident he had solved the conundrum, Brown confronted the duplicitous Ewbank. "Weeb, I know what's going on now, and I'm sorry about the way this thing has gone. Tomorrow you go over to Baltimore's table and draft for them."

MOTIVATIONS

While there is no written account from Ewbank admitting to this act of betrayal, Brown stated that his assistant thereafter confessed his part in the plot, saying, "I did it for my wife and family."[2] This undoubtedly implies Ewbank did it for the money, and while there is almost certainly a touch of truth to this statement, it would be foolish to think that Ewbank was not also motivated by wanting to assemble the very best team possible in his inaugural season as a head coach. After all, two of the Browns' targets that the Colts landed in the 1954 draft, wide receiver Raymond Berry and defensive end Ordell Braase, received eight Pro Bowl nominations between them.

Money, though, is certainly a primary motivator for many who have decided to betray their teams. As strange as this may seem in light of the large NFL salaries, many players find themselves with severe financial problems. Gambling is one reason for this. Broncos wide receiver Kenny McKinley was one NFL player who suffered from this problem and found himself so in debt and so desperate for a way out that he ultimately committed suicide in 2010.

Players from lower-income backgrounds trying to help their families are also particularly vulnerable, as they can quickly spend an entire year's salary or more attempting to support an extended family living below the poverty line. Coach Bill Parcells explained, "I can give you twenty cases of players whose parents negatively affect them with unreasonable financial demands. I've had Polynesian players caught in a dilemma because of their family village; you can get ostracized if you don't give enough, so these kids can get caught in the middle. One kid made $1.3 million as a twenty-year-old, and had to borrow $30,000 to get through the year. Between taxes, the family, and what the village took, he didn't have anything left."[3]

As financial troubles build, current and former NFL players can turn to desperate means, such as bankruptcy, health care fraud, drug trafficking, theft, and even suicide. Others with financial problems or in need of money find another, though no less dark, path out of their troubles—providing insider information.

Not all who turn traitor, though, are motivated by money. For others, revenge is the main motivating factor. For released players and coaches, telling their new team all about the secrets of their former team usually satisfies the need for revenge. But what happens when former employees are not picked up by a new team and have unusually strong feelings of anger? And what about those hurting for money who have suddenly lost their jobs? Upon occasion, these former players and coaches have been motivated or manipulated to serve as informants for rival teams.

DEBRIEFINGS

Players switching teams are routinely debriefed (as discussed in chapter 8), but occasionally so are players who are released and not picked up by another team. Typically, teams hoping to gain a leg up on an opponent initiate these debriefings using money or revenge as their motivational tools. Owner-coach George Halas of the Bears used to call players cut by Green Bay to see if they would divulge any secrets that might prove helpful when the two teams next met. For example, when the Packers released quarterback Babe Parilli after training camp in 1959, Parilli received a phone call from Halas to see what the quarterback was willing to share about the Bears' rival.

Upon occasion, released players and coaches are even bloodthirsty enough to contact another team's staff to offer information about their former team. In 2004, Bills offensive line coach Jim McNally received a phone call from an opponent's offensive line coach several days before the two teams were scheduled to play. In retaliation for being fired, the unnamed offensive line coach informed McNally of some defensive anomalies the Bills would encounter during the game.

TEAM MATERIALS

Passing along team materials is another way released employees have taken revenge on their former teams. In 1972, two weeks after being cut by the Los Angeles Rams, Karl Sweetan attempted to sell a copy of his 1971 Rams playbook to the New Orleans Saints for $2,500. The Saints refused and notified the FBI instead.

PRACTICE COLLECTION

Not all players depart their former teams with harsh feelings. Many, in fact, depart on excellent terms, especially if a player retires with a team. These players are often allowed to continue hanging around team facilities and practices, even though they are no longer part of the team. While this sounds Hallmark-movie-wonderful in theory, such Pollyannaesque allowances can be problematic, as players who have lost their inflated NFL paychecks are vulnerable to monetary overtures from rival teams. For instance, in 1957, the Lions under head coach George Wilson paid a former Browns player to spy on the practices leading up to the NFL championship game between Detroit and Cleveland. The player, desperate for money, provided the Lions with all the plays the Browns planned to run in short-yardage situations. As a result, Detroit not only knew the plays but also knew in what order Cleveland would call them. This bolstered a 59–14 rout by the underdog Lions.

CURRENT EMPLOYEES

Former employees are not the only ones targeted to provide insider information in the NFL. Current employees, although typically those in the process of shifting teams, are targeted as well. For example, in 1960, when Tex Schramm accepted the job as the Cowboys' general manager and departed the Los Angeles Rams, he asked 49ers and former Rams scout Gil Brandt to come along with him. Schramm said, "We're going to have a team in Dallas and I'm going to be the general manager. Steal all the information you can from the Rams so we know who to go after." As Brandt had switched from the Rams to the 49ers two years prior, it is unlikely Brandt still had anything of value from the Rams, although he obviously could have taken information from the 49ers had he so desired. Stealing paperwork was likely beside the point, though, as any information of value regarding prospects was likely contained between Brandt's two ears already.[4] He was renowned for his tremendous recall of data pertaining to college prospects. While Brandt was unable or unwilling to provide Schramm the paperwork he was looking for, the Cowboys' general manager still managed to acquire the desired information by paying Rams owner Daniel Reeves $5,000 for a list compiled by Rams scouts. This was a rather unusual arrangement to say the least.

TRUST

While teams are always looking for additional information about their opponents, trusting anyone who volunteers a tempting tidbit does have its risks. There is always the possibility of being fed false information from an opponent. What might appear to be a bad football breakup may not be a breakup at all but rather a clever bit of theater. After all, passing along misinformation is a staple countermeasure in the NFL. For this reason, coach Hank Stram was barely willing to take diagrams of plays allegedly drawn by Raiders quarterback Daryle Lamonica prior to the Chiefs playing the Raiders in the 1969 AFL championship game. Stram was half-convinced the Browns fan who had retrieved the discarded drawings was a spy sent by Al Davis to trick him. Luckily for Stram, he decided to use the information, and it proved beneficial defending against a new look by the Raiders' offense. The information could have just as easily been a ruse, though, and negatively impacted the Chiefs' chances of winning the game. In the high-stakes game of NFL football, where lying, cheating, and stealing are all too common, the only certainty is that there is no certainty.

A PLANT

Because of the issues with trusting those who volunteer information, particularly former or current employees of an opponent, planting a source inside a rival's staff is the ideal means to procure the services of a trusted insider. Players, coaches, assistants, and staff members constantly rotate teams in the NFL, and new personnel are always breaking into the league. This leaves open the very real possibility that a team could manipulate one of its current, former, or prospective employees to go to work for an adversary for the purpose of sending back valuable information. The most likely motivations to be leveraged to get someone to act as a spy inside another team's organization are loyalty, money, and the thrill of being a spy. Certainly, a lifelong fan of a team just might be ecstatic about doing something like this to help their team win. After all, most hardcore fans would love to be able to help their team in some shape or form. Wouldn't you?

For this reason, there is a great deal of paranoia over potential spies working from within NFL organizations. For instance, when Bryan Harlan went to work for the Bears in 1984, several of the coaches wondered if Harlan might be a spy sent by Green Bay. After all, Harlan's father was the president of the Packers, and Harlan had even once been a Green Bay ball boy. Harlan related that he was asked about his allegiance on several occasions. "A couple of coaches on [Mike] Ditka's staff, Johnny Roland and Steve Kazor, would say when I walked out to practice, 'Hey you're not spying.' I'd say, 'Yeah, I'm spying. We've beaten 'em like eight straight times. I must be doing a helluva job spying for them.'"[5]

COUNTERMEASURES

To help safeguard against threats of espionage from within an organization, teams take precautions to minimize possible damage. Restricting access to sensitive areas of a team's facilities and utilizing safes that are accessible to only a select handful of coaches and executives are a couple of the common security measures meant to safeguard against those within and without an organization, and some teams take more extreme measures too. Under Scott Pioli, the general manager of the Chiefs from 2009 to 2012, Kansas City staff members who had a view of the practice field from their offices—including the team president—were required to lower their window shades during practice hours. A security guard wandered around checking that employees complied with this policy and would even interrupt meetings to do so. This was certainly a rather draconian measure, but teams are just that paranoid and just that committed to doing "whatever it takes" to win.

Part Two

THE CORE OF THE PLAYBOOK

7

ADVANCE SCOUTING

As a football coach I spent a lot of time studying peoples' [sic] *backsides. As a sportscaster I am similarly preoccupied. It is not an idle interest, but more a professional obsession. Such hindsight, if you will, can prompt the knowledgeable observer to considerable foresight. It is not quite like reading tea leaves or divining for water, but the leeward side of an offensive line can tell you quite a lot about what is going to happen in the next few seconds.*[1]—Hank Stram with Lou Sahadi

BRONCOS D EATS WELL

The Broncos' rousing defeat of the ballyhooed Panthers in the 2016 Super Bowl shocked fans and pundits alike. After all, Carolina was led at quarterback by 2015 league MVP Cam Newton and had mauled opponents all season long, racked up pinballesque scores along the way, and finished the regular season as the NFL's top-scoring offense.

Denver's offense, in comparison, had hobbled through the regular season, and its record-setting attack from 2013 was nothing more than a fading memory now, largely because of the waning arm strength of quarterback Peyton Manning. Seemingly overnight, Father Time had caught up with the five-time league MVP and reduced him to a mere mortal. Fortunately, the Broncos had a spectacular defense, but few thought it capable of corralling Newton, who could confound opponents with both his arm and his legs.

While pundits lionized the Panthers and critiqued the Broncos in their analyses leading up to the game, Denver's coaching staff quietly busied itself with finding ways to stifle the Panthers' high-powered attack. It poured over Carolina's game footage in a three-day, bleary-eyed slog and successfully identified a couple of the Panthers' offensive tendencies, which led to the debunking of several myths that had plagued the rest of the league.

Firstly, it discovered Panthers quarterback Cam Newton rarely ran the ball while scrambling, in spite of being a prolific runner and carrying the ball frequently on designed run plays. This finding was important because thus far opponents had been hesitant to blitz Newton as they posited the quarterback would scramble for large amounts of yardage if he broke containment. Film study, though, revealed this fear appeared to be unfounded. Secondly, the Broncos discovered the Panthers' offensive line was not nearly as formidable as opponents assumed. While stout, the line lacked quickness and could be beaten using speedier defenders in one-on-one matchups. To compensate for this weakness, the Panthers often used a tight end or running back to double-team defensive linemen.

Armed with this knowledge, Denver defensive coordinator Wade Phillips crafted a defensive game plan to take advantage of these findings. Whenever Carolina's offense committed extra men to block, the Broncos would blitz to neutralize the extra blocker and prevent the use of double-teaming. This highly pressurized style of defense, sending more personnel rushing the quarterback than the offense could handle, was the cornerstone of the 46 defense that Buddy Ryan had made famous with his '85 Bears.

Fortunately, Phillips had learned the intricacies of the 46 defense during his time as the defensive coordinator in Philadelphia, and while it was true that some teams had since found ways to counter this scheme by employing quick passes with the West Coast offense popularized by Bill Walsh, Phillips had the luxury of an all-star supporting cast. Firstly, he had great cornerbacks who had performed magnificently earlier in the playoffs against the Steelers and Patriots, two teams with better receivers than Carolina. Phillips was confident his cornerbacks could handle the Panthers' receivers one-on-one. Secondly, the Broncos had even more talented pass rushers who had sacked Tom Brady four times and hit him on 20 of 56 passing attempts in the AFC championship game just days before.

While all of this sounded great in theory, Newton made a habit of shredding defensive game plans. Super Bowl L, however, proved to be an exception. Phillips's game plan worked to perfection—it was his magnum opus. As film study had indicated, when impromptu opportunities to scramble presented themselves, Newton eschewed these in favor of remaining in the pocket, and the combination of Broncos outside linebackers Von Miller and DeMarcus Ware left one-on-one was devastating. Time and again they unleashed on Cam Newton with the speed and ferocity of two bulls released from a pen, hell-bent on knocking their riders to the ground. When Newton avoided being crushed by tossing the ball out quickly, the standard answer to a blitz, All-Pro cornerbacks Aqib Talib and Chris Harris were there to hog-tie the receivers before they could even get started.

The defense was superlative and they knew it. They danced after sacks and popped up from tackles spooning up pretend mouthfuls of food—as in "you just got ate up." When the dust settled, the Broncos had forced five three-and-outs, sacked Newton seven times, intercepted him once, recovered three fumbles (one in the end zone for a touchdown), held the Panthers to a measly 10 points (a distant second to the 24 the Broncos had earned), and done all of this against an offense that had averaged 31.3 points a game during the regular season.

HISTORY AND FUNDAMENTALS

As this anecdote highlights, sometimes doing "whatever it takes" entails spending endless hours studying your opponents through advance scouting—and film study is but a modern form of this. Advance scouting dates back to the inception of the league and is truly the backbone and starting point of every team's collection efforts. While advance scouting and the other permissible collection techniques that will be covered in part 2 of this book may not be as flashy as some of those discussed in part 1, they are the core of most teams' collection efforts and are essential to winning.

Ultimately, advance scouting consists of nothing more than observing an upcoming opponent, taking notes, and organizing the captured information to assist coaches in the development of game plans. In the NFL's infancy, advance scouting consisted almost entirely of coaches watching the games of opponents from inside a stadium. Later, advance scouts took over this job. Although this practice may seem disreputable, it is permitted. In fact, league franchises are required to make press box seats available to scouts for games featuring teams' next two opponents.

While the live scouting of games continues to this day, its importance was vastly diminished with the introduction of televised games. The first broadcast of an NFL game took place in 1939 on NBC and featured the Eagles and the Brooklyn Dodgers. Coaches soon realized the potential advantages of watching games on film and thus began recording them. Coach Paul Brown, whom the Cleveland Browns were named after, was the first to utilize this method. While competing coaches initially mocked Brown's analysis of game footage, his success soon changed their mockery to imitation. As games began being televised more frequently and to broader audiences, and particularly after the digitization of game footage and its availability through the NFL Dub Center, coaches and scouts began watching opponents from the comfort of their own homes and offices. Game footage is of more value today than ever due to the improvements in filming, zoom, picture clarity, and features such as slow-motion viewing.

In preparation for the upcoming schedule, teams watch at least three games of each opponent, preferring to use the same scout or scouting team for purposes of continuity and to verify that findings are consistent. Additionally, scouts prefer to watch opponents play against stiff competition in order to get a good sense of their true style, strategy, and capabilities. Scouts also focus their efforts on watching recent games so that the evolution of opponents over time and injuries sustained do not render older scouting reports inaccurate and misleading.

Certainly, older games can still contain some information of value, and many teams thus scout key rivals for a much longer period than their last three games. For playoff games, and particularly for the Super Bowl, some coaching staffs have been known to watch films of an opponent's entire season. This is precisely what happened prior to the 2008 Super Bowl, when the Giants' staff watched the entire Patriots season time and time again.

In addition to merely watching game footage, many coaches today use a service provided by Pro Football Focus to study film. Pro Football Focus breaks up data and video of games for teams to make information and footage easily searchable. With this service, teams can search for plays involving particular players, specific offensive or defensive formations, and plays run by down and distance. These searches not only provide data but also offer links to the video footage of the associated plays.[2]

As information requirements vary from staff to staff, scouts alter the focus of their collection efforts based upon the requests of their coaches. For instance, a team that throws the ball 70 percent of the time is going to be less concerned with an opponent's run defense than a team that is primarily run oriented. Some coaches also want information that would be completely useless to others. One coach, for instance, might want to know if an opposing team reenters the locker room after warming up. This appears a rather inconsequential bit of information, but if a team is attempting to sneak a spy into opponents' locker rooms before games in order to search for game-relevant paperwork—such as the Patriots were accused of doing during the Spygate era—this could be a rather vital piece of information.

The amount of information desired also varies by coach. Some coaches only want scouts to provide the essential keys to victory. Other coaches want to know as much as possible about opponents. Prior to the availability of film study, coaches had to be very careful about overloading scouts with too many demands. Scouts attempting to pay attention to too many details at once during live games inevitably gathered nothing of real value. Today, the availability of game footage allows coaches to demand a great deal more from scouts, who can watch opponents play the same games over and over. The drawback with too much information, though, is paralysis by analysis. Collecting and reporting on low-priority or irrelevant information not only wastes valuable time, but a glut of information can be detrimental to formulating a game plan.

Once scouting reports have been given to the coaching staff, it is the job of the staff to decide what information to pass along to the players. Coaches typically request more details for formulating game plans than they wish to pass along to the players who need to make split-second decisions. Former Eagles coach Doug Pederson only stressed four points to his players so that they had a clear focus on what was truly important and could retain the information.

FILM STUDY BY COACHES AND PLAYERS

While scouts are responsible for studying opponents, they do not take on this responsibility alone. Television and the recording of game footage allow coaches and players to also scout opponents before playing them. Film study is so important to putting together game plans that many coaches spend endless hours watching game tape. That's right, coaching is one profession where watching tons of television can actually make you better at your job and lead to promotions, but before you exchange your briefcase for a whistle it should be noted that watching game footage is far more tedious than, say, binge-watching *Game of Thrones*—well, minus the last season. Yet some coaches still love this aspect of the job nonetheless. No coach enjoyed it more, or spent more time at it, than Sid Gillman. One night during the twilight of the 1960s, Gillman and his defensive coordinator were up late watching film when the Chargers' coach exclaimed, "Hey Bum, this is better than making love."

Now Bum Phillips liked watching film as much as the next coordinator but believed Gillman had clearly gone off the deep end with this comment. In his Texas twang, Phillips delivered one of the great lines in NFL history. "Sid, either I don't know how to watch film, or you don't know how to make love."[3]

Clearly, Gillman was passionate about watching film—perhaps a bit too passionate. He became so engrossed with it he often forgot about the little things in life, like putting on his pants. See, Gillman had a proclivity for studying film late at night while wearing nothing more than boxer shorts and a T-shirt at the Chargers' headquarters in the Lafayette Hotel. The problem was that when he became hungry and wanted food from the lobby, he occasionally had difficulties remembering to put his pants back on.[4]

Before you write Gillman off as a complete nutjob, realize that he was one of the most brilliant minds ever to coach the game of football, revolutionized the passing attack, and is a member of both the Pro Football Hall of Fame and the College Football Hall of Fame. Even though Gillman and the Chargers won an AFL championship in 1963, his loss of the 1955 NFL championship game while coaching the Los Angeles Rams and his losses of the 1960, 1961, 1964, and 1965 AFL championship games while coaching the Chargers weighed heavily on him. These losses were the driving force that pushed him to spend endless hours studying film. Looking at game footage was simply his way of doing everything in his power to help his teams win. He just liked to do it with a bit less clothing on than most coaches. To each their own.

As obsessed as coaches are with film study, even they can grow weary of it. Sometime between the mid-1960s and early 1970s, Jets coach Weeb Ewbank took a short trip into Tijuana, Mexico, and was approached by a local with what appeared to be two cans of 16 mm film. "Movies, feelthy movies?" the man asked. "Show 'em to you cheap?"

"Christ, no," the coach replied, continuing ahead without a second's delay. "I've been looking at movies all week."[5]

As film study is a tedious and time-consuming task, many coaches divide up this responsibility. For example, the Jets under Rex Ryan assigned one coach to study opponents' tendencies by down and distance, another pored over passing routes, and another examined play tendencies by personnel groups. Every coach had a different assignment and after watching film would share what he had learned with the rest of the staff.

Parceling out responsibilities in this manner is often necessary given the level of detail some coaches expect their teams to extract from film study. Browns defensive assistant Phil Savage learned this the hard way under the tutelage of coach Bill Belichick. Savage recalled, "He proceeds to go through all these little intricacies on the game film . . . and it's 20 minutes on one play. Twenty minutes! In my immature mind I'm sitting there in the dark doing the math: Three games to break down on each side of the ball, 60 plays in each game, 20 minutes a play means I can get through three plays in an hour. My god, I'll never sleep again. And I didn't."[6]

As part of their preparation, NFL players also study game film of their next opponents with the assistance of their coaches. Players watch film with the entire team or by positional groupings, depending on what coaches want to emphasize. Watching film by positional groupings is fairly standard as it allows players and groups to focus on what is specific to them. For example, offensive linemen need to coordinate picking up blitzes and stunts—a pass rush maneuver where two defensive linemen essentially trade places after the hike of the ball.

For some players, film study ends with the team-mandated sessions, but serious players spend additional hours watching film on their own. Typically, quarterbacks and middle linebackers watch the most footage, as they need a greater understanding of their opponents to move players around like chess pieces and take advantage of situations as they arise. Players at both of these positions often put in incredibly long hours.

Peyton Manning of the Indianapolis Colts, and later the Denver Broncos, became one of the greatest quarterbacks to ever play the game thanks in large part to his understanding of defenses through film study. Here is what he said about preparing for the Seattle Seahawks prior to the 2014 Super Bowl: "I think it's worth it to take time to get as familiar as you possibly can with what I would call an unfamiliar opponent. We played them in the preseason. We have not played them in the regular season. That's a lot of games that are out there, that are available to study. You try to get to know their schemes. You try to get to know their personnel. There is plenty out there to study."[7] Among some of the most common items to study are opposing players, team strengths and weaknesses, tells, and tendencies.

SCOUTING COLLECTION TOPICS

A key area of focus when scouting an opponent is identifying strong and weak players so that weak players can be exploited and strong players can be countered. However, simply labeling players as strong or weak is not enough. The specific attributes and techniques that make players struggle or excel must be determined. Additionally, even strong players have weaknesses and weak players have strengths, and teams look for these to exploit and neutralize.

For example, before the inaugural Super Bowl versus Kansas City, veteran Packers wide receiver Max McGee identified a weak link in the Chiefs' secondary. Before the game he told CBS commentator Ray Scott, "I've been studying film and I've found me a cornerback. I'm gonna have him for breakfast, lunch, and dinner." That he did. He gained

138 yards on seven passes. McGee believed he would have finished with twice as many catches if Bart Starr had only targeted him more.[8]

Just as players have strengths and weaknesses, so do teams. Identifying these is key to formulating strategies to counter opponents' strengths and to take advantage of their weaknesses. Targeting weaknesses is a time-tested tactic that has been used throughout the history of the NFL, and while it would appear to be the simpler strategy to implement, many coaches have made a name for themselves by instead focusing on negating an opponent's strengths. Rams and later Redskins coach George Allen frequently employed this tactic. He said, "We believe that if we can take away our opponent's best weapons, we can have reasonable success against the remainder of their attack."[9] Patriots coach Bill Belichick is another proponent of this strategy. He is one of the best in the history of the league at designing defensive strategies to take away what opposing offenses do best. For example, Peyton Manning of the Colts was a rhythm quarterback who had established impeccable timing with his wide receivers. So, when the Patriots played the Colts in the AFC championship game in January 2004, Belichick had his cornerbacks jam the Colts' wide receivers at the line of scrimmage. This threw off the timing of the Colts' offense and stifled one of the league's all-time great offenses.

TENDENCIES

Another one of the main reasons that teams watch opponents' games is to learn their tendencies, especially for offenses, whose strategies do not frequently change from game to game. Scouts take on the lion's share of this work by annotating the details of every play opponents run. Once this information is collected, scouts perform statistical analysis to identify trends, such as the percentage of runs versus pass plays, the percentage of runs versus pass plays called by down and distance, the percentage of runs or passes out of different formations, the percentage of runs through the various gaps in the offensive line, the percentage of plays run out of specific formations, running distribution by backs, passing tendencies by routes, and passing distribution percentages and rates of success. Armed with this data, coaches and players can make educated predictions about an opponent's upcoming actions based on distance, down, position on the field, and time remaining.

The identification of tendencies can be immensely beneficial. For instance, the Broncos defeated the heavily favored Packers in the 1998 Super Bowl largely because Mike Shanahan's coaching staff identified two particular tendencies after three straight days of grueling film study in the lead-up to the game. First, the Broncos identified the conditions under which Packers star safety LeRoy Butler blitzed. He blitzed only when opposing teams lined up two wide receivers on the same side of the field and one of his fellow linebackers covered the slot receiver. When instead a cornerback covered the slot receiver, Butler would guard the opposing team's tight end instead of blitzing. With this knowledge, the Broncos used formations with wide receivers Ed McCaffrey and Rod Smith on the same side of the field, and John Elway audibled as needed based upon whether Butler would blitz or not, as dictated by the defender covering the slot receiver. This vital piece of information allowed the Broncos to minimize the damage done by Butler's blitzing, a huge advantage as the safety had wreaked havoc on opposing quarterbacks all season long.

The other tendency the Broncos identified prior to the game helped Denver's offense punch in a critical touchdown from the goal line. Film study revealed the Packers' defense always blitzed on third-down plays when the opposing offense was a yard or less away from the Green Bay goal line. Fortuitously, this is exactly the position the Denver offense found itself in for the first play of the second quarter. Unfortunately, Broncos Hall of Fame running back Terrell Davis had just come out of the game at the end of the first quarter suffering from a migraine headache that rendered him nearly blind. Blind or not, Shanahan decided he needed Davis in the game and convinced Davis to play along by saying, "Just do this. You don't worry about seeing on this play because we're going to fake it to you on Fifteen Lead. But if you're not in there, they won't believe we're going to run the ball, okay?" Being a consummate team player, Davis agreed to go along with the coach's plan. Talk about taking one for the team. With Davis back in the game, John Elway faked to his running back, bootlegged, and ran the ball into the end zone.[10] Shanahan had correctly determined Elway would have an unobstructed path, because he knew from film study that the Packers' safeties would be up on the line of scrimmage.

Another reason that teams watch film of opponents is to identify tells—conscious or subconscious behaviors that give clues as to what is about to happen. Think of a poker player always scratching his nose when bluffing. This is a quintessential tell. A team-based tell can be as simple as how much time an offense spends in the huddle. If, for example, a team spends an extra five seconds in the huddle when pass plays are called versus run plays, a sharp opposing coach or scout will pick up on this.

Individual players also have tells, many of which are common to their positions. For example, wide receivers frequently fiddle with their gloves when they anticipate a pass coming to them on the next play. Terrell Owens had this bad habit. Another common tell among wide receivers is charging out of the huddle for pass plays and moseying out for runs. The Jets' receivers routinely made this mistake when quarterback Mark Sanchez played in New York.

Although tells can be identified while playing or watching live games, tells are most easily spotted via film study, where players' actions can be scrutinized at length. Alan Branch, a journeyman defensive tackle in the NFL from 2007 to 2017, noted just how obsessive NFL players can be looking for a tell. "Sometimes I'll watch just the first second of a play for five minutes, just so I can see the steps a lineman takes and try to get some kind of an edge or an advantage."[11] If Branch spends five minutes watching one second of game film, imagine how much time he spends watching the entire game. This is just the level of dedication required, though, to survive in the NFL.

COUNTERMEASURES

Just like teams collect on opponents' tells and tendencies, they also collect on their own tells and tendencies via self-scouting and often institute countermeasures to address these once identified. One of the most common ways teams deal with tendencies is to buck identified trends, such as by altering a play. The Saints did this before their 2006 Week 12 matchup with the Falcons in order to take advantage of Atlanta's familiarity with the New Orleans offense. For one play the Falcons were familiar with, the Saints' offense ran a double in with both an inside and outside receiver. In the past, Atlanta defended this by having a safety cover the middle receiver and having the cornerback lined up against the middle receiver switch to double-team the outside receiver as soon as the ball was snapped. The Saints recognized the big play potential of having a safety matched up one-on-one versus a receiver. So, instead of doing their regular routine, the middle receiver Devery Henderson ran a deep post route, caught the safety who had been expecting a double in route off guard, hauled in the pass from quarterback Drew Brees, and sprinted 76 yards for a touchdown.

Other times, bucking trends can simply mean changing up play calls typically used in certain downs and distances. To cap Miami's perfect 1972 season, coach Don Shula took advantage of coach George Allen's well-deserved reputation as a scholar of opponents' tendencies against him during the 1973 Super Bowl. Allen was a film aficionado and conducted statistical analysis of opponents to figure out their tendencies. Knowing Allen would show up to the game with a cheat sheet of the Dolphins' tendencies for down and distance, the Dolphins abandoned their usual play calls. For instance, where the Dolphins had run on first down all season, they now passed out of play-action fakes. The strategy worked as planned, resulting in several big plays—including the first touchdown of the game—and helped propel the Dolphins to football immortality.

Another method that teams use to avoid the exploitation of tendencies is to disguise virtually the same play using multiple formations. For the AFL championship game in 1963, Chargers coach Sid Gillman used this strategy to mask running essentially the same play calls over and over again. Chargers assistant Tom Bass explained the strategy used by Gillman. "Let's say we're going to run off tackle with [Ron] Mix leading, we could double-team block it and kick out with the fullback. That's one way. Another would be for Ron to block down along with the tight end, then pull for the kick out with a guard. Or we would block down with the tight end and pull Mix for the kick out. It's all the same play, going to the same area, but with three totally different looks. It was confusing as hell for the defense."[12] This strategy helped the Chargers clobber the Boston Patriots 51–10.

The easiest way to forecast what is about to transpire on the field is by watching the players who are shuttled on and off the field. An offense that replaces a bunch of fast, skinny guys with players who have their own zip codes is tipping its hand that a run is likely to ensue. An offense that uses the same personnel on varied downs and distances is far less predictable, and therefore some coaches try to run most of their plays out of one personnel group. Tony Dungy, who was a head coach in the NFL from 1996 to 2008, noted the difficulties of playing teams that use this strategy: "The guys most difficult to defend are the ones that do not fall into a pattern. The toughest teams are the ones that can do everything out of one personnel group, who can run the same play on third-and-6 with the same personnel that they run a play on first-and-10. They give you three or four runs that look so alike and then play-action pass off those plays. That's tough."[13]

Avoiding tendencies is another strategy that teams employ. The 1999–2001 Rams earned the moniker "the Greatest Show on Turf" for their exciting offense designed by Mike Martz. Besides being incredibly quick and talented, what made this offense so unique was its unpredictability. Offensive plays were seemingly called with no regard to down and distance. A 30-yard pass attempt was as likely to be attempted on third-and-1 as on first-and-15.

Tells can be every bit as deleterious as tendencies, and coaches are typically very diligent in ensuring that these are squashed as soon as they are identified. Every once in a while, though, coaches are not as security conscious as they should be, and players have to be the voice of reason. For example, in 1993 Packers head coach Mike Holmgren wanted his receivers to line up two yards wide of the numbers to give them some extra room to run their routes before they reached the sideline on a particular pattern. This would create a little additional time for quarterback Brett Favre to find them with the ball. So Jon Gruden, who was Green Bay's wide receiver coach at the time, tried to convince the Packers' receivers to follow Holmgren's instructions, but he was consistently met with stiff resistance. Sterling Sharpe and Mark Clayton complained that doing this would tip off defenses. Sharpe told Gruden, "I line up on the outside edge of the numbers on every play. Runs, passes, inside routes, outside routes, I'm on the outside edge of the numbers. Period! That's what I do, that's my deal. I'm on the outside edge of the numbers. That way I have no split identification for me. I'm like a thief in the middle of the night. I don't give away nothing."

Clayton was equally vociferous in his complaints: "Hey, man, when I line up two yards outside the numbers, why don't I just give the corner a Hallmark greeting card and say, 'Hey I'm runnin' an inside route'?"[14]

While some tells, such as where a wide receiver lines up, can be easily adjusted, others are not so easily altered. For example, the knuckles of offensive and defensive linemen often give away their upcoming actions, as white knuckles indicate more pressure being placed on them while red knuckles indicate less pressure. It is well known in NFL circles that when defensive linemen are prepared to pass rush, their knuckles are white, and when they are about to drop back into pass coverage, their knuckles are red. Likewise, when offensive linemen are run blocking, their knuckles are white; when pass blocking, their knuckles are red. For just this reason, most linemen in the NFL now wear gloves.

Another option to deal with tells is to exploit an opponent's knowledge of them. One such instance took place in 1942, when the Bears learned that the Packers had identified a tell of their quarterback, Sid Luckman, who bent his knees when calling out pass plays and stood erect when calling runs. Armed with this information, Luckman repeatedly fleeced the Packers' defense by bending his knees when calling runs and standing tall when calling passes.

While countermeasures such as these might seem rather insignificant in the overall outcome of a game, a small advantage such as being able to determine whether a play will be a pass or a run is often the tipping point in a battle between two teams. In the modern NFL where the salary cap and the draft have created a great deal of parity among teams, and the difference in player talent is often razor thin, any advantage gained by film study, or defended through countermeasures, is of vital importance.

8

DEBRIEFS

I don't care if we're playing them in preseason or in the Super Bowl, we're going to know everything we can about our competitors. It's almost to the point where we want to be sleeping with the enemy.[1]— Mike Shanahan with Adam Schefter

TREASONABLE OR REASONABLE?

Week 7 of the 2012 season was pivotal for Vikings head coach Leslie Frazier. His scrappy team was 4–2 and gaining momentum, but as any NFL coach could tell you, a 4–2 start was just that, a start. Just one year before Frazier had taken over in Minnesota, the 2009 Broncos under coach Josh McDaniels had started the season out 6–0, only to lose eight of the last 10 games and miss the playoffs. A similar wave of misfortune could happen to any team. All it took was a few injuries.

While a calamitous collapse such as that was unlikely, even a mediocre 8–8 finish could prove ruinous for Coach Frazier. Like the Norsemen for which the team was named, and whose descendants dotted the bucolic Minnesota countryside, Vikings fans were not known for their patience, and they were desperate to reclaim rule of the frigid NFC North. If this meant usurping their current leader, well, so be it.

Frazier was well aware of the volatility of the job. He had risen to power on the back of an uprising when head coach Brad Childress was axed three-quarters of the way through a disappointing 6–10 season in 2010. Frazier had escaped unscathed at the time, but when the Vikings finished the next season 3–13 the blame had fallen squarely on his shoulders. Another year like that and Frazier would be facing the same fate as Childress.

Sure, the Vikings had suffered some rough seas during his tenure, but they would find solid footing once again. It was only a matter of time—time to restock the team with talent, time to reestablish a winning culture, and time to regain the city's support. Ironically, Frazier needed wins in order to earn the time to effect change. He was hoping to get one of those wins from Arizona, Minnesota's next challenger, but this was far from assured. The Cardinals were a tough opponent and would not go down without a fight. They were an identical 4–2 and, as their record indicated, fairly evenly matched with the Vikings. Frazier, though, had a plan to tip the scales in his team's favor.

Minnesota had signed cornerback A. J. Jefferson from the Cardinals just before the regular season began, and the young player was all too eager to help plot the demise of his former team that had demoted him and then traded him away. Therefore, the Vikings staff was currently helping Jefferson unload secrets, shuffling him between meetings where he was sharing what he knew of the opposition. Already Jefferson had supplied information about the tendencies of the Cardinals' offense and quarterback John Skelton. Jefferson had played against this offense every day in practice for two years and knew it well. With any luck, the information would provide the Vikings with the edge they needed to secure another victory.

MOTIVATIONS

While Jefferson's actions might seem traitorous, they are fairly typical in a league filled with players and coaches willing to do "whatever it takes" to win. Players and coaches released or traded from one team and picked up by another frequently share information about their old team with their new. While the motivation can vary from player to player, three primary reasons surface recurringly.

Firstly, released and traded members of a team are often jaded about not being retained and provide information as a way to get revenge. Players enjoy being fired as much as the rest of us. When asked if revenge was a factor in supplying the Vikings with information that helped seal a 21–14 victory against the Cardinals, A. J. Jefferson replied, "Oh, yeah. No question. Anytime you get traded away, you definitely want to put it on the team you're playing against."[2]

Secondly, for personnel added to the roster of another team, the most obvious reason for sharing insider information is that the newly acquired member of the team wants to win, and providing information gives his new team an advantage. Doug Evans, a journeyman cornerback who was drafted by the Packers in 1993, rationalized it this way: "It's not about loyalty in the NFL, it's about winning. If you can get an advantage by spying or giving away secrets about your old team, then you do that."[3]

Thirdly, when teams release personnel, they often sever any sense of loyalty the employee felt for the organization. Defensive end and linebacker Tim Green noticed this repeatedly during his career with the Falcons. He said, "When a player changes teams, whether he's cut, traded or bought, there is absolutely no loyalty left behind. . . . The fact that players will so quickly and thoroughly roll over on their former teammates tells you just how mercenary NFL players really are."[4]

While most players are willing, and often even eager, to spill the secrets of their former teams, there are exceptions. For example, in 2019 Rams safety Eric Weddle refused to provide any information about the Ravens, a team Weddle had played for from 2016 to 2018. Weddle defended his decision by saying, "I could tell them a lot of stuff, but that's just not who I am. So we're going to play it on the field, and the best team is going to win."[5] Of course, taking a stance like this is much easier when you are one of the team's key assets, like Weddle, who is a six-time Pro Bowler. Players barely clinging to a roster spot are much less likely to refuse to cooperate, especially if coaches encourage them to spill the beans.

DEBRIEFINGS

Debriefings such as A. J. Jefferson underwent prior to playing the Cardinals are routine in the NFL. Seattle head coach Pete Carroll confirmed this in 2010 after the Seahawks had debriefed former Chargers player Charlie Whitehurst before a matchup between the two teams, "as everybody does when you've got a guy on your team who's played for the other guys."[6]

Current information on opposing teams is so valuable that players recently released or acquired from a rival team are commonly brought in for the sole purpose of being debriefed. These last-minute signings often create headaches for opposing coaches. For example, the Jets' signing of safety Andrew Sendejo from the Cowboys' practice squad in 2011 is rumored to have caused Dallas defensive coordinator Rob Ryan to trash his game plan and start anew.

The signing of practice-squad players for debriefs is particularly common as it does not burn an active roster spot. Matthew Bowen, a journeyman safety in the NFL from 2000 to 2006, elaborated on this: "The practice squad is a revolving door in the NFL, and while there are young guys developing on it, there is also a reason a team will sign an opposing team's practice squad player. Teams will gladly hand out a practice squad check for the week to get some new info. We did it all the time."[7]

Periodically, teams even add coaches for the sole purpose of debriefing them. In 2011, the Jets brought in Don Martindale, the briefly unemployed former defensive coordinator of the Denver Broncos, to instruct the coaching staff on the intricacies of the AFC West offenses.

The value of the information acquired in debriefings can vary substantially and typically rests upon three main factors: the amount of time since the individual departed his former team, the amount of time until the two teams play each other again, and the individual's position. Regarding timeliness, teams desire information that will still be pertinent the next time they play an opponent. The more recent the information is, the more likely the information will prove beneficial. After all, over time teams change players, plays, and strategies, and employ countermeasures to defend against collection attempts.

Audibles, injuries, and game-changing gadget plays like fake punts and trick plays are examples of time-sensitive information that a team looks to exploit through debriefing a recently released player. Acquiring such information in a league based on parity can easily prove the difference between winning and losing. For instance, the 1982 49ers led by coach Bill Walsh missed out on the playoffs as a result of a blocked field goal during the last game of the season. The player blocking the field goal had closed down on the kicker unblocked as a result of a stunt the

49ers were not anticipating. As if struck with a premonition of what was to come, in the lead-up to the game Walsh had nervously asked his special teams coach if there were any plays the Rams' special teams might run that would catch the 49ers' kicking unit unaware. The assistant assured Walsh there was no reason to fret. This lack of information cost the 49ers the game and ended their season.

While all members of a former team will have some helpful information, not all individuals are of equivalent debriefing value. Besides the obvious attributes of intelligence and memory, an individual's position on his former team is critical. Coaches and coordinators are the ideal candidates as they can provide a wealth of information. Quarterbacks and middle linebackers are the gold standard for players as they must understand the roles of each and every player in their respective offensive or defensive unit. Players outside of these two positions typically have less valuable information, but long-employed franchise-type players will also have plenty to share. Camp fodder—players that typically are brought in during training camp for numbers, for competition, or in case of injury—are the least likely to have information of value. But no matter how little time players may have spent on their former team, they generally have some information their new team would be interested in knowing, as every little tidbit can be advantageous.

Even off-the-field information about players from other teams is valuable, as teams are always looking to acquire new players via trades and free agency. Thus, teams collect information about players throughout the league to determine if the team wishes to pursue players and the best ways to go about this, such as where players are from and have family, the importance players place on playing for a winning team or Super Bowl contender, drug and alcohol abuse, work habits, intelligence, willingness to accept coaching, and leadership skills.

COUNTERMEASURES

As debriefings pose a perennial threat, teams employ a variety of countermeasures to protect vital information from escaping by means of this collection technique. Arguably, one of the most effective ways to defend against secrets being leaked by former players is to treat players well while they are with the team. When Eric Weddle talked about his reasons for not divulging the Ravens' secrets, he said, "I have a lot of respect for that place, not only how it helped my career and rejuvenated my career, how they treated myself and my family. But it's a very tight-knit group, and what would I be—what kind of man would I be if I just turned my back on all of them?"[8]

Of course, it is unrealistic to think that just treating players kindly is a panacea. The desire to win and to ensure they are contributing to their new team's success is intoxicating to most players. Therefore, more drastic measures are typically used to safeguard team information, and some are quite extreme. For example, Gene Ronzani, the Packers' head coach from 1950 to 1953, limited the damage his players could do if signed by another team by not issuing playbooks. He forced his players to memorize all plays by displaying them for 10 seconds. This amount of time was sufficient to allow players to learn their responsibilities but was not long enough to allow players to learn the responsibilities of their teammates. Having formerly been an assistant coach under Bears great George Halas and likely aware of some of his old coach's tricks, Ronzani was paranoid Halas would end up with a Packers playbook if they were issued. Halas used a similar tactic, though not quite as drastic. He allowed only quarterbacks to see the entire playbook. The remainder of the team could merely access their individual assignments for each play.

Another countermeasure that has been used is to insert information and/or plays that a team wants shared with opponents in its playbooks. The 2011 Jets used this tactic by issuing playbooks with the Seminole play call, a wildcat play where the football was directly snapped to a speedy player other than the quarterback. The coaching staff purposefully did not tell the players that the Seminole play call would never be used in the regular season. Jets coach Rex Ryan hoped to bamboozle their Week 1 opponent, the Cowboys, into wasting time preparing for this play. He was certain the Cowboys would add one of the Jets' preseason cuts to the team. While a tactic like this might seem rather inconsequential in the overall outcome of a game, coaches scrap for every inch gained, just like their players.

9

SIGNALS COLLECTION

I know we're all trying to get signals. We're all looking for an edge and that's about all I can say.[1]—Jon Gruden

DO YOU UNDERSTAND THIS SIGNAL, SHANAHAN?

It would have been perfectly understandable if Raiders owner and general manager Al Davis had been looking for an edge just before the opening Monday night game of the 1994 season. His opponent was the San Francisco 49ers, the gold standard of the NFL. With the exception of 1991, the 49ers had played in every NFC championship game since 1988 and had recently won back-to-back Super Bowl titles. They were led by future Hall of Fame quarterback Steve Young and supported by a dynamite cast including running back Ricky Watters, wide receiver Jerry Rice, and cornerback "Neon Deion" Sanders.

The Raiders were a strong team as well and had made the playoffs three of the past four seasons, but despite being frequent tournament participants they had been unable to reach the big game.

Simply put, they lacked the playmakers of the explosive San Francisco squad. Perhaps because of this, Davis wandered over to San Francisco's side of the field and lingered near the 49ers' huddle during pregame warm-ups. Conceivably, he was listening for a few nuggets of information, perhaps hoping to learn a couple of offensive play calls to give his team an edge. At least this is the purpose the 49ers' offense ascribed to his encroachment. Complaints soon reached the ear of 49ers offensive coordinator Mike Shanahan, who told his offense, "Guys we'll win the game. Don't worry about it. Don't let him bother you." However, while Shanahan refocused the offense, he also found Davis's close proximity disturbing. He thus pulled Steve Young aside and quietly instructed his quarterback, "Throw a go route. If you happen to hit that guy in the white outfit, you won't make me mad."

Of course, Davis was the guy in white. As instructed, Young went back out on the field and tossed his next pass in the direction of the Raiders legend. Nearly catastrophically, no one bothered to tell 49ers wide receiver Jerry Rice the plan, so he went sprinting after the ball headed straight for Davis. Neither Rice nor the Raiders' general manager seemed to realize their impending collision as the pass hung in the air. Reflecting on the situation, Shanahan confessed how nervous he was at the time: "Oh, my God. I wanted to scare him. I didn't want to kill him." Fortunately, Davis saw Rice barreling his way at the very last second and dove to the ground, narrowly avoiding the wide receiver. The ball, on the other hand, pelted Davis. This sent the 49ers' players and Shanahan into a fit of laughter. With his pride hurt more than his body, Davis stood up, stared coldly at San Francisco's offensive coordinator, and issued a signal that needed no deciphering—a one-finger salute.[2]

A TOUGH NUT TO CRACK

The practice of stealing signals, such as package signals, audibles, and spoken play calls (the latter was what Al Davis was potentially attempting to gather from the 49ers), dates back as far as the league itself. While some signals can be as simple as the obscene gesture Davis gave, they can be as complex as those given by a third-base coach in baseball: tummy pat, ear rub, nose tap, two blinks, and a chicken dance. Football signals take a variety of forms and often include hand signals, colors, symbols, signs, and even pictures. Trying to decipher these signals can be a very intensive, time-consuming endeavor, and success is far from guaranteed. More than one team has attempted to decode an opponent's signals with no better luck than the Japanese trying to crack messages passed along by the American Navajo code talkers during World War II. Still, week in and week out, the best minds in professional football labor away at this, trying to gain the upper hand on opponents.

PACKAGE SIGNALS

Before going into how teams collect on opponents, a quick synopsis of the types of signals teams utilize to communicate with their personnel and the benefits of deciphering these is in order. The most basic signals, and the easiest for opponents to decode, are package signals. They tell players who should be on the field prior to each and every play. One or more staff members patrol the sidelines shouting package calls at the same time another staff member holds up package signals to share this information with the players on the field who are likely unable to hear the package call. By knowing opponents' package signals, a team can create or attempt to prevent mismatches in personnel on the field. Also, by knowing an offense's personnel packages, a defensive coordinator can calculate the likelihood of a run or a pass play and whittle down the potential number of plays the offense is likely to call. Package signals are important enough that the very first item a defensive scouting report identifies is the person relaying these in for the upcoming opponent.

Package signals are especially vulnerable to collection because of their designed simplicity and the infrequency with which they are changed. Browns pro personnel scout Jeremy Green said he tracked the Steelers for five years, and they never changed their package signals during that entire time. In addition, assistant coaches who take a head coaching job elsewhere often use the same package signals as their previous team. So, by deciphering one opponent's package signals, a team might potentially gain knowledge of two, three, or even four teams' package signals.

PLAY CALLS

After getting the right players on the field, the next signals teams send in are play calls. Offensive play calls tell players exactly what their role is during each play, and the instructions are very precise. Defensive play calls differ from their offensive counterparts by only providing general guidelines, as defense is more reactive than offense by its very nature. They provide information such as blitzes and types of coverage, and as there are fewer defensive signals than offensive, they are also much easier to decipher.

Play calls can be relayed in a variety of ways. Firstly, a player on the field can issue a play. This was common in the NFL's infancy when quarterbacks, not coaches, chose plays and issued them in the huddle. A coach can also choose a play and have it relayed in to the players via a signal or by shuttling players onto the field with instructions. And lastly, in today's NFL, a coach can send plays to the quarterback on offense, and to a defender on defense, via headset communications.

AUDIBLES AND PLAY CALLS ISSUED AT THE LINE OF SCRIMMAGE

While teams usually execute the original play call, on occasion quarterbacks and defensive players call audibles—a change of play at the line of scrimmage—in order to counter or take advantage of the formation an opponent is showing. Players also occasionally issue play calls at the line of scrimmage sans huddle and without coaches' input, typically during hurry-up situations where time is critical. While the latter is technically not an audible, both will be referred to as audibles in this chapter for the purpose of simplicity, as the means to collect on and protect them are the same.

Audibles are usually issued vocally. As they can be overheard by opponents, teams give nonrevealing names to plays. With COVID restrictions producing football games in empty stadiums during the 2020 season, Las Vegas Raiders quarterback Derek Carr could be heard calling "Purple Walrus" and "Mom in Georgia."[3] As football stadiums are typically much louder, particularly when crowds try to drown out visiting offenses' communications by shouting, clapping, stomping their feet, and banging chairs, the use of verbal audibles is not always effective (as they can be inaudible audibles). For instance, during the 1989 Super Bowl, 49ers Hall of Fame quarterback Joe Montana attempted to call a verbal audible. Montana said, "I felt I was yelling as loud as I could, but no one could hear me." With the season riding on the outcome of the game, Montana depleted so much oxygen shouting that he nearly passed out when he dropped back to pass. He barely threw the ball away while suffering the effects of hyperventilation.[4]

To avoid situations like this, quarterbacks often use hand signals to call audibles when noise is a factor. Sometimes quarterbacks use a mix of verbal calls and hand signals to communicate information. For instance, Packers quarterback Aaron Rodgers often calls out audibles for his linemen at the line of scrimmage and flashes hand signals to receivers out of earshot.

THE VALUE OF SIGNALS COLLECTION

Since teams first began using signals to send in plays, opponents have attempted to decipher them by matching signals—including spoken play calls—with the plays run. And, done right, signals collection can completely overwhelm even a strong opponent. For example, quarterback Peyton Manning of the Denver Broncos was famous for his ability to diagnose defenses at the line of scrimmage and to call effective audibles. This ability helped the Broncos set the all-time NFL scoring record during the 2013 regular season and to reach the 2014 Super Bowl. Yet in the championship game versus the Seahawks, Denver's record-setting offense was virtually shut down, only managing to score 8 points. After the game, Seahawks cornerback Richard Sherman explained the reason for Denver's struggles. Prior to the Super Bowl, the Seahawks had deciphered the hand signals used by Manning. The Seattle secondary was thus aware of where the Broncos receivers would be running and jumped their routes anytime Manning issued an audible. With two weeks to prepare for the game, one or more of Seattle's defenders likely memorized the Broncos' hand-signaled audibles, or the Seahawks' coaching staff could have devised a wristband cheat sheet for a defender to reference during the game, a strategy formerly used by the Steelers under Bill Cowher.

COLLECTION STRATEGIES

The simplest way to collect on opponents' signals is to acquire their recently released players, as discussed in chapter 8. These individuals can either be debriefed for their knowledge of an opponent's signals prior to the game or can sit near a coach during the game to decipher signals in real time. Patriots coach Bill Belichick often signs opponents' recently cut players or practice-squad players for just this purpose.

While Belichick's use of this strategy is well known, it was being used in New England even before his arrival. In 1997, under head coach Pete Carroll, former Dolphins fullback Keith Byars taught the Patriots' defense Miami's hand signals prior to a first-round playoff matchup. Byars did his job so well that the Patriots' defensive players were able to repeat the Dolphins' signals to one another during the game in order to ensure all members of the defense were aware of the upcoming play. With this aid, the Patriots won the game in convincing fashion, 17–3.

Sometimes even not-so-recent signees can prove beneficial in deciphering signals. In 1991, Kansas City played San Francisco, and Chiefs quarterback Steve DeBerg realized partway through the game that he was able to decipher the offensive signals of the 49ers. DeBerg had played for the 49ers from 1977 to 1980, and San Francisco, led by coach Bill Walsh, had not bothered changing the signals in over a decade. DeBerg thus began feeding his coaches the incoming calls of every 49ers offensive play. Yet, even knowing what was coming, the Chiefs' defense could not stop the 49ers' offense, quarterbacked by the legendary Joe Montana.

Other times, players, and even coaches, have information about an opponent's signals because occasionally coaches do not bother to change signals when they change teams. Mike Shanahan made this mistake when he left his job as offensive coordinator of the Denver Broncos to become head coach of the Raiders in 1988. When the two teams faced off that season, Broncos head coach Dan Reeves realized Shanahan was using his former team's offensive signals and fed Broncos defensive coordinator Joe Collier the Raiders' offensive play calls before Los Angeles's offense snapped the ball. Unfortunately, knowing the exact call proved overwhelming for Collier, who eventually asked of Reeves, "Don't tell me the play, just tell me whether it's a run or pass." Even with this advantage, the Broncos were still beaten by the Raiders.[5]

Another way to decipher the signals of an opposing team is to painstakingly study them. One of the main tasks of an advance scout is to capture the opposing team's signals, commonly hand signals. Scouts attend games, watch the action from press box seats with binoculars, and record their observations with the aid of audio recorders. To aid in the deciphering of signals, scouts note the time in the game during which the play occurred, the down and yardage, signals made, and the resulting play that was run. This method is far more difficult than relying on a player with inside knowledge, as hand signals are relayed very quickly. One NFL scout explained the difficulties. "You can only talk [into the recorder] so fast and then to try to come up with the gestures they are doing, it's tough. They do it fast. They are used to doing it."[6]

Once scouts have collected this raw data, scouts and coaching staffs study it to look for trends. A single sighting of a play associated with its corresponding hand signal means little. The information needs to be corroborated, as scouts can easily record false or incomplete data if only seeing a signal a single time. Once a coach is certain he knows a play call associated with a specific hand signal, a player or assistant watches the opposing coordinator for the known hand signal.

For one game, NFL journeyman and offensive lineman Ross Tucker was chosen to watch Cowboys defensive coordinator Mike Zimmer for one particular signal that identified a blitz by the strong side and middle linebackers. Tucker was never informed of how the team gleaned the information, but he had a few ideas. "My guess is that the signal had been decoded by an advance scout who had attended a prior game, or perhaps another member of the coaching staff had previously worked with the other team's defensive coordinator."[7]

Advance scouts are also concerned with collecting package signals. They begin by searching for the coach whose job it is to send in packages. Locating this coach is not overly difficult as he typically wears something distinguishing to make him easily recognizable on the sideline. Scouts then watch and record the signals and make note of which players come on and off the field. Eventually this information makes its way into a report and is filed away for later use.

Watching film is also utilized to aid in the deciphering of signals, as teams can match the corresponding signals issued to plays run. Prior to 2006, teams were allowed to record their own video of opponents' signals and were only limited by the locations from which their videographers were allowed to film. Some teams really took advantage of this. For example, in 1980 Bears owner George Halas decided the Chicago staff should focus on deciphering the Packers' play calls communicated via hand signals. Bears director of player personnel Bill Tobin was given the assignment. After an offseason of film study, Tobin had matched the plays to the signals. Even with this knowledge the Bears still had difficulty exploiting what Tobin had learned because, during their next game against the Packers, Green Bay used two people to send in signals, with one person sending in dummy signals. This system stumped the Bears. However, after a delay-of-game call resulting from the confusion caused by having multiple signal callers, the Packers abandoned the dummy signal caller, and the Bears successfully deciphered the plays signaled in by Green Bay assistant Zeke Bratkowski for the remainder of the game. Tobin noted that this gave the Bears quite the advantage. "Whether it was going to be run or pass, which way, whether it was going to be a draw or screen—we had the whole bit.[8]

Because of examples like this, particularly relating to the Patriots, league executive Ray Anderson issued a memo in 2006 that stated that recording signals was henceforth a violation of league policy. While this made signals collection from film study more difficult, teams still find publicly available game footage with recorded signals on them. For example, former Steelers offensive coordinator Bruce Arians is convinced that the reason the Steelers lost a game to the Ravens in 2011 was because of audibles being picked up by the television broadcast of the game. He said, "We lost home-field advantage because Baltimore had somebody who was sitting and listening to all the TV copies. They tried to match those up to a play. We had an audible that was a quick screen and Terrell Suggs stepped up and intercepted it. That was going to be a walk-in touchdown. And they had the code word, and they got it off the mics."[9]

While having time to learn opponents' signals from debriefs and recordings is ideal, some signals, such as defensive play calls and package signals, are simple enough that they can be learned in a short amount of time just by watching an opponent sending them in during the course of a game. Spotters with binoculars are frequently assigned to coaching booths where they scrutinize and attempt to decipher opponents' package and defensive signals during games. Even players get in on the action occasionally. When Doug Pederson was a journeyman quarterback backing up Brett Favre in Green Bay, he routinely deciphered opponents' defensive signals by around the third series of the game by writing down the hand gestures and correlating them to the defense that was played. With the aid of a headset, Pederson would inform Favre of the defense's plans before most snaps. Pederson noted, "It was a big help to us offensively. I could tell him when a blitz was coming or what coverage, whatever it might be, based on the charting. It was all about trying to gain the competitive advantage."[10] Pederson added this was just one of the little things he learned to do in order to ensure he latched onto an NFL roster. He wrote, "Playing in the National Football League was a dream of mine, and I didn't want that dream to go away. So I did whatever it took to fight and scratch and make that roster."[11]

COUNTERMEASURES

Because compromised signals, particularly play calls, can be utterly devastating, teams implement a variety of countermeasures to protect them. A tactic once used to confuse scouts attempting to collect on package signals was to run players halfway onto the field before having some of them return to the sideline, while others proceeded to the huddle. This tactic is no longer quite as effective due to a rule change. Offensive players must now proceed to the huddle once they pass the numbers on the field or be penalized. Even with this restriction, teams still utilize the occasional personnel feint. Jets defensive coordinator Mike Pettine used this strategy in a game versus the Broncos in 2011. He treated his players like a yo-yo, sending a batch of them out a few steps, just far enough to be spotted and to confuse the Broncos' assistant calling in the Jets' package changes, and then yanking some back to the sideline once again. Another method used to counter signal collection efforts is to display multiple signals for each play call, with all but one of the signals being dummies—signals that are to be ignored by the team issuing them and shown simply to confuse opponents. In the '70s and '80s, defensive coordinator Tom Bass used a system like this where he sent in multiple signals with every play call. On first down, the first signal he relayed would be the correct one. On second down, the second signal would be the correct one, and so on. Other teams use more than one person to relay signals. One person relays the true signals while the others relay dummy signals.

Chip Kelly's Eagles took the use of multiple signal callers to a whole new level in 2014 and had five staff members send in signals for every play. To compound the difficulty of deciphering this system, the Eagles apparently gave their quarterback the option of selecting from multiple plays on any given down, allowing the quarterback to select the play that fit what the defense was showing. To further confuse the situation, it is believed the various signals provided different information to different groups of players. Thus, the offensive linemen might have been receiving instructions from one signal while the wide receivers received instructions from an entirely different signal. And of course, there is always the very real possibility that Coach Kelly used dummy signals as well. Confused? So were the Eagles' opponents.

Another countermeasure utilized is to issue signals at the last possible moment. Former Buccaneers defensive coordinator Tom Bass felt it was important to wait until only approximately 15 seconds remained on the play clock before relaying in a defensive signal. Using this technique, even if his team's defensive signals had been compromised, an opponent would have insufficient time to translate the signal, relay the play call to the offensive coordinator, and have the offensive coordinator send a new play call in to the quarterback.

Of course, a quarterback able to effectively audible could change plays quicker than this. Thus, when Wade Phillips's defenses would pair off against Peyton Manning, they waited until only 10 seconds were left on the play clock to get into their defensive alignments. Phillips instructed his defense to do this because Manning was so good with his presnap analysis and alteration of offensive play calls to take advantage of weaknesses in defensive alignments. Phillips figured 10 seconds was an insufficient amount of time for Manning to change the play call and get the snap off on time.

When a team strongly suspects or knows its signals are compromised, its coaches can also attempt to deceive their opponents by using their knowledge against them. For instance, in 2009 the Cowboys took advantage of Chargers linebacker Kevin Burnett, who had spent the previous four years with Dallas. Thinking he knew the play Tony Romo had just audibled, Burnett told teammate Stephen Cooper that the Cowboys had called a draw. Cooper signaled to the rest of the defense that Dallas would run the ball. This appeared to be exactly what was about to occur when Romo stretched out his arm to hand off the ball to running back Marion Barber, but instead, Romo kept the ball and threw it into the back of the end zone. Burnett quickly realized he had been suckered and that Dallas had used his knowledge of the Cowboys' offense against him.

Even when an opponent does not know the other team's signals, a crafty team can make them think they do. In 2011, Jets inside linebacker Bart Scott, a former Raven, made a pregame plan to call out the Ravens' defensive signals that he knew his ex-teammates would know. He was fairly certain the Ravens' offense would recognize the calls, might believe the Jets used similar terminology, and could be hoodwinked into believing they knew what the Jets' defensive plans were for the upcoming play.

An additional measure of protection is calling false audibles, so opponents that have or might have deciphered a team's audibles cannot be certain whether the audible or the original play call will be the upcoming play. Teams issuing the audibles know whether they change the upcoming play or not by the use of an indicator signal. Teammates know to ignore a quarterback shouting an audible who has not issued the correct indicator signal. As indicator signals are a last layer of defense, they are highly valued by opponents. Coach Bill Parcells wanted to know the indicator signals of opponents above all else. When journalist Michael Lewis asked Parcells what he would want to know from a hypothetical spy inside the Redskins, the coach replied, "I'd like to know their mechanism on audible. I'd like to know how they were changing the plays."[12] To prevent teams from figuring out this last line of defense, indicator signals are changed frequently.

To reduce the possibility and extent of compromise, teams also change their play call signals periodically. As former Falcons defender Tim Green noted: "You can't rely too heavily on secret information, because a savvy team will almost always change signals carried away to another team by a traitor."[13]

While one might think that all teams would change signals at least annually, and without fail, this is not the case. In 2014, the Packers changed their entire list of play call signals between training camp and the regular season for the first time since coach Mike McCarthy took over in 2006. Waiting so long might seem like a lapse in operational security, but coaches have to weigh the threat of having signals stolen with the threat of players not knowing what they are doing because of their unfamiliarity with newly issued signals. Consider that on 90 percent of plays at least one of the 11 players on any given team is not executing his role as assigned. Changing signals only increases the likelihood of mayhem and confusion. Also, the longer players are together and the more consistency there is with signals, the more a team can expand the number of play calls that can be relayed via signals.

The most common time for teams to issue new signals is at the start of a new season, frequently between final cuts and the start of the regular season. While issuing new signals earlier would be great to give players lots of time to learn them, waiting until after cuts are made prevents opponents from acquiring signals from recently released players.

In-season changes are difficult to implement, as teams usually only have a week between games, and hasty changes can be more damaging than beneficial if players are unable to remember the changes made. Thus, during the season itself, teams rarely change all the signals at once. Many teams, however, do alter a few signals every week and gradually change all their signals over time in this manner.

Still, teams do upon occasion feel the need to make major midseason signals changes if they deem the threat of vital secrets being used against them is imminent. Facing opponents that are very active and very successful at collecting signals, such as Bill Belichick's Patriots, is one reason for initiating such change. When Miami played New England in 2005, Dolphins coach Nick Saban ordered all defensive play signals to be changed prior to the game, stating, "They'll get them."[14]

Likewise, when teams play an opponent replete with their former players or coaches, they are also likely to change signals. The amount of change needed typically depends on the knowledge of the former coach or player. Quarterbacks, for example, tend to know all the calls for offensive linemen, wide receivers, and running backs, and a quarterback's transfer to an opponent is much more likely to result in major changes than an opponent acquiring a wide receiver who only knows his piece of the puzzle. Because of this, when the Bills acquired former Panthers backup quarterback Joe Webb, who was intimately familiar with the Panthers' offense, Carolina coach Ron Rivera ordered that all play calls and signals be changed after the 2017 preseason in order to prepare for a Week 2 matchup against the Bills. Just like that, the Bills lost what they probably assumed would be a big advantage, but disappointments like that are a fact of life in the NFL.

As this chapter's anecdotes have illustrated, teams spend a lot of time and effort attempting to collect other teams' signals and working to protect their own. Scouts and coaches spend seemingly endless days and sleepless nights at this, just for the hope of giving their team a game day advantage. While these efforts go completely unnoticed by fans, they can be as valuable as any contributions made by players on the field.

10

OPEN-SOURCE AND MEDIA COLLECTION

Why should I talk to you? I don't know where you're from. You could be from Florida! Or Afghanistan![1]—Al Davis in response to an unrecognized reporter's question

BEATEN BY THE MORNING PAPER

Denver's Mike Shanahan was closing in on a second league title as a head coach. The few coaches who had already achieved this feat were heroes of legend, and their names read like a Who's Who in the NFL Hall of Fame: Bill Walsh, Don Shula, Bill Parcells, Chuck Noll, Joe Gibbs, Jimmy Johnson, Tom Landry, George Seifert, Tom Flores, and Vince Lombardi.

They were the greatest coaches of their generations, but they had not won championships on their own either. Their teams had been replete with talent, and most had shared Shanahan's good fortune of being blessed with an elite quarterback like John Elway. Walsh had Joe Montana; Shula, Dan Marino; Noll, Terry Bradshaw; Johnson, Troy Aikman; Landry, Roger Staubach; Seifert, Joe Montana and Steve Young; Flores, Jim Plunkett; and Lombardi, Bart Starr. Only two coaches had ever won multiple Super Bowls without a marquee quarterback—Joe Gibbs and Bill Parcells—and Parcells had enjoyed the services of linebacker Lawrence Taylor, arguably the greatest defensive player ever. The advantage of an elite quarterback was not wasted on Shanahan. The Broncos' entire organization realized just how special Elway was and hoped he could deliver a second Super Bowl victory in what everyone assumed would be his final season before riding off into a Rocky Mountain sunset.

Of course, some pundits claimed Elway was past his prime, and it was true, his legs could no longer run the open plains of NFL stadiums as they once had. But he still possessed a rocket of an arm and a decade and a half of experience to compensate for whatever physical prowess might have been left behind in his youth. Perhaps he was no longer the quarterback who had carried the Denver franchise on his back and led them to three Super Bowls under head coach Dan Reeves, but he no longer needed to be that guy either. The Broncos had come a long way since then and were now stacked with talent. Their stars included running back Terrell Davis and tight end Shannon Sharpe, perennial Pro Bowlers and future Hall of Famers.

As talented as they were, Shanahan and the Broncos were taking nothing for granted as they headed into the championship game against the Atlanta Falcons. Talented teams lost all the time in the NFL, and complacency was one of the primary reasons for this. Because of this, Shanahan was constantly searching for any little advantage he could find. One way he did this was by gleaning information from the media. Of course, all teams engage in this practice to an extent, but Shanahan was on a whole different level. He had established an informant network that stretched the entire length of the United States and included contacts in the home cities of every NFL team. These contacts faxed local articles to Broncos' headquarters that contained helpful information regarding recent roster moves, injuries, and various other tidbits.

While the information garnered was certainly nothing earth shattering, it was often helpful, and the morning of the 1999 Super Bowl was an excellent case in point. Shanahan woke to read that Falcons free safety Eugene Robinson had been arrested the night before for soliciting an undercover prostitute. To make matters worse, earlier that same day Robinson had received the NFL's Bart Starr Award for demonstrating tremendous character.

This had several feasible implications. There was the possibility Falcons coach Dan Reeves might bench Robinson. The chances of this seemed remote, though, as Robinson was a star safety and had just been selected to his third Pro Bowl. Likely, Reeves would decide he was simply too good to leave out of the lineup. If this was the case, would Robinson be up to the task? His mental and physical readiness were questionable at best. After having been processed by the police, he had spent the night in jail and almost certainly had not benefited from a restful night's sleep. Furthermore, he would be distracted, wondering how his relations with family, friends, and teammates might be affected by his indiscretion. Realizing that Robinson would likely be struggling physically and emotionally with this ordeal, the Broncos' coaching staff altered their game plan and made a point of targeting Robinson early and often.

This decision returned huge dividends. The Broncos galloped for 121 yards on the ground by targeting Robinson's side of the field over and over again, and Elway completed an 80-yard touchdown pass to wide receiver Rod Smith with the safety in coverage. When the final whistle blew, Denver had 34 points to Atlanta's 19, and Coach Shanahan joined the ranks of an elite few.

COLLECTION

Intelligence gathering from publicly available information, such as the Broncos did before the 1999 Super Bowl, is known as open-source collection and is widely used throughout the NFL. Teams routinely scan the internet, newspapers, radio broadcasts, and television programs looking for information about opponents that might prove useful during an upcoming game. Really, open-source collection consists of little more than what you might do to see what your frenemies have been up to: a bit of research on Facebook, Instagram, or Twitter. Yes, NFL staffs check these sites for information as well. The only difference is NFL frenemies have national media exposure.

Particularly in today's day and age, the media spreads information more quickly than a wildfire, and one slip of the tongue can almost instantaneously provide an opponent with an unintended advantage. For instance, in 2018 Eagles middle linebacker Jordan Hicks divulged to a reporter that Nick Foles would be starting at quarterback over Carson Wentz for Philadelphia's season opener against Atlanta. This news quickly spread and was soon being reported on NFL Network. In cases like this, the media can prove to be a huge liability for teams with indiscreet players and at the same time a huge asset for opponents able to take advantage of the misfortune of their rivals.

In addition to sensitive information that team members accidentally let slip, media members with better access than most sometimes release information they have gleaned from talking to a coach in confidence or from watching closed practices. One such instance occurred before the 1976 AFC championship game between the Steelers and Raiders. The Pittsburgh media reported overly detailed information describing Pittsburgh practicing without the injured running back duo of Franco Harris and Rocky Bleier. This reporting tipped off the Raiders, who came prepared to face Pittsburgh's one-back formations to the immense frustration of Steelers coach Chuck Noll.

As this anecdote demonstrates, while teams love reporters and journalists for the information they can provide on opponents, they equally dread them for the threat they pose to their own interests. Above all else, reporters and journalists are feared for the possibility that they are spies, collecting information on behalf of an opposing team. After all, reporters would make great secret agents. In fact, investigative reporters are trained to collect information discreetly and even work under cover. Additionally, they are located in every NFL city, collect information for a living, and can ask a team's staff just about any football-related question under the guise of reporting on a story.

If the fear of a spy working on behalf of an NFL team seems far-fetched, consider this. Under the leadership of Al Davis, the Raiders maintained regular contact with sports journalists and sports broadcasters such as Will McDonough from Boston and Jerry Magee from San Diego as a way to collect information on opponents from around the NFL. Davis understood that if he gave a little information about his Raiders to reporters he would in return acquire some information about opponents. Of course, one can rest assured Davis carefully weighed the pros and cons of releasing any information and quite possibly disseminated misleading information as well.

Another reason that teams hesitate to share information with the media is because many television broadcasters are former NFL players, coaches, and executives who might potentially jump into a coaching or front-office position in the near future and use the information to the benefit of their new team. Such moves can create headaches for teams that have talked too much. This is precisely what happened in 2017 when former All-Pro safety John Lynch transitioned from the broadcast booth to being general manager of the San Francisco 49ers. During previous seasons, the NFC West rival Seattle Seahawks under coach Pete Carroll had shared a great deal of information with Lynch regarding opponents and the inner workings of the Seahawks' organization. Carroll said, "I don't think there's any question, the way he went about finding his information and getting answers to things. He was in depth beyond where most guys go. He wanted to know why and what were you thinking. Those kinds of things. I didn't really put it together. I thought he'd be doing *Monday Night Football* or something. . . . He was adding up his background and reservoir of information at the time. It makes sense it came out to get him a GM job."[2]

As if coaches need another reason to distrust reporters, upon occasion team personnel have even had the audacity to impersonate media members as well. Coach Paul Brown of Cleveland and later Cincinnati sent low-level members of his staff to pose as reporters during practices. Additionally, when Al Davis was an assistant coach with the Chargers in the early 1960s, he pretended to be a reporter during an interview session with a Bills player in order to ask about the details of a play Buffalo had used to score a touchdown against the Chargers. The player was even kind enough to sketch out the play for the wily assistant. The next time the two teams met, the Chargers used this exact same play against the Bills to score a touchdown of their own. Measures such as these just highlight the win-at-all-costs mentality that pervades the NFL.

COUNTERMEASURES

For all of these reasons and more, coaches have a long history of strained relations with the press. Certainly, the main reason for this is the media is constantly striving to gain more information about NFL teams, and those same teams are struggling to protect as much information as possible in order not to give competitors an advantage. As a frequent spokesman for the team, the head coach is often placed in a difficult situation. He is required to speak to the media per NFL policy but has to fend off questions from the media that he cannot or does not want to answer.

A rather humorous example of this took place during a pre–Super Bowl press conference in 1968. Half-joking about the level of coaching paranoia, sports journalist Jimmy Cannon asked Raiders coach Johnny Rauch, "If I held a gun to your head and you had to answer the question, 'What do you do more on offense, run or pass?' What would you say? Remember there's a gun at your head and you've got to answer."

"I'd say we tried to balance our offense," Rauch replied.

In unison, four media members shouted, "Bang."[3] Coaches are even seemingly willing to suffer hypothetical deaths to keep information from the media. "Whatever it takes," right?

While questions like this might seem innocuous, the incessant interrogation from the media wears on even the most patient of coaches, especially since divulging information is typically counterproductive to the team's goal of winning games. The choleric Bill Parcells is one coach who had a rocky relationship with the media, as he viewed news reports as a means for opponents to glean information about his team. He made this quite clear, once saying, "We're in the business of collecting information. We're not in the business of exchanging information."[4] In order to restrict the flow of information, Parcells even enacted a policy of not allowing his coordinators and assistants to speak with the media. This eventually proved problematic for the league. By 2007, so many of Parcells's former coaches had become head coaches and instituted similar media policies that the league decided to go on the counterattack and instituted its own policy requiring assistants to be available for interviews with the media on a weekly basis. After all, these interviews are free publicity for the NFL, and the league is as determined to succeed as players, coaches, and teams.

Just as teams are cautious in their exchanges with reporters, teams are also guarded with what they allow reporters to see and often restrict access to practices, or at least portions of practices. Reporters allowed inside a facility to observe closed practices are typically warned not to report on anything that could be considered strategic or give an advantage to opponents. Reporters generally abide by these requests, and those who do not find they are no longer welcome. Such was the case in 1977 when John Clayton of the *Pittsburgh Press*—the same guy you probably watched give draft analysis on ESPN until recently—reported the Steelers had been practicing in pads during the offseason, a practice in clear violation of the league rules. Steelers coach Chuck Noll thus accused Clayton of working on behalf of one of Pittsburgh's opponents, saying, "The thing that made it very bad was that the story was of no news to the people of Pittsburgh. So I have to assume that [Clayton] is working for the competition. He certainly wasn't working in the interest of the paper or the fans. As far as I'm concerned, he was working for the other people. The only way I can read it is espionage. I know for a fact that other people use other media for their interests, to spy."[5]

Teams are also very cautious about letting the media film any footage of a practice, as sensitive information can be leaked in this manner as well. Such an incident occurred prior to the 1994 Super Bowl. Cowboys coaches were hanging out watching a newscaster report on the upcoming game from the site of a Bills practice when they saw Buffalo quarterback Jim Kelly throwing shovel passes—short, underhanded tosses—to Thurman Thomas in the background. As the Bills had not used a shovel pass all season long, the coaches believed they had spotted a foreshadowing of what was to come. As a result of this serendipitous viewing, Cowboys coach Jimmy Johnson tweaked the defense, and the Bills' lone attempt at a shovel pass resulted in a Thomas fumble when the running back was hit quickly after catching the ball near the line of scrimmage.

While teams attempt to limit their exposure to the media as much as possible, this is often easier said than done. The demand for around-the-clock football news and updates is constant in today's information-sharing age. Teams, players, and coaches are bombarded with requests for interviews. The most intrusive reporters request nearly unlimited access at times. Such is the case with the HBO show *Hard Knocks*, which follows an NFL team around during training camp chronicling the highs, lows, challenges, and successes of NFL players, staffs, and teams. Due to the potential for disclosure of sensitive information, as well as the disturbance such filming creates, teams are reluctant to have the HBO film crew around. Arguably the best defensive end of his generation, J. J. Watt of the Houston Texans, learned the Miami Dolphins' snap count as a result of watching the show. Watt was kind enough to disclose this to the media but not before the Texans sacked Dolphins quarterback Ryan Tannehill twice and intercepted him three times in the 2012 season opener. Because of problems like this, teams routinely fight not to be featured on the show.

Another problem that teams encounter when dealing with out-of-town media is determining whether these visitors can be trusted. While coaches typically deal with the same local reporters over and over again, upon occasion, especially before big games where national media attention is attracted, unfamiliar out-of-town reporters with dubious loyalties roam the premises stalking their next story. When unsure of the loyalty of certain media members, one option is simply to have them removed from the premises. For instance, the Raiders escorted Denver journalist Woody Paige out of a Raiders practice held at the Oakland headquarters prior to the 1977 AFC championship game out of fear Woody might be a spy for the Broncos.

Teams also keep a close eye on players' social media posts in order to avoid critical leaks of information. For example, in the days leading up to a 2018 match between the Jaguars and the Jets, Jacksonville running back Leonard Fournette, who had been listed as "questionable," posted on Twitter that he was "happy to be back" for the game. He promptly deleted the tweet, undoubtedly after a frantic call from one of his coaches.

Perhaps the subject coaches are most tight-lipped about with the media and take painstaking steps to keep confidential is player injuries, and rightfully so. Being able to anticipate injured personnel in advance can greatly assist coaches with their game planning. For instance, during the 1993 Super Bowl, the Bills blocked a punt as a result of determining that Dixon Edwards, a Cowboys lineman on the punt unit, was injured and would likely be unable to play in the big game. As Buffalo had suspected, Edwards was on the bench for the first Dallas punt, and the Bills put their top special teams player, Steve Tasker, to go against Edwards's replacement. As Buffalo had hoped, Tasker took advantage of the matchup, slipped free inside, and got a hand on the ball.

Up until 1960 anything went, and teams took any measures they wanted to safeguard information about injured personnel. For example, on one occasion Packers coach Vince Lombardi along with team physician Dr. Nellen escorted star quarterback Bart Starr to the Saint Vincent Hospital to have an X-ray to see if Starr's finger was broken. X-ray technician Robert Strom met them at a fire exit as instructed by Lombardi in an earlier phone call. Dr. Nellen convinced Strom not to make a record of the visit, took the only copy of the X-ray once the appointment was complete, and hinted that Strom should make no mention of this visit to the media if any reporters came asking for information.

Injury protocol, or lack thereof, changed in 1960 after a dramatic shift in the gambling point spread of an upcoming Steelers-Redskins game sparked rumors the game would be fixed. An NFL investigation concluded a nationally published photograph of injured Pittsburgh quarterback Bobby Layne had caused the shift in the point spread; because of this, the NFL formalized an informal policy that had been implemented under the previous commissioner, Bert Bell, requiring teams to report injured personnel to NFL headquarters every Tuesday and Thursday during the season.

While this policy led to more transparency overall, coaches still employ a variety of tactics to safeguard player injury information. During his time with the Panthers, coach Ron Rivera made a point of not visiting the training room on Mondays before press conferences, thus limiting his knowledge of player injuries and ability to answer any questions on this subject.

Other coaches simply give vague responses to questions about injuries. After all, a quarterback with a known injured right shoulder might receive a few extra hits to the right side of his body from opponents in an attempt to aggravate the injury. A team might even shift its star defensive end from the right to the left side of the line in the hopes of facilitating those hits.

Coaches also occasionally exaggerate the degree of injury suffered by players to confuse their next opponents about players' availability and health. Patriots coach Bill Belichick is renowned for listing an abundance of players on injury reports in order to help conceal which players have serious injuries. He is far from the first to use this strategy. Weeb Ewbank of the Jets used it way back in 1968 while preparing for Paul Brown's Bengals. Prior to the matchup, Ewbank placed 14 of his players' names on the injury list that included everyone with a cut, bruise, scratch, or bump. Ewbank even included Randy Rasmussen, who had merely sustained a minor poke in the eye during the previous game. Such stratagems led Redskins coach George Allen to say, "You get reports, you know, about injuries and things like that, or some injury that's supposed to be worse than it is. Even if you get a report you don't know whether to believe it, and you can't bank on it anyway.

"The worst thing we could do is believe some of the propaganda that comes out. We could get psyched out. Too many players who are supposed to be injured end up playing."[6]

Saints coach Sean Payton had to learn this lesson the hard way in 2009. All week long the media had been reporting that Cowboys defensive end DeMarcus Ware had a neck injury and would not be playing when the teams faced one another. Confident Ware would be sitting out, Payton did not bother to game plan around one of the best defensive ends to ever play the game. Ware, however, did play and appeared unfazed by the injury. All game long he created headaches for the Saints and helped Dallas end New Orleans's run at a perfect season.

Other coaches leave injured personnel off injury reports. In October 2006, a Cowboys injury report listed only one player, a third-stringer. Even in the early parts of an NFL season, teams always have at least a handful of players banged up, but apparently not that day. When coach Bill Parcells was asked why offensive tackle Flozell Adams, who was not listed on the injury report, was gimping, Parcells sheepishly replied, "That's just how he runs." Another glaring omission from the injury report was defensive back Aaron Glenn, who was slated for arthroscopic surgery in just over a week's time.[7]

Another method that teams employ that goes beyond simple exaggeration of injuries to counter the risk of leaking potentially damaging information through the media is to facilitate the dissemination of completely false information. This not only can provide a temporary advantage if an opponent believes this information to be true and game plans around it, but also makes opponents hesitant to trust or utilize any future reports by the media. Weeb Ewbank used this strategy of issuing false information during his stretch as the Jets head coach from 1963 to 1973. He once asked reporter Larry Fox to insert into a Jets-Dolphins pregame article a blurb about how the Jets' trap plays were critical to the success of the team's offense. They weren't. When Fox asked why Ewbank wanted this added, the coach replied that he hoped Dolphins defensive lineman Manny Fernandez would read the bit and not be as aggressive in his rush to the ball as a result. The effects of operations such as this are usually minor at best, but in a league where the gap between victory and defeat is often paper thin, coaches would be foolish not to use every tool at their disposal.

Part Three

THE DRAFT AND FREE AGENCY

11

DRAFT PROSPECTS

It's not the size of the dog in the fight, but the size of the fight in the dog.[1]—Archie Griffin

SCOUTING BIG GAME AT THE WATERING HOLE

The Tampa Bay Buccaneers were on the clock in the 2012 NFL draft with the fifth overall pick. Although some of the top collegiate players had already been snatched off the board—such as quarterbacks Andrew Luck and Robert Griffin III—there were still plenty of jewels for the taking. Wide receiver Justin Blackmon, cornerback Morris Claiborne, safety Mark Barron, quarterback Ryan Tannehill, and linebacker Luke Kuechly were just some of the elite prospects who were still within reach of Buccaneers general manager Mark Dominik.

Tampa Bay had already spent endless hours scouting these prospects and countless numbers of their peers. Scouts and other members of the staff had visited their campuses, practices, and games; spoken with their friends, professors, and coaches; evaluated them; ranked them; and even compared them to players on the Buccaneers' roster. The question now was, Who was a good fit for Tampa Bay and ideally a value pick at No. 5?

As the Buccaneers prepared to select their newest team member, the Jacksonville Jaguars called and offered to trade the seventh overall pick and a fourth-rounder for Tampa Bay's fifth overall selection. Dominik quickly accepted the offer. There was a strong chance Tampa Bay would still be able to draft the prospect it wanted two picks later, and extra draft day capital is always helpful.

Several minutes later, league commissioner Roger Goodell announced the Jaguars had selected wide receiver Justin Blackmon out of Oklahoma State, a standout in college with dazzling potential. Blackmon had racked up an incredible 1,529 yards and 18 touchdowns in 2011 and could run a 40-yard dash like he was shot out of a cannon. Additionally, he had the prototypical size and strength of an elite NFL receiver. He was the complete package, at least on the field; off the field, though, was another story.

Wary of investing a high first-round draft pick on Blackmon, Dominik had sent a Buccaneers scout up to Stillwater, Oklahoma, to snoop around. The scout had camped out at Blackmon's favorite watering hole, sitting there from 3 to 11 p.m. for days on end, noting how many times the young wide receiver went in and out and monitoring how much he had to drink. The reports from the scout had not been favorable for Blackmon, and the Buccaneers had removed Blackmon from their draft board because of the receiver's propensity to imbibe.

Coming off a 4–12 season in 2011 with 10 straight losses, the Buccaneers needed to restock their roster with players that would be around for the long haul. From what he had learned about Blackmon, Dominik was not so sure the young wide receiver would last long in the league. NFL players work long hours, have stressful jobs, and spend lots of time far from home. For all of these reasons, NFL players and coaches alike frequently turn to the bottle for solace. Drafting a college prospect who was already engaging in heavy alcohol consumption was a recipe for disaster. Dominik and the Buccaneers had no need of players who were constantly three sheets to the wind.

The Buccaneers needed players who could be counted on to help turn the ship around for new head coach Greg Schiano. Since 2002 and the franchise's first Super Bowl victory under head coach Jon Gruden, Tampa Bay had been unable to sustain a long-term winning tradition and instead remained an enigmatic and inconsistent team. Winning seasons were almost always followed by losing seasons and vice versa, and some of those dark seasons had been really dark. The Bucs had gone 5–11 in 2004, 4–12 in 2006, 3–13 in 2009, and most recently 4–12 in 2011. If the

Buccaneers were going to leave those dismal seasons behind them, they needed successful drafts. Prospects like Blackmon were simply too risky to be counted on to develop into franchise players. The Jaguars were in a similar situation, as well, but perhaps Jacksonville's scouts had not dug up what Tampa Bay's had. Or maybe the siren's song of Blackmon's abilities had been irresistible to Jacksonville. After all, there was always a team willing to roll the dice for his kind of talent.

ASSESSING PROSPECTS

While the means used to assess Blackmon's draft status may seem atypical, going to such extraordinary lengths is not at all that unusual for assessing high first-round draft choices. In the case of Blackmon, the Buccaneers and Dominik avoided a bunch of trouble by not drafting the wide receiver. After being drafted, Blackmon was soon arrested twice for drug- or alcohol-related incidents. As a result of his troubles, rehab, and numerous arrests and NFL suspensions, Blackmon played only slightly more than a full season in the NFL. He was a disaster of a first-round pick, and the Jaguars felt the repercussions of this selection for many years.

Making smart draft choices is essential for teams to be successful in the NFL, because although preparation and game planning are important, typically the team with the best players wins, regardless of all other factors—including spying on opponents. For this reason, NFL teams focus a lot of their intelligence-collection efforts on draft prospects in order to make well-informed draft selections. Because just as the effectiveness of national-security-related decisions depends upon accurate intelligence assessment, and accurate intelligence assessment relies upon effective intelligence collection, success in the NFL draft depends upon both the collection and assessment of intelligence. Though draft collection is not as heavily focused on opponents' activities as the topics previously covered in this book, draft-related collection is every bit as vital to teams' success and often involves techniques every bit as stealthy, sly, and secretive.

Because of the draft's importance, teams dedicate a tremendous amount of resources to gathering information on prospects, as whiffing on just a single top draft choice can set a team back for years, and conversely, drafting an elite talent can turn a team into a perennial winner. One need only look at the fortunes of the teams lucky enough to have drafted star quarterbacks Peyton Manning, John Elway, or Dan Marino to see what a difference one player can make. Finding a marquee player is not all that easy, though. Often prospects who excel in college fail miserably in the pros, and likewise, unheralded college prospects can thrive in the NFL. While drafting well is no easy feat, salary-cap restrictions designed to promote parity and the sizable investment teams make in top draft choices only accentuate the need for successful drafts. While the importance of making good selections in the first and early rounds of the draft cannot be overstated, later selections are equally important. As of 2011, more than half the players in the league were drafted in the fifth round or later.

The process of assessing prospects has changed substantially since the implementation of the draft in 1936, but the core principles remain the same. Coaches are first and foremost searching for prospects with the necessary football skills and attributes to compete at the very highest level. While prospects' college careers are a good indicator of future NFL success, many additional factors need to be considered before teams can make their selections, including physical characteristics, mental characteristics, character, and medical history. Teams even delve into intangibles because while it may be easy to determine "the size of the dog in the fight," it is much tougher to figure out "the size of the fight in the dog." Thus, teams research everything about prospects in excruciating detail because these details are often the difference between success and failure in the NFL.

However, the process of assessing draft prospects was not always as refined as it is today and took years to gain a semblance of professionalism and decades more to mature into its current pseudoscience. During the first NFL draft in 1936, none of the general managers showed up with scouting reports. Rams owner Dan Reeves started the first real scouting department in professional football in the early 1940s. Most teams were woefully unprepared in comparison. During the 1940s, some teams attending the draft brought college football magazines to help them decide which players to select. General managers and coaches quickly realized that the teams that invested the most time and money in scouting were outperforming their peers in the draft, as well as contending for championships, and thus began emulating their examples.

While scouting has always been a function of NFL teams, it was very limited in the infancy of the league. Due largely to budgetary constraints, scouts could not always be sent to assess talent around the country, and therefore players tended to be from the same general region as the team that drafted them. NFL coaches also relied heavily on word of mouth from trusted players and collegiate peers to select draft prospects. Additionally, coaches watched what limited film was available to help them decide. When all else failed, coaches selected prospects from the All-America Team.

By the midpoint of the 20th century, scouting was still overwhelmingly an amateurish affair. For example, in the 1956 draft the Steelers selected Gary Glick, a second-team All-American defensive back from Colorado A&M, with the No. 1 overall pick based solely upon his reputation and a letter of recommendation sent by his college coach. A letter of recommendation was also the impetus behind the Colts signing Hall of Fame quarterback Johnny Unitas. Unitas had been cut from the Steelers in his rookie year and was playing for the semipro Bloomfield Rams when Colts coach Weeb Ewbank received an anonymous letter touting the skills of the young quarterback. The Colts signed Unitas shortly thereafter, and the rest is history. Looking back on the letter, Ewbank suspected Unitas himself had written it. When Ewbank asked Unitas about the matter, the quarterback only grinned. Talk about a man willing to do "whatever it takes."

While the scouting process was still maturing in the 1950s, it was leaps and bounds more organized and professional than in the NFL's nascency. During this period, the Rams employed the first full-time scout, and other teams soon followed suit. Jack Vainisi, who was in charge of scouting for the Packers from 1950 to 1960, elevated NFL scouting to a whole new level. He began collecting information on players from college coaches who provided Vainisi with written reports in exchange for a $25 fee. Furthermore, Vainisi took to the road frequently to see promising prospects in person. From reports and his scouting trips, Vainisi ranked thousands of prospects and created 18 large binders of prospect dossiers. All of Vainisi's methods spread throughout the league in time.

The 1960s saw the introduction of computers to help facilitate drafting. Tex Schramm started this trend by hiring IBM employee Salam

Qureishi in 1962 to design a computer program that would be better at selecting draft choices than humans. He quite possibly succeeded. During the 1964 draft, aided by Qureishi's program the Cowboys selected three future Hall of Fame players. What is truly remarkable, however, is that two of the players were selected after coach Tom Landry had already gone home due to the perceived lack of college talent remaining on the board. Aided by Qureishi's program, Tex Schramm grabbed Bob Hayes in the seventh round and Roger Staubach in the 10th. Both men would be selected into the NFL's Hall of Fame, along with Cowboys second-round pick Mel Renfro.

As late as the early 1970s, some teams still relied almost entirely on a single scout to run their college scouting operations. Naturally, trying to monitor the best college players from around the nation with a barebones staff was unrealistic. The enormity of the task, combined with the expense, led teams to band together in their efforts to assess draft prospects. In 1960, the Cowboys, Rams, and 49ers joined together to form Troika, an alliance to share the cost of computer-assisted prospect evaluations. In 1963 the Bears-Lions-Eagles-Steelers Talent Organization (BLESTO) materialized to share prospect information. Years later the Dolphins also joined BLESTO out of fear that if something happened to head scout Joe Thomas, Miami would be in real trouble. BLESTO soon encountered competition when the Colts, Browns, Packers, and Cardinals formed the Central Eastern Personnel Organization for the same purpose in 1964.

In the 1980s, videotape began replacing 16 mm film and made the job of scouts easier. Videotape technology allowed universities to replicate game footage with relative ease, and universities began sending out film more freely to NFL teams. Prior to this, college scouts had to spend a great deal of time on college campuses across America watching footage of prospects on 16 mm film. NFL scouts would bring their own Kodak film projectors and were often stuffed into a room with as many as 10 of their counterparts, running 10 discrete projectors at the same time. Occasionally scouts would get lucky, and a university would send game footage to them, but even then most film had to be returned within a couple of days.

While the limitations of film distribution hindered most scouting operations, for others it was an opportunity. For instance, Alabama A&M wide receiver John Stallworth caught the eye of the Pittsburgh staff leading up to the 1974 draft. Because Stallworth had attended a small and lesser-known college program and had run a slow 40-yard dash, he was not considered a top prospect by most NFL teams. Steelers scout Bill Nunn felt the slow run time was due to the long grass at Alabama A&M and managed to acquire the only film reel of Stallworth from the university. To prevent any other teams from having the opportunity to view Stallworth's film, Nunn purposefully delayed returning the reel. This effort just might have made the difference, as Stallworth slipped all the way to the fourth round, where the Steelers grabbed Coach Noll's top choice. Stallworth went on to become one of the best wide receivers in league history and helped Pittsburgh to four Super Bowl victories.

Today, most teams commence the scouting process by identifying draft-worthy talent with the use of BLESTO and/or National Football Scouting Inc. (more commonly known as "National"). Only a few modern-day teams eschew the use of outside scouting services. The Raiders under the late Al Davis were one such team preferring to perform all scouting activities in-house without any assistance or bias.

Outside scouting services lay a strong foundation for NFL teams assessing collegiate prospects, as they provide a ranked listing by position based upon an amalgamation of scouting grades accumulated at junior days held by NCAA teams. These listings serve as a starting point for scouts performing their talent hunt. They are not, however, relied upon to be the end-all-be-all, as some prospects experience meteoric rises just a few weeks into the NCAA season, and experienced scouts are already aware of most of the prospects with NFL-level talent in their area of responsibility.

This is because most NFL talent comes from predominately the same universities year in and year out, and regional scouts typically frequent the same practice fields, stadiums, and locker rooms multiple times a year. This helps keep scouts updated on prospects' progress and reduces the chances of scouts only seeing prospects on a particularly good or bad day. These scouts work tirelessly and are on the road up to 200 days a year. Jack Vainisi, an incredible talent scout who provided the Packers with a wealth of talent in Green Bay, took his honeymoon in 1952 by going through key football states signing college players. He must have had one angel of a wife. Most wives would have likely signed with another husband.

Out on the road, scouts spend a lot of time watching prospects and talking with college coaching staffs. Watching practices is crucial to obtaining an understanding of prospects' willingness to work hard, while games obviously provide the best opportunity to see prospects in action against competition. Scouts also continue to watch footage of prospects, of course, but no longer have to do so from the confines of small college film rooms.

Since approximately 2010, the digitization of game footage has made the job of scouts much easier. College teams now digitally upload all games to the NFL Dub Center using standardized NFL Competition Committee–approved formatting. The Dub Center then formats and packages the games before placing them on the T3 system, which can be accessed by all NFL teams. In addition to team-supplied footage, the Dub Center also provides televised footage of games.[2] Scouts are thus able to watch recordings of every major Division 1, 2, and 3 college game, approximately 1,500 games per year, from anywhere on the planet with an internet connection. How do we order that sports package?

While it might seem logical that teams would focus their scouting efforts based on team needs and draft position, teams evaluate all prospects who have the potential to play professional football. Just because a team has the 32nd pick in an upcoming draft does not mean scouts get to skip the evaluations of prospects likely to be drafted at the top of the first round. The star player of an NFL team might suddenly get arrested, suffer an injury, die, or even retire unexpectedly, and a team might find the need to move up in the draft in a hurry. Likewise, the team with the first pick cannot ignore prospects expected to go in the middle portion or tail end of the first round. After all, an opponent might offer a king's ransom in picks to move up the draft board.

Such fortune befell the Browns in 2016. In trades with the Eagles and Titans, Cleveland exchanged the draft's second overall pick and a conditional fourth-round draft choice for the 15th overall pick, two third-round selections, first- and second-round picks in 2017, a second-rounder in 2018, and additional lower-round picks.

After scouting assessments have been confirmed and tweaked as required and the offseason begins, coaches and general managers begin taking a look at prospects. They look over written assessments, watch film, and scrutinize prospects over the course of numerous postseason events. The first is the Senior Bowl. Here teams get their first opportunity to interview the top senior prospects from around the country over the course of a week of practices leading up to the game.

The National Invitation Camp, better known as the National Combine, is the next opportunity to observe and interview prospects. The camp began in 1982 and is held every February. The Combine gives prospects the opportunity to show off their football skills and their physical abilities. While evaluations vary somewhat by position, nearly all prospects are tested in the 20-yard shuttle, 40-yard dash, broad jump, vertical jump, and bench press. Additionally, prospects undergo the Wonderlic test, an assessment that captures their ability to learn and problem solve. You can even take the test yourself if you wish. It can be found online along with the results of your favorite players.

Medical information on prospects is also supplied to teams at the National Combine. Before the 1970s, teams did not conduct physical exams of prospects, but all of that changed in 1976 when the Jets started bringing players to their headquarters to receive an orthopedic physical by a team physician. Soon other teams began doing the same, and this resulted in quite a lot of unnecessary travel for draft prospects and excessive expenses for teams. To alleviate the need for all NFL teams to conduct medical evaluations on the same prospects, draft prospects now undergo a thorough physical with input from a medical committee prior to the National Combine, and the medical results are shared with every NFL team.

Teams are also given the opportunity to interview prospects at the National Combine in an organized, structured, and scheduled environment. Interviews are conducted in hotel rooms and given a 15-minute time limit. Some teams' interviews are very informal, while others purposefully grill draft prospects with stress-inducing questions to see how they will react. The interview process is also commonly used as a way to ask prospects about weaknesses in their games and any character issues that might have arisen in their past.

Prospects have an interest in putting their best feet forward and often try to hide any indiscretions. Out of desperation to make a team or to get drafted higher, some flat out lie, but this can quickly backfire if teams suspect that a prospect is not being honest with them. Falcons general manager Thomas Dimitroff explained, "Every year, you're gonna have a handful of players that are gonna have a knack for being coy and getting themselves out of trouble. One of the major black marks next to a name is when someone is perceived as being a con guy. . . . If you're full of crap, you're truly fighting an uphill battle."[3]

Various NFL teams hand prospects psychological tests to answer at the National Combine, and some of the questions on these can be very strange. Prospects have been asked if they are attracted to their mother and when they lost their virginity or requested to list all the possible uses for items such as bricks and paper clips. One of the questions the Giants are notorious for asking is, "If you were a cat or dog, which would you be?" Most questions like this are simply meant to see how a player thinks on his feet or reacts to a stressful situation, but some odd questions have a more direct purpose. Offensive lineman Chris Myers was asked about his parents' height and weight in the hopes of understanding if he was still likely to grow or increase the size of his frame. He declined to respond to the question about his mother's weight. "I didn't want to disrespect my mom, so I left that question blank."[4] Smart man!

To limit some of the shenanigans that NFL teams put prospects through at the Combine, the league issued a warning in 2022 that inappropriate interviews could cost teams a draft pick in the first- to fourth-round range and a fine of no less than $150,000.

Some teams even go beyond psychological testing and bring in psychologists to interview players at the National Combine. Bill Polian began using psychologists during his stint as the general manager of the Buffalo Bills from 1986 to 1993 in order to gauge how a prospect would react under pressure and how they would best learn new information. This just goes to show, teams truly use every tool at their disposal to assess prospects and ensure they have the best chance possible of hitting with their draft picks.

After the National Combine, teams only have two remaining opportunities to view and interact with prospects. The first is at university senior days. These are basically minicombines held by each of the universities, which give prospects a chance to perform in a more familiar and relaxed environment. They also afford prospects an opportunity to improve results from the National Combine and provide prospects who were injured at that time an additional opportunity to be tested.

Coaches then have a final opportunity to interact with prospects by bringing them to team facilities for workouts and interviews. Prospects who are brought to a team's facility are likely draft targets of that team, but of course, prospects can also be brought in just to throw opponents off the scent of a team's intended targets. Teams often fall in love with certain prospects and do anything they can to prevent their interests from being known.

For those prospects considered worthy of a first-round pick, and often lower picks as well, anyone from the team who comes in contact with those prospects is debriefed. Joe Banner, the president of the Eagles from 1995 to 2012 and chief executive officer of the Browns from 2012 to 2013, elaborated on some of the questions frequently asked of staff members coming into contact with top-tier prospects. "Was he friendly? Was he on time? Did he sound like he wanted to be here? Did you feel like he's a solid guy? What did he talk about?" As another means to assess prospects, teams often mess with them just a little bit to see how they will react. For instance, a driver may purposefully arrive late to pick up a prospect from the airport.[5] A team might remove a prospect from the draft board who flies off the handle or is disrespectful in such a situation.

Upon occasion, teams turn to private companies to assist them in assessing prospects. Scott McCloughan, a longtime evaluator of talent with multiple NFL teams, started up Instinctive Scouting in 2014 based on his reputation for finding draft gems. Teams pay McCloughan up to $75,000 for player evaluations.

NFL teams also look into prospects' backgrounds. This practice dates all the way back to the founding father of the NFL, Bears owner-coach George Halas, who researched every prospect he targeted. In the modern NFL, scouts conduct the first level of background investigations on prospects and interview people who have coached, played with, or dealt professionally or personally with prospects, in order to learn all about them. Talking to those within a prospect's circle of contacts is vital because scouts are restricted by NCAA rules from talking with prospects during their NCAA careers, thus leaving teams with only several opportunities to hear directly from prospects before the draft.

Good scouts have a wealth of sources, as many as journalists, who are capable of providing information on prospects. Teams even interview their own players if they played with prospects in college. For instance, before the 2004 draft the Falcons asked quarterback Michael Vick about DeAngelo Hall, a former Virginia Tech teammate of Vick's. In hindsight, the Falcons probably would have been better off getting a character reference from someone who did not operate a dogfighting ring.

Football coaches are the most common target for interviews, but trainers, former teammates, NCAA compliance directors, employers, resident advisors, neighbors, professors, tutors, law enforcement officials, friends, and family are often interviewed as well. In the early 2000s, the Falcons under the leadership of general manager Rich McKay asked scouts to interview a minimum of three sources about potential draftees and ideally at least five. McKay further encouraged scouts to interview people outside of football to get a well-rounded picture of prospects. When you consider teams are looking at hundreds of prospects, this quickly becomes a never-ending job, but this is the dedication required to succeed in the ultracompetitive NFL.

The task is further complicated by the reluctance of many college coaches, staff members, friends, and family to say anything negative about prospects, particularly when it comes to character. For this reason it is important for scouts to cultivate relationships with college football staffs. Former Bills general manager Tom Donahoe said, "You need guys you can trust that will tell you if someone is a good character guy or no. If you have developed those right relationships, you'll get an honest evaluation."[6]

Coaches in particular are often reluctant to speak ill of prospects. Penn State under the leadership of coach Joe Paterno took the approach of being less than frank in providing player assessments, with the rationalization that having players selected high in the draft benefited Penn State and that providing negative information would only hurt the university's football program. As some college staffs, like Penn State's under Paterno, are unwilling to share any negative information on prospects, successful scouts must be adept at picking up on subtle cues indicating when additional research needs to be conducted.

For example, during the lead-up to the 1988 draft, the Steelers spoke repeatedly with the Eastern Kentucky head coach about Aaron Jones, a defensive end the Steelers were very interested in drafting and ultimately picked in the first round. However, every time a Steelers representative talked to the coach, he diverted the conversation to John Jackson, another player on the team. Jones went on to have a rather pedestrian NFL career, and the Steelers' staff regretted not picking up on the cues given off by the Eastern Kentucky coach. Tony Dungy, the Steelers' defensive coordinator at the time, said, "If I had been a seasoned coach, I would have picked up on that. And I think Chuck [Noll] knew better, but he drafted him in the first round." Luckily for the Steelers, they also drafted John Jackson in the 10th round, who ended up being a complete steal.[7]

When confronted with staffs that are reluctant to speak candidly about prospects, scouts often look for coaches and staff members hoping to eventually move into the NFL ranks themselves. Sometimes such individuals are willing to provide honest assessments with the belief that their helpfulness will one day be rewarded with NFL employment. Just as players are willing to do "whatever it takes" to make a team, members of college staffs are just as hungry to join the ranks of the NFL elite.

While all prospects' backgrounds are checked out to a certain extent, those considered potential top draft prospects are examined more thoroughly than most. Character checks for such prospects go back as far as junior high. Scouts frequently talk with former teachers, academic advisors, and principals. Prior to picking wide receiver Mike Williams in the 2010 draft, the Buccaneers even interviewed his kindergarten teacher. Warren Sapp had his academic record examined all the way back to the eighth grade and was amazed at how thoroughly teams combed through his past. "I heard about some of the stuff they found and I thought, 'Damn, how deep can they dig on me.'"[8] Every bit of information teams find is analyzed, down to how many speeding tickets prospects have received and whether they were paid in a timely manner.

Teams even go so far as to hire private investigators to surveil prospects. This occurred in 1987 with the Lions' first-round pick, defensive tackle Reggie Rogers. As teams grew nervous of this talented defender's off-field antics, one team—not the Lions—employed a private eye to follow Rogers around Seattle. Such efforts just might have saved the team from drafting the troubled player, who would spend a year in jail for killing three teenagers in an alcohol-related crash.

Of course, these detailed investigations to research prospects' backgrounds are expensive. In 1996 a *Sports Illustrated* article revealed that New England spent approximately $1 million per year on this type of collection. This is just small change, though, for NFL teams that are willing to fork over hundreds of millions of dollars in salaries and team-related expenses.

Starting around 2011, teams also began examining prospects' social media sites. When Eric Mangini coached the Jets, the team checked on prospects' Myspace pages for potentially troubling information. If any was found, the team would print it out and bring it to an interview with the prospect to discuss. Some teams use interns, low-ranking staff members, or scouts to look through social media accounts, with instructions on what to look for. Other teams, such as the Panthers, use software that is capable of searching through, identifying, and monitoring all prospects' social media sites. As prospects update their social media accounts, the software records this in a consolidated and easy-to-review fashion. The software can even sift through social media posts using keyword searches. Thus, if teams want to know if prospects are posting about gang activity, drug use, or alcohol abuse, terms relevant to these activities just need to be entered. Additionally, even times of posts can be monitored to see if prospects are routinely out late at night. Getting this type of software working on behalf of teams is as simple as knowing the names or handles of prospects.

These social media checks can be very revealing and give teams a good indication of the type of person they are considering drafting. For example, a social media check of a first-round prospect in 2011 revealed a photograph of an apparent pile of cocaine on one account.

Some teams even have team security personnel conduct research as part of the background review process. The use of team security directors to help vet prospects began in 1997 under Jets coach Bill Parcells and his head of security, Steve Yarnell. Other teams quickly followed suit. Team security directors, typically former law enforcement or FBI officials, do much more than just examine social media sites. They use a variety of means to search for any hint of a troubled past that scouts might have missed. Security directors interview or reinterview people, conduct criminal background checks, and coordinate with law enforcement officials. The latter is particularly important, as law enforcement officials will often share information with security directors they are unwilling to share with scouts: records that were sealed, intelligence about criminal charges that were dropped, or even rumors of criminal activity. The law enforcement background often makes all the difference.

Clearly, teams spend a tremendous amount of time and effort assessing prospects, and while there are more misses than hits in the draft, teams work around the clock to maximize their chances of success, identify potential pitfalls, and locate the next draft day steal. So, keep that in mind the next time your team drafts an unknown, unheralded player in lieu of the next "sure thing" and you are cursing at your television set. Your team's draft gurus very likely know something you don't.

12

OPPONENTS' DRAFT TARGETS

We tried to hide our interest a little bit. I never spoke with Patrick; I never zoomed with him. I told our coaches, "Don't call him." I told our scouts, "Don't call, don't Zoom." I didn't go to Alabama pro day. This is a kid we targeted; this is a kid we wanted.[1]—Broncos general manager George Paton on drafting Patrick Surtain II

KNOW THE COMPETITION

The Cowboys were determined to address their defense in the 2005 NFL draft. After all, it had been the team's Achilles' heel last season, and the lowlights included surrendering 35 points in Week 1 against the Vikings, 41 in Week 7 versus the Packers, 49 in Week 10 against the Eagles, and 39 in Week 13 against the Seahawks. Over the course of the season, only five teams had conceded more points than Dallas.

Fortunately, there was hope. In spite of the Cowboys' defensive struggles the team was improving. The year 2003 had been the first time since 1998 Dallas had won more games than it had lost, and in spite of the team having regressed in 2004, the upcoming 2005 season held promise with coach Bill Parcells now in his third year on the job. Parcells was a well-respected coach in NFL circles and renowned for his ability to turn around struggling franchises. He had brought the Patriots all the way to a Super Bowl in New England and more recently resurrected a seemingly hopeless Jets team. Parcells had already shown some of the same magic in year one with the Cowboys, and everyone on the

Dallas staff was excited for year three, especially with two first-round draft picks to bolster the squad.

Big changes were underway, and none bigger than the Cowboys' transition from a 4–3 to a 3–4 defense. This was no small endeavor and meant shifting some players to new positions and finding all new players to fill others. Most critical of all, the Cowboys still needed to add the secret sauce to the new defense, outside linebackers big enough to battle offensive tackles, yet fast enough to cover tight ends. Needless to say, they were a rare breed.

National scout Jeff Ireland and the rest of the Cowboys' scouting team had been hard at work on this issue, though, and felt they had found a star in the making in defensive end DeMarcus Ware out of Troy University. Problematically, Parcells had his eye on another target, defensive end Marcus Spears, who had just led Louisiana State University to a national championship. While both sides liked both Ware and Spears, each felt their choice was superior. As a result, neither side was willing to budge, and the Cowboys were facing a good old-fashioned Texas standoff.

The tiebreaker, as it always does in Dallas, went to Cowboys owner Jerry Jones. He happened to agree with Ireland and the Cowboys' scouting staff that Ware was the better prospect. Jones, however, had promised Parcells final say in the operational control of the football team, and that included matters relating to player personnel. This had been one of the coach's stipulations for taking the job in the first place. Of course, as the owner and general manager, Jones could do as he pleased, promises be damned. He had made difficult choices before, and nettling Parcells over a draft choice was small potatoes compared to some of the other dust storms Jones had kicked up in Dallas.

Upon taking over the organization, Jones had fired Cowboys legend Tom Landry, who had coached the team for 29 straight seasons, brought the team to five Super Bowls, and won two NFL championships. He had also ousted Cowboys general manager Tex Schramm around the same time. The man was nearly as storied as Landry and had assembled some of the greatest teams in NFL history with his revolutionary scouting methods.

Jones's replacements for Landry and Schramm were equally controversial. Head coach Jimmy Johnson came from the University of Miami with no professional coaching experience and was a former teammate of Jones's at the University of Arkansas. Many saw Johnson's appointment as nothing more than a misguided, nostalgic, let's-get-the-band-back-together, ill-reasoned decision that was destined to fail. For the general manager position, Jones selected none other than himself—a man who had never played, administered, or coached a minute of professional football.

All of this is to say, Jones was comfortable making difficult and unpopular decisions, and while his methods were certainly unusual, it was tough to argue with the results. The Dallas Cowboys had won three Super Bowls since his taking of the reins. Only the Patriots had done as well. He had even made the Cowboys into "America's Team," and he planned to keep it that way, even if it meant chapping Parcells's hide.

The night before the draft, Jones watched footage of Ware and Spears one last time and reconfirmed his preference for Ware; he then held a meeting the next morning where Parcells was informed, "Coach, we're going to pick Ware." Parcells, or the Big Tuna, as his players affectionately referred to him, was livid and fumed for hours after being given the news.

Ireland attempted to placate Parcells by saying, "Coach, don't look at it as Ware or Spears. It's Ware and Spears." Ireland then unveiled a draft day plan to lasso both prospects but stated Ware would need to be selected first in order to pull this off. Ireland based this belief on his knowledge of team needs throughout the NFL.

Parcells doubted this was possible and said, "I don't think you're right, but we'll see." Much to Parcells's shock and delight, Ireland's plan worked. The Cowboys corralled both their targets, selecting Ware with the 11th overall pick and Spears with the 20th.[2]

COLLECTING ON OPPONENTS' DRAFT TARGETS

The above anecdote illustrates the importance of knowing the wants and needs of other NFL teams. Without this information, the Cowboys might have missed out on either Ware or Spears. Even worse, the Cowboys might have tried to trade up in the draft to land both, needlessly wasting valuable draft picks. Because having knowledge of other teams' draft needs and targets is so vital, NFL teams collect on these to improve their odds of acquiring their desired prospects and having the best draft possible.

Knowledge of opponents' draft targets can tell a team if a prospect will be available when it picks; if the team will need to move up to select a prospect; or if the team can move down, acquire additional draft picks, and still acquire the same target. Teams are always trying to obtain maximum value for their draft picks, and the further along in the draft that teams can select their desired prospects, the better off they will be. However, if teams wait too long, they risk losing their prized targets to an opponent. Falcons president Rich McKay looks at it like a business transaction. "You want to buy wholesale. You'll pay retail, but you never want to pay the marked-up price."[3] For this reason, teams spend a lot of time collecting on how other teams rate draft prospects.

Patriots coach Bill Belichick said this about the draft: "It's such a process, and part of it is knowing what the league thinks. We have players on our board and we look up there and say, 'We're probably higher on this player than any other team in the league.' You see mock drafts out there and the player is not mentioned in the first round. In any of them. Scouts talk, and you kind of get a feel that no one else sees the player, quite like we do. On the flip side, there are guys that we might take, say in the third round and we know someone's going to take him in the first. So, again, it comes back to homework."[4]

As Belichick alluded to, much of the information about how opponents view prospects is gathered on regional scouting circuits. These circuits are relatively small with generally the same universities turning out the bulk of NFL talent year after year. Furthermore, a tremendous number of scouts and coaches from across the league are brought together during the Senior Bowl, the Combine, and university senior days, providing additional venues of collection. As scouts from opposing teams spend a lot of time in the same locales, they inevitably talk to one another, establish friendships, share assessments of prospects, and build up trust in one another's opinions.

Some scouts even use their counterparts' opinions to help verify their own assessments. Former scout and current Cowboys director of college scouting Lionel Vital tells why this is the case: "When I was a young scout, my first five years, I was guessing some, because you have no history to gauge. When you get in this for ten years or twelve years, now you have twelve drafts to compare it to. But in your first couple of years, you really don't know. You've got to be confident, and you've got to act like you know and all that, but you're guessing your ass off."[5]

While sharing information in this manner might seem harmless, good scouts can turn such seemingly innocuous conversations to their team's advantage. Ron Wolf, a scout for Al Davis's Oakland Raiders during the 1960s, was so good at piecing together bits of draft information that he would routinely predict draft selections of other NFL teams throughout all the rounds of the draft. He even accounted for the intelligence of the other teams' staffs when predicting draft picks. While Wolf was in a class of his own in this regard, it should be noted he was no ordinary scout. He was a former army intelligence officer who had operated in West Berlin during the height of the Cold War.

Another method that teams use to identify opponents' draft targets is to analyze requests for trades leading up to and during the draft, particularly at the top of the draft where the best prospects are typically drafted in a fairly predictable order. This tactic helped the Broncos land quarterback John Elway in 1983.

Elway was the consensus No. 1 draft pick that year, and the Broncos under head coach Dan Reeves exchanged several phone calls with the Baltimore Colts, hoping to trade for the top spot in the draft, but to no avail. The Colts wanted too much in exchange for the Broncos moving up three picks, including two or three future first-round draft picks in addition to players already on the Broncos' roster. Denver thus refused the offer. The Colts countered with a potential trade to swap the fifth and fourth picks in the first round if the Colts could manage to acquire the fifth overall pick. Reeves replied that he would consider this exchange if it indeed became a possibility; however, the Colts did not find any suitors willing to trade into the No. 1 spot and thus drafted Elway, while the Broncos chose Northwestern University offensive lineman Chris Hinton.

Just when matters with Elway appeared to be settled, ESPN announced that the top-rated quarterback refused to play for the Colts. By the second round the Broncos were in full war-planning mode trying to figure out a way to land Elway and began assessing what they would need to give up to obtain the prized quarterback. Reeves realized that the Colts were likely interested in Chris Hinton by virtue of Baltimore offering to swap the fourth and fifth picks and focused a trade strategy around the Broncos' new lineman. Five days after the draft ended, Denver arranged a deal with Baltimore that sent Elway to the Broncos in exchange for Hinton, backup quarterback Mark Herrmann, and a future first-round draft choice.

While all the methods discussed thus far are considered fair game, teams also resort to more creative and duplicitous tactics to decipher opponents' draft plans. In the 1949 draft, Redskins owner George Marshall walked around the draft room exchanging greetings with personnel from various teams while attempting to covertly glance at the paperwork splayed out all over the tables of each team's station. Unfortunately for Marshall and the Redskins, everyone at the draft quickly figured out what Marshall was up to and made sure nothing of value was visible when he passed by. Marshall's desire for opponents' draft knowledge is understandable, as Washington relied mainly on *Sport* magazine for its draft assessments at the time.

In an even more nefarious act, the Colts enticed Browns assistant coach Weeb Ewbank, soon to be the Colts' head coach, to supply them with the Browns' targets for the 1953 draft. The Colts then selected the Browns' targets at every available opportunity because Cleveland and Coach Brown were renowned for their superlative drafts.

COMPILING INFORMATION

Once teams acquire information on opponents' draft needs and targets, they begin to organize this intelligence for use. The Patriots have a "needs book" for every team in the NFL. As the name indicates, this is a record of team needs by player and position, from starters to the very last backup. The Patriots list players who will likely be replaced in the offseason and record prospect visits to every NFL team. When the draft arrives, these books assist the Patriots in determining the targets of other teams and whether the Patriots need to move up or stay put or whether they can even slide back and still draft their desired targets. Additionally, by knowing which prospects teams have fallen in love with and are eager to draft, the Patriots are able to play hardball and demand a little extra from opponents attempting to move around in the draft to grab their prized prospects. Being so well organized and understanding the needs of other teams are the key reasons the Patriots are able to routinely pull off favorably lopsided draft day trades.

Teams also integrate the information they have learned about opponents' targets onto draft boards. Coach Bill Walsh of the 49ers kept a list of all players deemed worthy of being drafted and assessed when he felt that a prospect would be drafted based upon his ability and information gathered on opponents' needs. This board helped Walsh land Hall of Fame quarterback Joe Montana late in the third round of the 1979 draft. Confident in his assessment that no other team would pick Montana in the third round, Walsh traded the 56th spot in the draft to the Seahawks for the 82nd pick and a Seattle linebacker. Walsh then used the 82nd pick to select Montana, even though he would have been perfectly willing to draft him with the 56th pick.

COUNTERMEASURES

Aware that opponents are collecting on their assessments of prospects and their team needs, teams take various countermeasures to safeguard their prospect evaluations and draft day plans. To prevent a situation like the Colts using Weeb Ewbank to supply Browns draft information, teams are very strategic about when they replace personnel involved in the evaluation of draft prospects and draft planning. Bills owner Terry Pegula waited until hours after the 2017 draft to fire general manager Doug Whaley. Regarding the draft, Pegula said Whaley "put the whole thing together" and added, "The decision [to fire Whaley] was made now because this is the end of the scouting year."[6]

Teams are also very tight lipped about who they plan to draft. For instance, New Orleans coach Sean Payton would not even tip his hand when President Bush asked who the Saints would be drafting with the No. 2 overall pick the weekend before the 2006 draft. Apparently not even presidents have the requisite security clearance for NFL draft secrets.

Such paranoia is common, and the closer the draft nears, the more close-mouthed teams become. Teams make a point of warning scouts, coaches, and staff not to give away any hints about targets their team might draft. Some coaches, including Bill Belichick and Bill Parcells, do not even allow their assistant coaches to speak to the media on this topic for fear they will give something away.

Additionally, teams also try to hide their interest in the prospects they hope to draft. Al Davis worried teams would learn who he was targeting, so Raiders strength and conditioning coach Marv Marinovich often flew to interview prospects during the very last days leading up to the draft. "I'd have to go check guys and he'd always wait until the last possible minute to send me 'cause he thought people were watchin' where I was goin' and would know who he wanted. With Ray Chester, I went to draft day."[7] On occasion, teams also purposefully avoid interviewing certain prospects at the Combine and eschew bringing them to team facilities in order to mask their interest.

In the 1956 draft, the Rams went a step further and started a deception campaign to conceal their true draft targets by stoking false interest in little-known Hamline player Dick Donlin. The junior scouts went so far as to leave a message on the desk of general manager Tex Schramm stating, "We gotta get more film on this prospect, Dick Donlin. Unbelievable talent out of Hamline in Minnesota." Schramm and head scout Eddie Kotal then started reaching out to contacts all over the Midwest asking about Donlin. Word soon leaked to the far corners of the NFL that Donlin was a rising star. Rams scout Gil Brandt recalls seeing the Colts' delegation approach the Rams' table at the draft that year and being told, "Ha ha, you didn't think we knew about him, did you? Well, we found out!" The Colts had spent the draft's 21st overall pick on Donlin, a player they had never even seen, based solely on the fallacious rumors spread by the Rams' scouts. The Colts realized their mistake at training camp when they discovered Donlin was neither fast enough nor strong enough to play in the NFL and cut him before their first regular-season game.[8] This just goes to show, even opponents are surprised from time to time at the lengths their competitors are willing to go to gain an advantage.

When teams have obvious needs, masking their interest in prospects who are an obvious fit is difficult. Such was the case in the 2020 draft with the Denver Broncos. They were in need of a speedy wide receiver, and the University of Alabama's Henry Ruggs III was the obvious first-round candidate. So, when local journalist Mike Klis went on the radio several weeks before the draft and announced the Broncos' wide receiver board was different than the rest of the NFL's, the rest of the league was left to wonder if this was a smokescreen (plenty of teams have used this tactic of spreading false information via the media) or a legitimate report.

Once team draft boards showing prospect rankings are posted, teams become even more paranoid about protecting draft information. Bill Polian, a former NFL scout, personnel director, general manager, and team president, explained how one team he worked for protected the team's draft board. Only coaches and executives with a say in who the team would draft were ever allowed to see the draft board. When not being used, the draft board had a screen placed over it that was locked in three separate locations. Only one key was made for the screen, and only three keys to the draft board room were given out, all to team executives. Only one copy of the draft board was ever made, and this was kept secure in a safe. On draft day, the board was only unlocked for use when the team was ready to draft and immediately locked up again after the team drafted a player. Obviously, these are extreme defensive measures, but some coaches and team executives feel they are absolutely necessary. After all, espionage is a 24/7 business in the NFL, and spies can be everywhere, even on one's own team. Furthermore, an opponent's knowledge of a team's prized draft day target can easily cost a team that prospect, and one player, one good draft pick, is sometimes all it takes to turn a franchise around or lift a team to the heights of success in the NFL.

13

PRO SCOUTING

He doesn't let anything pass him by. He knows who's up for trade and who's unhappy.[1]—William Kilmer on George Allen

TWEETS WITH CONSEQUENCES

Teams had been bird-watching Falcons wide receiver Roddy White for quite some time. Drafted in the first round of the 2005 draft, Atlanta's swift wide receiver had developed in the Falcons' aerie into one of the best in the business in just a couple of years. From 2007 to 2012, he glided for over 1,500 yards receiving annually and perched at the Pro Bowl for four consecutive years between 2008 and 2011. Unfortunately, White was also attracting attention for reasons other than his play.

In 2007, he celebrated a touchdown by showing off his "Free Mike Vick" T-shirt worn underneath his jersey. The Falcons quarterback would soon be a caged bird as he had been sentenced earlier that day to almost two years behind bars for operating a dogfighting ring. While supporting struggling teammates is generally lauded in NFL circles, this act ruffled feathers and caused talent evaluators around the NFL to question White's maturity and moral compass. Then in 2009, he attracted additional criticism by holding out in training camp and refusing to play out his rookie contract, but it was his incessant chatter on Twitter that really took wing and attracted the attention of NFL teams.

On February 12, 2013, White tweeted the following insensitive message: "Out of all the sports the Olympics could've dropped they dropped wrestling they are retards." A few months later, White tweeted another head scratcher in response to a discussion on *Sunday NFL Countdown* about Aldon Smith's DUI arrest: "Aldon Smith isn't right in any way form or fashion but come on guys don't act like you never did it you just got away with it." White appeared to be accusing the hosts, former NFL players, of having driven under the influence and was apparently suggesting this was just a normal part of life in the NFL. Many, of course, wondered if White was speaking from personal experience.[2]

Then in 2014, White posted another doozy of a tweet that made national headlines for all the wrong reasons: "I'm probably going to lose my fantasy football matchup this week cause all day can't play Sunday for disciplining his child Jesus help us." This post reflected White's frustration over "All Day," Vikings running back Adrian Peterson, having been deactivated by the Vikings while the running back faced child-abuse charges in Texas.[3]

Regardless of whether Peterson had done anything wrong or not, teams inevitably construed the callous words as evidence of White being immature and self-centered. Had White truly valued his fantasy football team over the welfare of a defenseless child? Perhaps White had just been shocked that Peterson had been arrested for using a switch made from a stripped tree branch to discipline his child. After all, Peterson had been subjected to similar punishment growing up, as had many kids of his generation. Nonetheless, the photos of Peterson's child did not bode well for the elusive running back, nor for White, who now had one more mark against him in scouting circles.

ASSESSING INTERNAL TALENT

So much hoopla is made of the NFL draft that fans often underestimate the importance of free-agent signings and trades. These often have a much bigger short-term impact than incoming draft picks, who frequently need a year or more to assimilate, learn the playbook, and put on the requisite weight and strength to compete in the pros. Therefore, teams continuously evaluate and update assessments of NFL players from every team so that they have a proper feel for players as they become available via trade and free agency. Keeping track of social media posts, such as Roddy White's, is but a small part of this.

Before teams can evaluate if bringing a player in from another team is worthwhile, though, pro scouts must first assess the players of their own team. They thus spend hours and hours watching game and practice footage of the team's roster and grade the players using codes. For instance, some teams use colors that serve as an easy reference tool to talk about the general ability level of players. The 2013 Saints used blue to represent an elite player, red for an All-Pro talent, yellow for a quality starter, green for a quality backup, gray for a below-average player, and brown for a camp body—a player who would never see action beyond training camp.

Additionally, players are labeled as either ascending or descending. Typically, rookie players are marked as ascending since they are young, still learning the nuances of professional football, and getting familiar with the playbook. Seasoned players are more likely to be marked as descending, as age begins to reduce their speed and strength and inhibits their ability to remain injury-free. Marking players as ascending or descending helps teams figure out how the strengths and weaknesses of their rosters will change over time. For instance, a team needing a starting-caliber linebacker might only need wait for one of its three ascending linebackers to develop, versus drafting another, making a trade, or signing a free agent. On the flip side, although a team might currently have an All-Pro defensive tackle, marking him as descending because of age will help identify that a replacement will be needed in the not-so-distant future.

FINDING NEW TALENT

Armed with an understanding of the talent on their own team, scouts search for suitable candidates to replace existing players in order to maintain or upgrade the quality of the team roster. Teams look to fill their rosters not only from the college ranks but also from players on other NFL teams, from professional talent in other sports, and from people off the street—typically former professional or college football players, but not always. Additionally, teams search for talent from other professional football leagues, as some of the NFL's all-time greats started their careers elsewhere. Quarterbacks Warren Moon, Joe Theismann, Doug Flutie, and Jeff Garcia all played in the Canadian Football League (CFL). Quarterbacks Steve Young and Jim Kelly, running back Herschel Walker, and defensive end Reggie White came out of the United States Football League (USFL). Quarterback Kurt Warner played in the Arena Football League.

While all teams are searching for talent, not all teams' efforts to identify talent are equal. To be frank, some teams want to win more than others, and it shows. From 1960 to 1971, the Chargers under coach Sid Gillman were known for finding talent among athletes participating in a wide variety of sports from across the globe. This led NFL security journeyman Don Klosterman to joke that when warfare erupted in the Katanga province of Africa, the only non-natives who remained behind were two missionaries and a scout from the Chargers. Although this was clearly an exaggeration, it stemmed from a truth that the Chargers were working harder than most of their opponents to identify talent.

While some players are found abroad and playing a multitude of sports, most of the talent that pro scouts assess are current NFL players. While the free-agency status of every NFL player is publicly available today, for much of the NFL's history the status of player contracts was a closely guarded secret, and teams had to work hard if they wanted a jump start on the competition in signing available free agents. Even through the early 1970s, the details of players' contracts were kept under wraps, including the number of years that players had signed on to play. Even teammates were often kept in the dark. Thus, knowing when players from around the league would become free agents took a great deal of work. Only those coaches who ate, drank, and breathed football mustered the dedication needed for this tedious task.

Al Davis of the Raiders was one of those. He knew the ins and outs of both the AFL and NFL rosters. In a 1965 *Sports Illustrated* article, an AFL coach noted, "Davis always acts like he's got some kind of secret information nobody else knows about and much of the time that's true. He knows the members of every taxi squad in both leagues and what players are having trouble with their coaches, and he's always ready to make a deal, although you'd better look out when you deal with him."[4]

Former Raiders coach Mike Shanahan recounted how Davis acquired information on players throughout the league. "Preparation. He left no stone unturned. He knew personnel so much better than anybody else in the league, it wasn't even a contest. I could see how he did it. He used to call me at home at 11:00 P.M., when most people were sleeping and say, 'Mike, I think I can trade for this guy,' or 'I think I'm going to sign this guy,' or 'What do you think about this guy?'"[5]

ASSESSING EXTERNAL TALENT

Today, teams rank all players in the NFL on an annual basis in order to assess them and to determine if their addition would be beneficial. Rankings and records of players are updated continually, as decisions often need to be made expeditiously. For example, in 1986 the Bills' director of pro personnel, Bob Ferguson, kept a ranked and continually updated list of all NFL players by position. Additionally, each assistant coach under Buffalo head coach Marv Levy kept his own such list of talent around the NFL for the position he coached. Thus, when a player became available through free agency, trade, or the waiver wire, the Bills' coaching staff already had an opinion on him and could potentially act quickly. Obviously, ranking all the players in the league is a tremendous amount of work, but this is a necessary undertaking to stay competitive.

Many of the players pro scouts assess are two years or less removed from playing college football and have not yet solidified a long-term spot on an NFL roster. For such players, pro scouts consult with the team's college scouting section to see how the players were graded coming out of college and to learn about the system they played in while there. Some promising players are thus quickly dismissed based on character or medical issues from their past. Pro scouts might also learn the reason a player did not stand out in college but flourished in the NFL, such as a lightweight, pass-catching tight end asked to primarily block for a run-heavy college football team. While the input of college scouts is helpful, ultimately pro scouts must be able to see a player for who he is and not who he was. Players often dramatically change in the formative years immediately after college, both physically and mentally.

Even their character can change. After all, bad apples can turn their lives around as a result of maturing, being removed from a bad environment, or becoming financially secure. Similarly, young men with no issues in college can have difficulties making responsible choices after latching onto NFL rosters, having cash burning in their pockets, and with women screaming their names.

To assist with assessments, teams conduct interviews to vet players, especially players considered to be high risks. Prior to the Broncos signing free-agent cornerback Dale Carter in 1999, Denver conducted extensive interviews with people who knew him best, former coaches, and former teammates. Their testimony convinced Denver to take a chance on Carter, who had been arrested three times since 1993. He lasted one year in Denver before being suspended by the league for missing at least two drug tests, resulting in the Broncos eating $5.14 million in salary cap costs for cutting Carter in 2001. Clearly the vetting process is not perfect.

Another way teams research players' character is through their social media sites. While no one needed to monitor Roddy White's social media account to learn of his post concerning "All Day," most posts do not attract the spotlight of the national media. Therefore, teams track players' social media sites to keep tabs on personnel they are interested in adding to the team. While this might seem like an invasion of privacy, to teams striving to put together the best rosters possible, this is simply a reality of competing in the modern NFL.

KEY TIME PERIODS FOR ADDING PLAYERS

Preparing for free agency—an offseason period where a host of players become available to sign with any team—is one of the key jobs of pro scouts. While the draft usually fills numerous holes in a team's roster, it does not typically fill them all. Once scouts identify possible free-agency targets, they write up reports on these players and discuss them with the coaching staff to ensure coaches agree with the scouts' assessments and that they are the type of players the team is interested in adding. If the coaching staff does not feel a player is a good fit, that is typically the end of the conversation. Former pro scout Mike McCartney explained, "At the end of the day, I can be excited about a player, but if you're a coach and you're not excited and you don't think he fits the scheme, it's probably not going to be a real good match."[6]

Preparing for preseason cuts is another key job of professional scouts. During the preseason, teams are required to gradually trim their rosters from 90 to 53 players. The final cut day leaves a tremendous number of players available at the same time—864 to be exact. Pro scouts thus spend a lot of time researching other teams' players, as well their own, looking for possible upgrades. Pro scouts must be familiar with other teams' rosters in order to know which players are likely to be cut. Once cut-down day arrives, pro scouts have already identified targets and have discussed these with coaches and management, and teams have formed a plan of attack to promptly sign released players who they believe will improve their team. Sometimes finding an upgrade at a position of weakness on cut-down day is not realistic, and knowing opponents' rosters can help identify when this is the case. For example, a team needing a cornerback might have its eyes on a likely opponent cut, but if 10 other teams also need a cornerback, arranging for a trade might be a better course of action.

Pro scouts pay particular attention to the rosters of teams having undergone a recent coaching change, especially of teams making a major shift in offensive or defensive scheme. Such teams often release starting-caliber players who no longer fit the new scheme. Also, new staffs often have insufficient time to properly assess their own rosters and can mistakenly cut quality players. Mike McCartney stated it this way: "You have to know your football team. If you don't know your own football team, first and foremost, you're gonna make mistakes. . . . I know when we were at the Eagles, we always put extra attention on new staff. New coaching staffs—sometimes they're making their full evaluation on their 53-man roster without seeing their team play a true game. So, new staffs can make mistakes with existing players that get off to a slow start with the new scheme or whatever. So, we put a little bit of extra attention on teams with new staffs."[7]

Teams also gather information on players whom opponents might be willing to trade due to player unhappiness, a player being in the coach's "doghouse," or contract issues. The salary cap is another reason why teams are often forced to dispense with players. To take advantage of this, Mike Shanahan's Broncos maintained a list of opponents' salary cap situations to look for players whom opponents would not be able to keep due to fiscal limitations. In 1997, this method helped the Broncos identify and acquire Tony Jones from the Ravens—a team the Broncos knew was under heavy salary cap restraints—for a second-round pick in order to replace their retiring offensive tackle, Gary Zimmerman. Clearly, one team's misfortunes can be another team's gains, and teams are too busy trying to win to have any pity on the less fortunate.

Once the season is underway, pro scouts stay busy preparing for changes to next year's roster and assessing players who are still available, in case of injuries or suspensions. Players who they think could step in and contribute if needed are added to the ready list. Former scout Dan Hatman stated, "To get on that list, it means that someone in the pro department starts the process, liked them, graded them well. Then, the director and assistant director both qualified that, said they liked him, and, depending on the GM, they might have also taken a peek to sign off on that. That ready list is gonna have the grade, it's gonna have where the player's home base is, who his agent is, agent's phone number, what have you, all there, and that ready list is available at the drop of a hat."[8] Teams are so prepared, in fact, that if a player sustains a serious injury during a game, a team representative will likely be making calls to the agent of a player on the ready list during the game.

In order to gain more information on players being assessed for the ready list, teams bring in players for off-day workouts. Teams are thus able to vet what they have seen on film, become acquainted with players, answer any unknowns, and obtain updated information. Mike McCartney related that teams conduct workouts to "get updated height, weight, body type, because guys do change—you can see what kind of shape they're in. Say there's a running back you like, but haven't seen in the pass game enough—you can throw him some balls, see how he moves and catches the ball. Then, as much as anything, it answers: 'What kind of shape is a guy in? Is he ready to play?' Because if they've been out of football for a couple weeks or longer, that becomes a concern." Teams also conduct a medical exam when players are brought in for workouts. When teams like what they see, they add the player to the ready list and line everything up so that if the team suffers an injury all that needs to be done is to contact the agent and sign the contract.[9]

Clearly, teams do not waste time grieving over injured players. Football is a business, and players are commodities. There is a reason "next man up" is such a hackneyed phrase in the NFL. Teams go about their business no matter how badly players are injured and regardless of the dreams that are crushed when careers abruptly end. This is simply the reality of the NFL and part of what it takes to win. Nobody's position is safe in the wake of tragedy, and one player's injury is another player's opportunity to fulfill a childhood dream.

14

THE AFL AND NFL FIGHT OVER PLAYERS

The words "cunning, shrewd, devious" don't have a bad connotation to me. Look at the history of people in positions of leadership. They've said of every one of my time that he's devious—from Roosevelt and Churchill to Eisenhower, Kissinger, and Mao.[1]—Al Davis

THE NFL FIGHTS TO SURVIVE

In 1920 George Halas took over a football team for the A. E. Staley Company, a starch manufacturer in Decatur, Illinois, that played in an industrial league. He immediately began bolstering the squad by virtue of being able to offer players a job with the company. Additionally, he had the advantage of knowing players hungry to play the game, having played for the revered Robert Zuppke's University of Illinois squad in college and the navy's Great Lakes football team during World War I.

With the team shaping up nicely, Halas turned his attention outward to address issues that wre plaguing the loosely regulated midwestern industrial leagues, including the Central Illinois league that the Decatur Staleys had been a part of the season prior. Pay was the biggest problem. There simply was not enough. Teams attempted to collect donations from fans, but this typically generated no more than a pittance in revenue. Because of this, players shifted mercurially between teams in a perpetual attempt to maximize their pay. Additionally, teams brought in ringers from universities that played under aliases. This not only undermined the spirit of the industrial league, but also was a clear violation of collegiate rules.

Faced with these problems, Halas looked into the possibility of starting another league in late 1920, and reached out to Canton Bulldogs manager Ralph Hay about this. Before long, the men were meeting with representatives of 11 football teams in a car dealership in Akron, Ohio. Here the teams agreed to form the American Professional Football Association (APFA), renamed the National Football League in 1922.

The upstart league almost immediately began play, and Halas's Decatur team had a great deal of success, nearly winning the championship the very first season. While the on-field results were nothing to complain about, the team cost the A. E. Staley Company $16,000 in just salaries alone, an amount the company simply was not willing to continue spending for bragging rights and entertainment.

Looking for a viable option, the A. E. Staley Company offered Halas a deal. If Halas would move the team to the larger Chicago market and keep the Staley name, the company would pay Halas $5,000 to support the 1921 season. After that, the team was all his to do with as he wished. Without a lot of options and in no hurry to jump back into his work in engineering, Halas agreed.

He thus moved the team to Chicago, where it struggled financially for several decades. Other teams, many of which played in smaller markets, fared even worse and were forced to fold. In fact, 47 APFA or NFL teams dissolved in the 1920s alone, 15 more than the current 32 in the league today.

The Bears only escaped a similar fate through sheer grit and determination. When the stock market crash of 1929 reduced the value of investments to pennies on the dollar, Halas resorted to asking friends and family for loans. He even borrowed money from his children's college savings accounts. By 1932, the Bears were starving for funds and Halas was in such desperate straits that he issued IOUs to his players. The Bears were on the brink of collapse at this point, and if the players had balked at having their pay deferred, that would have been the end of the Chicago franchise, and perhaps of the entire league. The players accepted the IOUs, however. Perhaps they trusted Halas to pay them back. Perhaps they just loved the game too much to walk away. Or perhaps they had learned from Halas how to place the needs of the collective above their own.

As the owner of a team struggling to stay afloat and competing with others to win games and championships, Halas could have very easily taken a myopic, team-centric stance on league issues, but he realized the Bears were just a spoke in the wheel, one of many teams that relied on the league for their well-being and survival. So, while Halas employed chicanery, skullduggery, and sometimes full-bore cheating to win on the field, he also willingly succumbed to the needs of the league at times, even to the detriment of his beloved Bears team.

For example, when Eagles owner Bert Bell proposed the idea of a draft in 1935, Halas knew its implementation would impair the Bears' ability to sign college prospects. After all, Halas's team had already won three championships, built a strong reputation, and accrued more funds to work with than the vast majority of its competitors. Yet Halas supported the proposal because he understood a draft would help the less profitable, bottom-tier teams and thereby help the entire league as well.

Likewise, when the All America Football Conference (AAFC) collapsed, Halas did not complain about the inequitable division of AAFC players among NFL teams. He realized Bert Bell was only giving the weaker NFL teams more selections in order to help bring parity to the league. He knew the Bears only thrived if the league did as well, which is perhaps why he took the threat from the AFL so seriously. The battle with the AAFC had been financially disastrous for both leagues; fortunately, the NFL had managed to outlast its counterpart. The AFL, though, had the backing of some of the richest tycoons in America. It was a threat the likes of which the NFL had never seen before, and the league had seen its share, including World War II and the Great Depression.

The frustrating part was that the NFL had worked so hard to survive those lean times and to develop the professional game and its fan base. Only now, with games drawing large crowds and large-market clubs profiting from television revenue, were AFL fat cats getting in on the act, hoping to cash in from the foundation the NFL had laid. Finding this unacceptable and attempting to avoid a long, drawn-out battle, Halas and his NFL cronies devised a scheme to sabotage the inchoate league before it was even fully formed.

The AFL's inaugural draft was scheduled to take place on November 23, 1959, with participation from its eight franchises: the Houston Oilers, New York Titans, Boston Patriots, Los Angeles Chargers, Denver Broncos, Buffalo Bills, Dallas Texans, and Minnesota Vikings. All appeared in order until the day of the draft meeting, when the AFL owners learned that Minnesota was withdrawing from the league, having been offered a much-desired franchise with the NFL. AFL owners quickly realized they had been outwitted by Halas.

The AFL was now left with only seven teams, an awkward number for the scheduling of games and the formation of divisions. The defection also reflected poorly on the upstart league, which is precisely what the NFL and Halas had intended. Chargers owner Barron Hilton said, "Halas's strategy was that he wanted to show the college players that the nascent league was already falling apart."[2] What made the slight all the more embarrassing was that the AFL's draft was set to take place in Minneapolis, a city that had just abandoned the AFL. In spite of this, the AFL pressed ahead and the defection was far from the coup de grâce the NFL had hoped; rather, it proved to be the opening salvo of a war that would endure for 10 years and stretch the ingenuity and resources of both leagues to their very limits.

THE COMPETITION

While controversies like drug use, gambling, and kneeling during the national anthem and scandals such as Deflategate and Spygate have threatened and will continue to threaten the league's image and popularity, the greatest threat to the NFL has been and always will be that of an upstart league supplanting the NFL. Although the NFL is clearly the most popular and prestigious football league in the world today—and nearly as synonymous with the United States as apple pie and freedom—the NFL's place at the top was and is anything but assured. The NFL has been challenged by fledgling leagues throughout its history and has thus far survived competition from the AAFC (1944–1949), the CFL (1958–present), the AFL (1960–1970), the World Football League (WFL, 1974–1975), and the USFL (1982–1986), to name just a few.

The idea of another league competing with the NFL today in terms of talent and money seems almost preposterous, but this was not always the case. In 1948, arguably the three best teams in professional football all belonged to the AAFC, whose owners cumulatively shared more wealth than their NFL counterparts. Over the course of time, the NFL scrapped its way to the top of the heap, but the outcome was anything but a foregone conclusion.

Besides competing for franchise locations and ticket sales, leagues and teams battled to acquire the top prospects coming out of college. Team owners knew that wherever the best prospects went the fans would follow. The AAFC and the NFL participated in the first heated contest for top talent around the middle of the 20th century, and by 1947 the NFL was losing the college recruiting war. The NFL might have been in real trouble if not for the financial difficulties that ultimately capsized the AAFC.

While the NFL's battle with the WFL was short, lasting only from 1974 to 1975, it was equally intense. The WFL initially attempted to steal players away from the NFL by signing big names in exchange for lucrative contracts. Luckily for the NFL, a court injunction filed during the heat of the conflict prevented WFL personnel from further contacting and signing players currently employed by the NFL. The battlefront thus shifted to college prospects. Former Cowboys vice president Joe Bailey described the battle. "I spent five days at State College [Pennsylvania] trying to figure out whether [Heisman Trophy winner John] Cappelletti and all those guys were going to the World Football League. We had a bunch of espionage going on. It was an enormous drain on resources and created huge hurdles for Tex [Schramm] and the organization."[3]

Less than a decade later, the USFL created another scare for the NFL, once again competing for football's best talent. Donald Trump's purchase of the New Jersey Generals increased the competition for players between the two leagues, as Trump provided a huge injection of badly needed capital. However, the rival USFL ultimately collapsed under the weight of the increased salaries that Trump had pioneered.

While all of these challengers were worrisome, no one threatened the NFL more than the AFL. One of the main reasons for this was that the AFL's game was exciting. The new league was more passing based because of a pointier ball and benefited from innovative coaches like Sid Gillman, Al Davis, Weeb Ewbank, and Hank Stram and great quarterbacks like Joe Namath, Daryle Lamonica, and Lenny Dawson.

The AFL also rivaled the NFL on the issue of player talent. One way it did this was by drafting more black players than the NFL. While the NFL was integrated at the time, race was still a major factor for the league. Former Chargers offensive tackle Ron Mix wrote, "There was a rumor that there was an unwritten law in the NFL: no more than five black players [per team]. I don't know if it was true or not, but there weren't many black players in the NFL on each team." To highlight the extent of the NFL's bias at the time, the Redskins did not draft a black player until 1962, and only then under tremendous pressure from the federal government.[4]

Finally, the AFL was able to compete with the NFL financially. This allowed the AFL to lure much of the top talent coming out of college, as the upstart league often outbid its NFL rival. This was possible due to the wealthy backing of owners like Barron Hilton—of the Hilton hotel chain—oilman Bud Adams, and tycoon Lamar Hunt.

By the mid-1960s, once the AFL had become a legitimate threat, the two leagues fought hand, tooth, and nail over the top college prospects. Both leagues knew that attracting elite talent was vital, and thus both leagues routinely drafted the same players, with the draftees deciding for which league and team they would play. Attempts to sway draftees to one team or another often took the form of racing to meet and sign the players or engaging in bidding wars for their services. As the following anecdote demonstrates, competitions to sign players were often incredibly fierce.

In 1965 the AFL's Raiders and the NFL's Lions drafted Florida State University (FSU) wide receiver Fred Biletnikoff. Both were eager to sign the talented player but had to wait until the collegiate season finished to do so. Determined to acquire him, the night before FSU's last game—the Gator Bowl in Jacksonville, Florida—both the Lions and Raiders were jockeying for position to sign the wide receiver. Raiders defensive backs coach Charlie Sumner was with Biletnikoff in a hotel and kept shifting the wide receiver from room to room to make it difficult for Lions personnel to track him down. Lions general manager Russ Thomas became so frustrated searching for Biletnikoff all over the hotel that when he found Sumner he lifted the Raiders assistant off the ground and asked, not so politely, "Where's Biletnikoff?" Clearly, by this time the competition between the leagues was seen as a matter of life and death, and the gloves were just about literally coming off.

The next day, with the last few seconds ticking off the clock at the Gator Bowl, the Lions' Thomas, accompanied by Biletnikoff's mother, and the Raiders' Sumner, accompanied by a lawyer, both waited to rush the field and to attempt to sign the wide receiver. To get a leg up on the competition, Sumner pointed out the Lions' entourage to field security and said, "Hold those people back. They're not allowed on the field." This stratagem worked, and Thomas and Biletnikoff's mother could only watch as Biletnikoff signed a contract on national television, with the wide receiver's inconsolable mother screaming, "Don't sign it! Don't sign it!"[5]

BATTLE TACTICS

With the race to sign players so heated, the rival leagues used a variety of different tactics to tip the scales in their favor. The timing of the drafts was particularly important, as whatever league drafted first had a clear advantage. Because of this, the two leagues' drafts were usually scheduled closely together, if not simultaneously. If one league moved up the date, the other simply did the same. The only way around this game of calendar leapfrog was to move up the date of the draft in secret, which is precisely what the NFL arranged in 1960—the year after the NFL had derailed the AFL's draft by luring the Minnesota franchise to the NFL. Undoubtedly, the NFL feared reprisals and attempted to once again outsmart its AFL rival. The AFL likewise held its own secret draft in 1962, a draft so secretive that not even AFL commissioner Joe Foss knew about it ahead of time.

The enmity between the AFL and NFL grew so intense that teams even engaged in intraleague cooperation just to ensure that prospects did not sign with the rival league, even if this meant trading away a good player for a fraction of his draft day value. For example, after University of Southern California offensive tackle Ron Mix was drafted by the AFL's Boston Patriots, the Patriots called him up, and Mix stated that if he had to go back east to play, it would be with the NFL, as the Colts had also drafted Mix. The Patriots understood Mix's implicit message that he preferred not to play for a team on the East Coast and asked, "If we traded your rights to the Los Angles Chargers, would you consider playing for them?" Mix agreed, and just like that he was a Charger in the AFL.[6]

Another strategy that teams used to secure prospects' services was to take advantage of the less affluent teams in their rival league. Al Davis did this by drafting the same prospects as the NFL's 49ers. The 49ers had financial difficulties at the time and did not even attempt to sign their top draft picks. The AFL had its own teams with pecuniary issues, such as the New York Titans and Denver Broncos. They also struggled to sign their draft choices and were undoubtedly taken advantage of by NFL teams.

As the threat from the AFL grew, Dan Reeves, the owner of the NFL's Rams, established a program to promote strong ties with prospects prior to the draft, to convince them not to sign with the AFL, and to hide players from the rival league once signed. When NFL commissioner Pete Rozelle learned of the Rams' tactics in 1964, he decided to implement them league-wide. The NFL selected Rams publicist Bert Rose to run Operation Hand-Holding using approximately 80 "babysitters." These individuals were typically businessmen aligned with the NFL elite. Even the governor of Oregon worked as an NFL babysitter at one point. They were paid for their services and received a "gold card" to fly on the NFL's dime on United Airlines flights, but most cared little about the money and perks. They simply enjoyed the adventure and the elitism that came with being associated with an NFL team.

NFL clubs provided the babysitters with the names and schools of prospects they were interested in drafting. The babysitters were then expected to travel to the prospects' locations in order to establish relationships with them. Once there, they started working on convincing the prospects that the NFL was the right choice for them. After the college season concluded, a babysitter's only constraints in signing a player and keeping him from the AFL were the depth of the babysitter's pocketbook and the breadth of his imagination. As Cowboys vice president of player personnel Gil Brandt noted, "They had the latitude to do anything they wanted with these kids. Leading up to the last game of the season, they couldn't offer them money or anything like that, but form a relationship with them. Then as soon as the last game of the season was over, the players were no longer under NCAA rules, they took care of the player."[7] In addition to taking care of prospects, NFL babysitters also routinely hid them away in hotel rooms prior to and even after the draft. In one instance, 27 prospects were squirreled away together in a hotel in Detroit.

Of course, the AFL felt the need to respond to the threat the NFL's babysitters posed. One way the upstart league attempted to sabotage the efforts of the babysitters was by calling a fake meeting in 1966. Davis, the AFL's commissioner at the time, recalled, "We got the names and addresses of all the babysitters. We sent them all a memorandum that on the day of the draft, you are to meet in Portland, Oregon, at 5 o'clock, at a certain motel." If the plan had worked, all of the NFL's top prospects would have been left unguarded on the day of the draft.

Unfortunately for the AFL, Cowboys personnel chief Gil Brandt uncovered the plan at the last minute after a tipoff from a college player in Oregon. The NFL's babysitters were quickly alerted to the ruse, with some already waiting to board their flights to Portland. Davis denied that the fake babysitter meeting was his idea. Gil Brandt believed otherwise. "Al was pretty good. He was really our only competition."[8]

The AFL also quickly followed the NFL's example by establishing its own babysitters club. Al Davis, of course, was at the forefront here as well. Pat Sarnese, who helped Davis squirrel players away, said, "He was getting calls from all over the country where different guys were bein' babysat. He had 'em hidden all over."[9] Davis truly ran a clandestine network, and Raiders babysitters were only given information about their specific assignments, just in case any of them were ever enticed to go to work for the enemy.

One of the reasons the competing leagues spent so much time and energy hiding players was that just because a team from one league signed a player first did not mean that the other league simply gave up. Whichever team failed to sign a player first would typically continue to press, hoping the drafted player would sign to play for them as well. In situations where two teams signed a player, the courts or the player had the final say. Thus, teams began hiding players after—and sometimes even before—they signed, starting a nationwide, high-stakes game of hide-and-seek. Memphis State offensive lineman Harry Schuh was one of the players dragged into this game. After the college season ended, Scotty Stirling of the Raiders retrieved Schuh, his wife, and their baby daughter and flew them to Las Vegas in an attempt to hide Schuh from NFL teams. Schuh and his family registered at their lodging under a false name.

Ron Wolf, a former army intelligence officer working for the Raiders, met Stirling in Las Vegas as part of Schuh's protective detail. In spite of the Raiders' best efforts to keep Schuh hidden, Hamp Pool of the NFL's Rams tracked down the offensive tackle. Not long after Schuh arrived in Las Vegas, two men approached him in a casino and plopped down a card with the Rams' logo. Schuh said, "I'll be with you in a minute." He then ran to Wolf.[10] Wolf quickly advised Al Davis of the situation and asked Schuh where he wanted to go next. Schuh picked Hawaii and then waited in a closet until the getaway car arrived.

Allegedly, Al Davis showed up and distracted Pool as Wolf quickly ferreted Schuh out the back of the hotel. Perhaps Davis was already in Vegas, or perhaps the story has simply been embellished over time. Either way, when the car showed up, the Raiders drove Schuh to the Los Angeles airport, where he flew to Hawaii. Schuh left in such a hurry that even the offensive tackle's wife and daughter were left behind, sleeping inside their hotel room. Imagine explaining that one to your spouse!

Unable to find Schuh, the Rams went to the local police and filed a missing person report. The police interviewed Schuh's wife, Joyce, but she had no idea where her husband had gone. Davis had been wary of calling her, as he feared her telephone might be bugged. Police then interviewed Schuh's parents, who assured the police that Schuh was fine. Al Davis had been kind enough to contact Schuh's high school coach, who passed along a message to the parents that Schuh was doing well. Unable to find Schuh, Pool sent a punny telegram back to NFL babysitter headquarters that read, "Boo hoo. I lost my Schuh."[11]

As the last anecdote clearly demonstrates, recovering a player hidden by the rival league was no easy feat, but it was managed from time to time. In 1965, wide receiver Otis Taylor was drafted by both the AFL's Chiefs and the NFL's Eagles. On Thanksgiving eve, Buddy Young and Wallace Reed, babysitters for the Cowboys, picked up Taylor from Prairie View A&M and hid him away at a Holiday Inn in Richardson, Texas, under the guise of being invited away for a Thanksgiving weekend. Like the AFL's Raiders, the NFL's Cowboys assisted the entire league with acquiring and hiding prospects at the time.

The Chiefs became suspicious when phone calls to Taylor's room at Prairie View A&M went unanswered. Kansas City general manager Don Klosterman then contacted Taylor's mom. To gain her assistance in tracking down Taylor, Klosterman told her he was afraid that her son might have been kidnapped. This undoubtedly terrified Taylor's mother, but such tactics were deemed necessary in the AFL-NFL battle for supremacy.

Kansas City put scout Lloyd Wells in charge of the operation to find and recover Taylor. From Taylor's girlfriend, Wells learned the NFL had the wide receiver under watch in Richardson. Wells drove out to the motel room where Taylor was staying. From here, the story is a bit murky, and two versions of events exist for what happened next. In the first, Wells convinced NFL security personnel he was with a magazine in order to gain access to Taylor. In the second, the Cowboys' babysitters never allowed Wells to see Taylor, but because a babysitter had fallen asleep with the help of one-too-many drinks, Wells was able to whisper to Taylor from the parking lot. Whichever the case, Wells managed to convince Taylor to abandon the Eagles and to join the Chiefs, by reminding Taylor of their lengthy personal relationship and their joint love of chasing women. Additionally, Wells pleaded that his job would be in jeopardy if Taylor did not return with him and upped the ante by stating that a red Thunderbird was waiting for Taylor in Kansas City.

Wells then briefly left the hotel, without Taylor, but returned at two o'clock in the morning, only to be spotted by NFL security. The NFL goons threatened to shoot Wells or have him arrested, and Wells thus fled with two NFL ruffians hot on his tail. Not only were the rival leagues no longer pulling punches, but guns were nearly coming out of their holsters at this point.

Wells ducked into a nightclub and convinced a waitress to pretend that they were out on a date and he was driving her home. This ruse fooled the NFL's security personnel, and Wells returned to the motel, hopped over a fence, and stealthily crept to the patio door of Taylor's room. Here Taylor reconfirmed his desire to leave with Lloyd but threw in a new wrinkle as well. He wanted to bring along Seth Cartwright, his best friend, who had been drafted by both the NFL and the AFL's Jets. Wells agreed and ferreted the two players out of the hotel and to the Dallas airport.

At the airport, Wells noticed two people he suspected of being NFL security goons asking questions at the check-in counter. So, he quickly smuggled the two players away to the Fort Worth airport and flew them out to Kansas City from there. As promised, Taylor received his red Thunderbird. One day later, the Chiefs sent Cartwright on to the Jets.

Another creative strategy used during the battle to sign college prospects was to destroy the contracts of the rival league. After all, if there was no contract, there was no proof a league had ever signed the prospect. The Colts almost certainly resorted to this tactic in 1964 while battling with the Raiders for the services of Arizona State University (ASU) running back Tony Lorick. Los Angeles–based journalist Brad Pye, serving as an intermediary for Al Davis, had already signed Lorick in a hotel in Southern California when Arizona State head coach Frank Kush knocked on the door and asked where Lorick was. "He's gone back to his room," Pye answered.

"Did he sign with the Raiders?" Kush asked. Pye nodded his head in confirmation. "Do you have the contracts?" Pye confirmed he did. "Then let me see them," Kush requested. Pye handed over the contracts. Kush then snatched them and took off running, taking Lorick with him during the escape. Likely, Kush had come on the behalf of Baltimore, as the running back went on to sign with and play for the NFL's Colts.[12]

Al Davis quickly learned from his mistake with Lorick and began signing players while they were still in college and before his AFL's Raiders had even drafted them. If a player refused to sign with the Raiders before the draft, Davis simply drafted someone else. After Lorick, the Raiders never again lost a first-round draft pick to the NFL, thanks to this tactic. Of course, some of their targets were still lost to AFL opponents in the draft. In such cases the Raiders simply made the presigned contracts disappear, as they did with cornerback Miller Farr's contract when Denver drafted him one selection ahead of Oakland in the first round of the redshirt portion of the 1965 AFL draft.

In spite of the fierce competition between the rival leagues, for the vast majority of the time that the NFL and AFL competed over college prospects, the two leagues managed to avoid clashing over already established professionals by not signing players from one league into the other. This changed on May 17, 1966, when the NFL's Giants broke the long-standing gentleman's agreement and signed AFL kicker Pete Gogolak from the Bills.

AFL commissioner Al Davis, who had only recently taken over for Joe Foss, immediately recognized the opportunity and launched Operation Takeaway to sign the NFL's top stars, particularly their quarterbacks and other skill-position players. The AFL even had a nest egg of cash stashed away for just such an occasion and tapped into this, aggressively signing NFL talent with offers too good to be refused. At the same time, Chiefs owner Lamar Hunt negotiated with the Cowboys' Tex Schramm about a possible merger of the leagues. This two-pronged attack led to an agreement to merge the leagues only three weeks after the signing of Gogolak. In the interim, though, the AFL raided the NFL's talent and generated a great deal of panic. Tight end "Iron Mike" Ditka from "da Bears," 49ers quarterback John Brodie, and Rams quarterback Roman Gabriel were among the most prominent players wooed by the AFL.

These signings resulted in NFL staff members, such as Gil Brandt of the Cowboys, hiding away players being targeted, while the AFL cached recently signed former NFL players. Willie Williams was one of the former NFL players acquired by the AFL. He was not only paid a princely sum to change leagues, but also given a few new suits by the Raiders before they tucked him away at the Edgewater Hotel near the Raiders' headquarters with instructions to keep his location a secret. The Raiders' Scotty Stirling later joined Williams in his room and wondered why he was removing labels from his newly purchased suits. "Why are you doing that?" Stirling inquired.

"Well, you told me not to tell anybody where I was," Williams replied.[13] In his train of thought, even suit-jacket labels had to be sanitized so as not to give away his general location.

Now that's dedication and paranoia at its finest.

These shenanigans did not last long, however, as the leagues soon agreed to merge. While nearly everyone was satisfied—if not thrilled—with the merger, Al Davis was not one of them. He had so much fun with the machinations of the interleague competition it is hardly surprising that he was disappointed when the leagues negotiated a shared draft commencing in 1967, and the full merger in 1970, putting an end to some of the most incredible and far-fetched intelligence operations in the NFL's history. After all, Davis was confident he could have dethroned the NFL if only given more time. And he just might have done it, too. He certainly proved he was as willing to do "whatever it takes," just as Halas and his NFL counterparts had been doing for decades.

Part Four

A CASE STUDY OF THE CHEATRIOTS AND THE LEAGUE THAT ENABLES THEM

15

SPYGATE

The game would be over. If I knew what was coming, that's the whole game.[1]—Steve Young

A FRIENDLY WARNING

For the opening day of the 2007 season, the NFL scheduled the division rival Jets and Patriots to play. The media hyped the game as a battle between Bill Belichick, the mentor, and Eric Mangini, the apprentice. The story line was inevitable, as Mangini had worked under Belichick with the Patriots, Browns, and Jets for a total of 10 years and had only recently landed his own head coaching job in New York. While the game was just one of 16 on paper, it was more than that in reality—a litmus test, not just for Coach Mangini, but for the entire Jets organization. If New York was to become a Super Bowl contender in 2007, the team would have to find a way past the perennial powerhouse Patriots.

The Patriots had won the AFC East every year since 2003, along with two Super Bowls. They guarded the path to the AFC's championship game with drilled precision and routinely fended off those who challenged their hegemony.

Beating them would be difficult, but not impossible. During the 2006 regular season, the Jets made a good showing in both of the dogfights they engaged in with their AFC East counterpart. The Jets lost a home game to the Patriots in Week 2, but only by a narrow 7-point margin. The Jets had rattled off 17 unanswered second-half points and fallen just one score short of tying the game. This comeback had left the Jets flying high and confident they could hold their own against New England.

Then in Week 10, the Jets pulled off a stunning upset of the Patriots at Gillette Stadium, where visitors almost never come away with a victory. New York appeared to have New England's number, but as fate would have it, the Patriots and Jets met again in the playoffs. There the Patriots left no modicum of doubt over who was the better team and shot the Jets out of the sky in a lopsided 37–16 New England victory.

Even though the Jets crashed and burned in the playoffs, they still had a lot to feel good about from the 2006 season. They may not have accomplished their mission, but Mangini had led his team to a very respectable 10–6 record in his first year, a steep ascension from the 4–12 record a season ago under Herman Edwards. Mangini, though, was not one to rest on his laurels. Yes, 2006 had been a great beginning, but there was still a lot more work to be done if the Jets were going to dethrone the AFC East champion Patriots and win the Super Bowl in 2007.

After all, the Patriots were consistently in the hunt for the title, were well coached, and had a strong roster including a future Hall of Fame quarterback; and to top it all off, they cheated, using their cameramen to illicitly tape opponents' defensive signals. Mangini was aware of the latter from his time spent in New England with the Patriots, and it was a matter that disturbed him now as the coach of an AFC East division rival. If New England taped the Jets' defensive signals in Week 1, Belichick and staff would inevitably match the signals to the corresponding defenses before the two teams played again later in the year. This would mean New York would be at a severe disadvantage during the teams' second matchup, as the Patriots would be able to predict every twist and turn of the Jets' defense.

Mangini was not willing to concede such a significant advantage. Not this year. Not against his Jets, and especially not on their home field. So, he picked up the phone to call Belichick. He would give his former mentor a friendly warning that taping signals would not be tolerated against the Jets. The questions was, what would he do if Belichick ignored him?

COLLECTION

The most infamous example of signals collection and of a team doing "whatever it takes" to win took place from the preseason of 2000 through Week 1 of the 2007 season, when the Patriots engaged in filming the defensive play call signals of their opponents during games. This was a methodical, deliberate, and well-organized practice that commenced almost as soon as Belichick took over as the head coach of the Patriots.

The first time New England engaged in recording opponents' signals was during a preseason game versus Tampa Bay in 2000. Weeks later, the teams met up again for the debut of the regular season, but not before Patriots backup quarterback John Friesz reviewed preseason footage of the Buccaneers' signals and associated plays and committed them to memory as instructed to do by the New England staff. During the game, Friesz watched the play call signals issued by Buccaneers defensive coordinator Monte Kiffin and deciphered them with the knowledge he had gained from studying the preseason footage. Former Patriots videographer Matt Walsh reckons that Friesz was able to figure out about 75 percent of the Buccaneers' defensive play calls with this system.[2]

As he deciphered the play calls, Friesz relayed them to Patriots offensive coordinator Charlie Weis. Weis then passed the information to quarterback Drew Bledsoe via their headset communications. To make maximum use of the system, the Patriots played a hurry-up offense much of the game, forcing the Buccaneers' defense to relay signals quickly. This allowed the Patriots to inform Bledsoe of defensive play calls before the headset communications between the Patriots quarterback and offensive coordinator shut off as dictated by league rules, 15 seconds prior to the play clock expiring.

The Patriots continued recording opponents' signals over the course of approximately 40 games and refined the process along the way. According to former Patriots videographer Matt Walsh, the quarterbacks were soon removed from the loop of memorizing signals and associated plays, leaving only a few in the know: the staff shooting the videos, select coaches, and the Patriots football research director. The latter, Ernie Adams, was really the brains of the entire operation. Adams is Belichick's go-to man for special assignments, and this appears to include deciphering signals. His role on the Patriots is kept purposely shrouded in mystery, even from Patriots staff and players. When former Patriots vice president of player personnel Scott Pioli was asked about Adams's job, he replied, "Some of that information is top secret."[3] This secrecy surrounding Adams goes back a long way. He also worked with Belichick on the Browns' staff, and just like in New England, no one really understood the role of Adams in Cleveland. Even Browns owner Art Modell was left in the dark. He once said, "I'll pay anyone $10,000 if they can tell me what Ernie Adams does.[4]

With the Patriots, Adams instructed the videographers on what he wanted recorded from game to game. Although recording defensive signals was the usual assignment for Patriots videographers, this was not always the focus of their collection, depending on the opponent. When the Patriots played at home against the Peyton Manning–led Colts, the focus of collection shifted to Manning's audibles. Even offensive play calls signaled in from the sideline were targeted on at least one occasion.

With the quarterbacks removed from the circle of trust, Adams took over the role of memorizing opponents' signals and their associated plays and passing these along to the coaches. Adams sat in the coaches' box and wore a headset with a direct connection to Belichick. Once Adams passed opponents' play calls up the Patriots' chain of command, a coach would either relay the information directly to Patriots quarterback Tom Brady or call an offensive play to exploit the defensive play call.

Naturally, teams around the league routinely change signals to counter collection. Thus, even with properly deciphered signals from recorded videos, Adams could not always be certain the intelligence he gained from reviewing films would be of use the next time the Patriots played the same opponent. One method the Patriots utilized to determine which signals were still valid was to send advance scouts to upcoming opponents' games. Scouts prepared spreadsheets of plays with matching signals. Adams would then compare these spreadsheets to his own findings from video recordings. A second method the Patriots used was to conduct player debriefings. The Patriots routinely signed players from opponents' practice squads, or who were recently cut, for the sole purpose of assisting with deciphering signals. A recently acquired player would go into Adams's office and be shown a recording of signals and associated plays, and the player's job was to tell Adams which pairings were obsolete and which were still valid. This method was used selectively, as the Patriots tried to limit the number of personnel with knowledge of the program.

As an additional security measure, Patriots video director Jimmy Dee provided training to videographers engaged in filming signals. Videographers were instructed on what to say if interrogated by opponents' staffs or league officials regarding the Patriots' use of a third videographer, when using only two was the standard around the league. Matt Walsh, a Patriots videographer from 1999 to 2002, said two excuses given to opponents were that Patriots coaches wanted footage from both end zones in order to see the fronts and backs of players for each play and that coaches wanted close-up footage of certain Patriots players in various situations. Jimmy Dee also ensured that videographers had a plausible reason prepared for having their video cameras pointed in the direction of opponents' sidelines. Walsh was primed to say he was filming the down-and-distance marker if asked. Additionally, videographers engaged in signals collection were told to dress like members of the media, as opposed to team employees. Patriots videographers thus used tape and turned clothing inside out to conceal their team logos. Credentials supplied to videographers read "Patriots TV" or "Kraft Productions." Patriots videographers using such vague credentials were instructed to state they were filming for a television show or something along those lines if questioned. The Patriots' staff also disabled the lights indicating when cameras were in use.

SUSPICIONS GROW

Although New England was engaged in the taping of opponents' signals all the way back to 2000, the preseason of 2006 appears to be the first time the activity started drawing league-wide attention. An assistant of the Giants noticed the Patriots recording signals during their final preseason game. The Giants apparently reported this matter to NFL headquarters, because one week later league executive Ray Anderson sent out a memo to every team warning against this practice. "Videotaping of any kind included [*sic*] but not limited to taping of an opponent's offensive or defensive signals is prohibited on the sidelines, in the coaches' booth, in the locker room, or at any other location accessible to club members during the game."[5]

By Week 9, word of the Patriots' ignoble signal-collection activities had spread throughout the league, and Indianapolis took the unusual step of not allowing any non-network cameramen on the sidelines when they played the Patriots. Then, during Week 11 of the regular season, Green Bay removed Patriots cameraman Matt Estrella from the sideline at Lambeau Field after catching him taping signals. The NFL was well aware of the Patriots' continued signal-collection activities, as multiple teams lodged complaints with league headquarters. The NFL responded by sending out a second letter to all teams prior to the 2007 season.

CAUGHT

While Mangini called Belichick before their Week 1 matchup, he also took a few additional precautions, just in case. He had two assistants relay dummy signals during the game to make deciphering signals more difficult and also tasked the Jets' security team to carefully watch Patriots videographer Matt Estrella.

In spite of two league warnings and Mangini's shot across the bow, the Patriots carried on as if it were business as usual and recorded the Jets' defensive signals during the game. With Jets security on the lookout, it was not long before Estrella was spotted in the thick of it. Jets security then waited a while, giving Estrella plenty of time to record damning evidence before apprehending him. The security members then turned both Estrella and the videotape over to NFL security. Estrella employed all of the Patriots' standard security protocols. He claimed to be with Kraft Productions, wore a special vest that identified him as an NFL photographer, and even had tape over the Patriots logo on his shirt. Not even all of these subterfuges were enough to save him this day, though.

THE LEAGUE RESPONDS

With conclusive evidence in league custody, NFL commissioner Roger Goodell contacted Belichick to get his version of events. During the conversation, Belichick admitted the Patriots had been recording opponents' signals since 2000 but told Goodell he believed he had been operating within the framework of the rules, arguing that videotaping signals was permissible so long as the taped material was not used during the game in which it was recorded.

With this admission and the evidence of the Patriots' wrongdoing, Goodell issued New England's punishment just four days after the Patriots-Jets game. The Patriots received a $250,000 fine, Belichick received a $500,000 fine, and the NFL stripped New England of a first-round draft pick in 2008. Additionally, Goodell ordered the Patriots to turn over all material pertaining to the recordings of opponents' signals and sent NFL general counsel Jeffrey Pash and league executive Ray Anderson to New England several days later to collect. There the Patriots handed over six videotapes and documents going back seven years. Pash and Anderson watched some of the footage before smashing the tapes underfoot and shredding the documents, per direction from Goodell. The league officials also conducted rudimentary interviews with Belichick, special assistant Ernie Adams, and video coordinator Jimmy Dee. During these interviews, Pash and Anderson asked about the impact the taped signals had made on the outcomes of games. The Patriots' staff assured the league officials that taping signals had not provided much of an advantage. The league thus washed its hands of the matter and hoped the controversy and media frenzy would quickly peter out. It would not be that easy.

WERE THE PATRIOTS THE SOLE OFFENDERS?

Patriots fans argued that the league had been unfair in its punishment and alleged other teams had surely engaged in recording opponents' signals as well. They were right, too. After this scandal broke (to be forever after known as "Spygate"), Jimmy Johnson admitted his team in Dallas had done the same: "Oh yeah, I did it with video and so did a lot of other teams in the league. Just to make sure that you could study it and take your time, because you're going to play the other team the second time around. But a lot of coaches did it, this was commonplace."

Johnson did not mention the other coaches involved by name but revealed where he obtained the idea. "Eighteen years ago a scout for the Chiefs told me what they did, and he said what you need to do is just take your camera and you go and zoom in on the signal caller and that way you can sync it up. The problem is that if they're not on the press box side you can't do it from the press box, you have to do it from the sideline. This was 18 years ago."[6]

Of course, in spite of this admission, there was no proof any other teams had engaged in recording opponents' signals after the issuance of the 2006 Ray Anderson memo. Still, Patriots fans felt the main reason their team had been punished was because of its success at deciphering opponents' signals and knowing how to effectively counter opponents' upcoming plays. The revelation that the Cowboys only ended the practice because Jimmy Johnson did not believe it helped only lent credence to this belief.

UNANSWERED QUESTIONS

Patriots fans were not the only ones disgruntled with the NFL's handling of Spygate. The league's swift handling of the scandal left many NFL coaches, players, and fans with more questions than answers. Undoubtedly the most significant unanswered question related to the benefit the Patriots received from conducting illicit signals collection. Belichick and Adams stated the collection activity had no meaningful impact on games, and some former Patriots coaches echoed this line of thought. One coach said, "Ernie is the guy who you watch football with and says, 'It's going to be a run!' And it's a pass. 'It's going to be a pass!' And it's a run. 'It's going to be a run!' It's a run. 'I told you!'"[7] NFL commissioner Roger Goodell publicly agreed with this assessment, stating the Patriots' activities had "a limited effect, if any effect, on the outcome of any game."[8] Others, though, were not so quick to dismiss the usefulness of a program that the Patriots carried out for over half a decade.

One anonymous Patriots employee claimed the signal deciphering program was of quite a bit of use to the Patriots when their opponents did not have much time to change signals between meetings, such as their second games versus AFC East opponents—the very reason that Jets coach Eric Mangini had felt compelled to confront Belichick over this issue. Along a similar line of thought, some former Patriots coaches felt the recording of signals was of most benefit against teams that did not change their signals routinely, such as Miami and Buffalo.

For some games it appears the Patriots knew all, or nearly all, of their opponents' defensive signals. After New England lost its opening game in 2000, Patriots offensive coordinator Charlie Weis told Buccaneers defensive coordinator Monte Kiffin, "We knew all your calls, and you still stopped us. I can't believe it, amazing."[9]

Some players and coaches around the league felt fairly certain that the Patriots' Spygate practices helped them win crucial games that led to Super Bowls and championships. Steelers wide receiver Hines Ward had this to say about the AFC championship game he played against the Patriots in 2002: "They were calling our stuff out. They knew a lot of our calls. There's no question some of their players were calling out some of our stuff." Some Steelers coaches also believe recording signals aided Patriots in the 2005 AFC championship game. Evidence pointing to this includes that the two teams had played previously in the year, and the Steelers did not change their signals all year, Matt Walsh stated he believed the Pittsburgh game earlier in the year had been filmed for signals, and a Steelers coach had several former Patriots players confirm they knew the Steelers' defensive play call signals for this game.[10]

In 2018 Steve Spagnuolo revealed he believed the Patriots used signals they had stolen to help them defeat the Eagles during the 2005 Super Bowl. Spagnuolo, who was the Eagles' linebacker coach at the time, developed this suspicion based upon misgivings voiced by Philadelphia defensive coordinator Jim Johnson during the game. Spagnuolo was skeptical when he initially heard the accusation, but after reviewing the game footage he was certain Johnson's suspicion was correct. "In hindsight, he was right," Spagnuolo argued. "When you go back and look at that tape, it was evident to us.

"I'm not crying over spilled milk here, but we believed that Tom [Brady] knew when we were pressuring because he certainly got the ball out pretty quick."[11]

Just how much Spygate activities benefited New England will likely never be known to any but a select handful wearing Super Bowl rings, but perhaps history can provide some insight as to the advantage recording signals can provide. In 1980 the video recording of signals was not yet prohibited by league rules, and the Chicago Bears attempted to take advantage of this. The Bears were aware that Packers assistant coach Zeke Bratkowski signaled in the offensive plays for Green Bay. The Bears thus videotaped Bratkowski during the first game of the season, and Bears personnel director Bill Tobin studied the Packers' signals prior to their next matchup later that year. In the second game, Tobin deciphered the signals for Bears defensive coordinator Buddy Ryan, and Ryan adjusted his defense accordingly. Tobin would go on to comment, "Let's just say it worked." How much of an impact did this technique make? In the first game, the Packers won 12–6. The Bears won the second 61–7.[12]

THREAT OF A SENATE INVESTIGATION

The NFL's handling of Spygate and the public's desire for a thorough investigation into the Patriots' activities resulted in an outpouring of criticism directed at the NFL and Roger Goodell. One of the most vehement and powerful critics was Senator Arlen Specter of the Senate Judiciary Committee. He questioned the thoroughness of the investigation and believed Goodell had a conflict of responsibilities by virtue of being both the person who issued punishments and also the person responsible for protecting the league. To further complicate the lives of the NFL's brass, Specter called for a congressional inquiry into the Spygate matter.

Gravely concerned about the possibility of congressional intervention, Goodell began requesting statements from senior NFL personnel indicating they were satisfied with the manner in which Spygate had been dealt with by the league; 49ers offensive coordinator Mike Martz was one such person that Goodell contacted. Martz stated that Goodell called him in a panic and said, "The league doesn't need this. We're asking you to come out with a couple lines exonerating us and saying we did our due diligence." Like many coaches around the league, Martz had major concerns and questions about the way the league had handled

Spygate but was also worried a congressional investigation might irrevocably damage the league. Martz thus complied with the commissioner's request and sent a memo off to NFL headquarters. Upon later reading his statement, Martz was baffled to find portions he did not write. "It shocked me," he says. "It appears embellished quite a bit—some lines I know I didn't write. Who changed it? I don't know." This accusation would be nothing compared to what Senator Specter would allege. He stated that a prestigious friend of his informed the senator that if he dropped the issue, he would be financially compensated.[13] Specter declined the offer, leaving everyone wondering if the NFL had tried to buy his silence. In the end, the Senate never launched an investigation. Of course, all of this only led to further suspicions that the NFL had conducted a cover-up of the Spygate affair and would do "whatever it takes," even deceive the public and bribe a senator, in order to protect the league.

LEAGUE IMPACT

While the NFL narrowly escaped a Senate investigation, the effects of Spygate were nonetheless dramatic and chilling. Perhaps the greatest impact of Spygate was a change in the way fans viewed the game. Spygate highlighted the drastic and untoward measures the Patriots had undertaken to reach dynasty status, and many believed New England had simply cheated its way to the top. Numerous fans, perhaps including you, felt their favorite teams had been swindled and were bitter with the Patriots and the league. After all, New England had won three Super Bowls during the Spygate era, and they were only receiving fines and the loss of one draft pick as punishment? Why had the NFL not rescinded New England's titles during this period, like the NCAA would have done if these were college football teams? For many fans, this was the first time they truly questioned if teams were actually playing on a balanced playing field, and they wondered if the NFL's handling of Spygate was just a massive cover-up to protect the image of the league.

Additionally, as a result of Spygate, in 2008 NFL teams voted to allow defensive coordinators to talk with a defensive player via headsets, just like offensive coordinators had been able to do with quarterbacks since

1994. This rule had almost gone into effect prior to the 2007 season as a result of rumblings around the league that the Patriots were involved in recording signals; however, a close vote, with Belichick voting against the change, defeated the proposal. The use of headsets has since greatly diminished the use of signals for play calling. Former Steelers coach Bill Cowher said the practice of deciphering signals in the post-Spygate era "isn't even an element anymore because of the communications that take place on the field to the quarterback, to the linebacker."[14] This is a bit of an exaggeration, since package signals and audibles continue to be collected on by opponents, and some teams even continue to signal in play calls instead of relaying them through headsets.

Chip Kelly's 2014 Eagles are a prime example of this. Philadelphia used signals to relay play calls in, in lieu of headset communications, as they allowed the coaches to pass along information to each member of the offense instantaneously. Players merely needed to look at the sideline to know the upcoming play, as the signals cut out the need for the quarterback to act as the middleman in the huddle. Using signals, the Eagles were able to speed up the offense's tempo and operate at a blistering rate that averaged a mere 15 seconds between snaps.

The Eagles' use of offensive signals and up-tempo pace created interesting problems for opponents. Among them was the inability of defenses to distribute play calls sent in by coaching staffs via headsets in a timely fashion. Green Bay experienced this exact problem, as headset instructions to linebacker A. J. Hawk simply were not arriving quickly enough for distribution. To counter the Eagles' frenetic pace, Packers coaches had to resort to using old-fashioned signals sent in from the sideline, allowing for the potential capture of defensive signals once again.

An additional situation where signals are still needed is when a team is playing in a really noisy environment, and players are having a difficult time hearing the quarterback's calls in the huddle, or the quarterback is having difficulties hearing instructions via the headset. Such an instance took place during a critical third-down play in the 1997 season AFC championship game between the Broncos and the Steelers. The crowd noise was so loud that tight end Shannon Sharpe was unable to hear the play call from quarterback John Elway as they stood in the huddle together. Sharpe left the huddle yelling, "What's the play?"

Elway shouted back, "Just get open!"[15] While a Hall of Fame quarterback can get away with winging a play like this, a signal to get everyone on the same page is the preferred method and helps to avoid giving the coach a heart attack.

THE NFL BLOWS ITS CHANCE TO UNCOVER THE WHOLE ENCHILADA

While the NFL aptly addressed the signals collection issue by allowing headset communications between a coach and defensive player, the league left other issues unresolved, including the question everyone wanted to know: What else had Belichick and the Patriots been up to? After all, teams had been complaining about the Patriots violating various rules for years. Many believed signals collection was just the tip of the iceberg, including members of the NFL's Competition Committee. The committee had discussed allegations made against the Patriots on a routine basis from 2001 to 2006 but had been unable to act without sufficient evidence. Spygate provided the smoking gun to justify a thorough league investigation of Patriots activities, but no such probe ever took place. Almost certainly, the Patriots thus escaped punishment for other illicit collection techniques, and many wondered whether this was an oversight or a deliberate attempt to conceal the extent of the Patriots' malfeasance from the rest of the league and its fans. After all, the NFL was a business, and Spygate was certainly not helping the league's image or its bottom line. Perhaps leaving a few secrets buried was just a price the NFL was willing to pay.

16

THE SKELETONS IN THE CLOSET

If you ain't cheatin', you ain't tryin'.[1]—Jerry Glanville

A NOT-SO-SUPER BOWL FOR THE RAMS

The Saint Louis Rams were heavy favorites heading into the 2002 Super Bowl versus the New England Patriots, and for good reason. The Patriots had finished the 2001 regular season with a solid 11–5 record, but this win-loss total belied New England's 24th ranked defense in yards surrendered and its 19th ranked offense in yards gained. Statistically, they were nothing more than an average team that had overachieved.

In comparison, the Rams had put together a stellar 14–2 season, had the top-ranked offense in the league in points and yards gained, and possessed the third-ranked defense in yards allowed. While the defense had been surprisingly stout all season, the Rams were renowned for their "Greatest Show on Turf." This offense was led by reigning league MVP Kurt Warner, their quarterback who had averaged just over 300 yards per game in the regular season. He was supported by wide receiver Torry Holt, who would finish his career with seven Pro Bowl nominations, and Isaac Bruce, a future Hall of Fame inductee. Furthermore, the offense also employed the services of running back Marshall Faulk, who had accumulated 2,147 all-purpose yards in the regular season, was the league MVP the season prior, and would be another future Hall of Fame inductee. With these weapons the Rams were lighting up scoreboards all over the league. Four times this season the Saint Louis offense had scored 40 or more points, and it had scored 30 or more points on 12 occasions. The Rams were confident they could butt heads with any team in the league and come away victorious.

Yet, as lopsided as the game was on paper in favor of the Rams, it was anything but when the teams clashed. The Patriots gave the Rams everything they could handle, and despite a late comeback that almost saw the Rams climb back from a steep deficit, New England narrowly defeated the heavy favorites 20–17. The Rams were absolutely stunned. They had locked horns, and they had lost. Their vaunted offense had been held to a paltry 6 points through the first three quarters. NFL pundits and fans alike were trying to figure out how this could be as Rams players watched the confetti fall in disbelief.

Rams running back Marshall Faulk was one of those left pondering where everything had gone wrong. Faulk's performance in the Super Bowl had been admirable. He had run 17 times for 76 yards and caught an additional four balls for another 54 yards, all in spite of being hit on almost every play, whether he was handed the ball or not. Yet somehow, the Rams had still come up short.

Perhaps if the gadget plays coach Mike Martz had designed had been more effective, it might have made the difference, but the Patriots had always seemed to know what to expect. When Faulk went back to receive a kickoff—something he had done only one other time all season—Adam Vinatieri had seemed to know he was back there and purposefully kicked away from him, pinning him on the sideline. When he caught a ball in the flat, and expected to see nothing but green grass in front of him, Patriots defenders had anticipated where he would be and were standing there waiting for him.

The Patriots' defense had been incredibly tough, and it was nothing if not well coached and well disciplined, but it also seemed omniscient at times—like with the red zone plays Coach Martz had installed just for the Super Bowl and the Rams had never used before. How had the Patriots known exactly what was coming? The Rams had intentionally thrown new looks and plays at the Patriots precisely because the entire league knew how good the Patriots were at film study. Yet the Patriots defense had known exactly what to do, even with the new plays and looks. How? There was nothing to study, and no way to know.

SPYING ON PRACTICES

Approximately six years after the game, on February 2, 2008, the *Boston Herald* ran an article after an unnamed source came forward and claimed that the Patriots had filmed a Rams practice prior to the Patriots playing Saint Louis in the 2002 Super Bowl.[2] Near the same time, former Patriots videographer Matt Walsh claimed to have new evidence of Patriots' spying activities. The two together sparked a wave of outrage and national interest in NFL activities, not witnessed since the Spygate scandal.

The claim run by the *Boston Herald* was not the first of its kind. NFL commissioner Roger Goodell admitted that the league had heard rumors of this before. "We pursued it and weren't able to get any information that was credible."[3] Many were convinced Walsh had the footage to damn the Patriots once and for all, and NFL fans and pundits alike were eager to hear what Walsh had to say. Goodell seemed less keen on the idea and took several months to iron out the terms of Walsh's testimony.

In the interim, Rams running back Marshall Faulk began speaking out about the Rams' Super Bowl loss: "I understand Bill is a great coach, but number thirteen [Kurt Warner] will tell you. [Former Rams coach] Mike Martz will tell you. We had some plays in the red zone that we hadn't ran. . . . We hadn't ran them the whole year. . . . It's either the best coaching in the world when you come up with situations that you had never seen before. Or you'd seen it and knew what to do."[4]Members of opposing teams also came forward, sharing stories about how the Patriots were prepared for plays they should not have been. Pittsburgh wide receiver Hines Ward felt the Patriots' unexplained knowledge of Steelers audibles and signals in the 2001 and 2004 AFC championship games had been vital to the Patriots' success. Additionally, an unnamed Panthers source expressed his belief that the Patriots taped Carolina practices leading up to the 2004 Super Bowl, saying "it was like [the Patriots] were in our huddle."[5]

On May 13, 2008, Goodell finally sat down and interviewed Walsh. Shortly after, he held a press conference and told the world what he had learned. Almost nothing. Walsh did not have the smoking gun videotape so many were hoping for, and there had been no major revelations shared.

Goodell did mention that Walsh and other Patriots employees had sat around and watched 30 minutes of the Rams' practice before the 2002 Super Bowl, while wearing Patriots attire and in full sight of the Rams' crew, in order to point out Saint Louis had been very aware of their presence and spotted no recording activities, or anything else untoward. What Goodell failed to mention—assuming Walsh did not hide this from him, and there is no reason to think that—is what came out later on the Senate floor after Senator Arlen Specter interviewed Walsh.

The Rams had indeed been foolish enough to let Walsh and other Patriots employees watch almost the entirety of the walkthrough practice, and during this practice Rams star running back Faulk had lined up as a kickoff returner and as a running back in the flat, two unusual assignments for him. The Rams had also practiced red zone plays (plays within 20 yards of the goal line) during the walkthrough. After the practice was over, Walsh located Patriots assistant coach Brian Daboll back at their hotel and briefed him on what he had seen. The information was pure gold. Red zone information is always highly prized, and Coach Belichick had been desperate to know how Faulk would be utilized for the Super Bowl, believing that stopping him was the key to derailing the Rams.

With the myth now debunked that the Patriots had taped the walkthrough practice before the 2002 Super Bowl, there was no longer much reason to believe the Patriots were involved in recording practices—even if they did spy on them—but then an incident in Denver threw everything back into question. In 2009, Patriots offensive coordinator Josh McDaniels joined the Broncos as their new head coach and took the unusual step of acquiring former Patriots videographer Steve Scarnecchia from the Jets. Nearly a year later, with the Broncos in the midst of a slump, Scarnecchia taped footage of a 49ers walkthrough practice. The Broncos' front office mysteriously managed to acquire the film and quickly launched an investigation. McDaniels and Scarnecchia were both interviewed by Broncos staff members, and McDaniels stated he had refused to view the tape when informed of its existence by Scarnecchia and had nothing to do with the recorded material. No one could prove otherwise, not even the NFL investigation and forensic sweep that followed, although many had their doubts. Most NFL experts assumed the recording of practice footage was simply a continuation of what the pair had learned in New England, especially since Scarnecchia had been involved with the recording of opponents' signals in New England as a video assistant from 2001 to 2005.

Whether or not the Patriots were involved in taping practices, many teams around the league still strongly suspected New England made a habit of watching opponents' practices and thus safeguarded their practices accordingly. For example, in 2019, Bills head coach Sean McDermott escorted two Patriots assistants—one of them being Brian Belichick, the son of Bill Belichick—off the field after they were spotted watching the Bills' warm-up session. The Patriots had already gone back inside the locker room at this point, and the reason the New England assistants were dawdling was unclear—which is to say, the reason was perfectly clear. Lingering outside of practices seems to be a Patriots habit, even if their involvement in taping practices remains a mystery.

FLIGHT STATUS CHECKS

The Patriots were certainly spying on practices and illicitly taping signals, but their collection efforts did not end there. New England even scouted teams traveling to play in Foxboro for missing players, as prior to 2005 NFL teams were not required to provide a list of the players who would be traveling to away games. By some means, in the early 2000s Belichick was able to inform his Patriots staff which opposing players had not made the flights for games. This knowledge gave the Patriots a few extra hours before kickoff to revise their game plan and account for the opponent's sick and injured players who would not be playing that week.

Now, the Patriots could have employed perfectly legitimate ways of garnering this information—such as sending a staff member or a fan to the airport to confirm or deny the presence of players—or the means could have been illicit if not illegal—such as asking, and perhaps paying, an airline member to check the names of certain players on the flight manifest and sharing this information with the Patriots.

LOCKER-ROOM COLLECTION

While acquiring information on opponents' flight status was certainly useful, it was nothing compared to the benefits of this next collection technique. Ex-Patriots assistant coaches who served under Belichick during the Spygate era claim the Patriots routinely stole opposing teams' play sheets during games at Gillette Stadium. While the visiting team was busy warming up, a Patriots employee allegedly slunk into the locker room and stole this paperwork. Why is this important? Play sheets typically outline the first 20 or so scripted offensive play calls of a game and can include reminders of what plays coaches want to run in certain circumstances. Former Patriots employees, including coaches, believed this form of intelligence gathering was even more useful than the team's infamous signals-collection program that was revealed during the Spygate scandal.

Intercepting opponents' play sheets prior to a game can be particularly valuable in knowing what offensive plays a defense will see early in the game, being able to predict the early mix of run versus pass plays, and possibly knowing the exact plays that a team will run in certain down and distance situations. During the 49ers' glory years, coach Bill Walsh's play sheets reflected the order in which he would call plays. Walsh typically only varied from the exact order of his scripted plays on short-yardage downs and then immediately returned to the scripted sheets. If the Patriots recovered any play sheets from teams that called plays in order like Walsh, New England would have known the majority of an opponent's offensive play calls for a quarter or more of a game. Talk about an advantage!

HEADSET MALFUNCTIONS

Another technique the Patriots are suspected of utilizing throughout the Spygate era, and up to the present, is interfering with opponents' headset communications during New England's home games. Teams that have no issues elsewhere have all too often experienced problems in Foxboro.

In a 2006 wild-card playoff game, the Patriots switched frequencies and "forgot" to tell the NFL frequency specialist about the change.

Remarkably, the Patriots changed to the same frequency the Jaguars were using for their coach-to-quarterback communications, leaving the Jacksonville offense high and dry for the majority of the first half until league personnel figured out the issue. The league looked into this incident and determined that the Patriots had not committed a violation.

The next season, Detroit also had issues in Foxboro. The Lions had an early lead in that game but lost their momentum due to reoccurring headset issues every time they launched a drive that started to build up steam. When coach Marvin Lewis of the Bengals heard what had happened to Detroit, he said the same thing happened to his team in New England as well.

In 2008, the Cardinals could not get quarterback Karlos Dansby's headset working the entire game versus New England, his only problem with a headset the entire year. Even backup quarterback Matt Leinart's headset was inoperable. When asked if Dansby thought the headset malfunction in Foxboro was a coincidence, he replied, "C'mon, man. It's not a secret. They gotta do what they gotta do to win, man. . . . It's just how they operate."[6]

In September 2015, the Steelers picked up interference on their headsets from a Patriots radio transmission, leaving the Pittsburgh coaching staff unable to communicate effectively with their players. Under the NFL's equity rule, if one side is unable to use headsets due to technical problems, the other side is prohibited from using their headsets as well, but when the NFL official finally walked over to order the Patriots to stop using their headsets, the Steelers' headsets coincidentally began working again. Strangely, as soon as the NFL official departed the area, the problem returned. The league later determined that the malfunction resulted from an electrical problem that was exacerbated by the weather.

Now, there are numerous theories about how the Patriots might be able to interfere with opponents' signals—both in the analog days, and since the implementation of digital protection in 2012—many of them quite technical and convoluted, but if the Patriots are doing this, most likely they are simply collecting signal frequency information on opponents and jamming those frequencies. Given the claims by former Patriots assistant coaches after Spygate that New England was collecting information, such as play sheets, from opponents' locker rooms and hotel rooms, there is the very real possibility that frequency information was also targeted during these missions. Such collection certainly seems within the Patriots' capabilities and modus operandi, and the Patriots switching to the same frequency used by the Jaguars for the 2006 playoff game is indicative of this type of collection having taken place. Still, it is worth noting that Coach Belichick had also complained about the Patriots having headset issues during home games, and problems with headset communications occur from time to time at other NFL stadiums as well.

HEADSETS AND THE 15-SECOND CUTOFF

The Patriots have also been accused of an equally heinous stratagem of using a second radio frequency to communicate with their quarterback. So, why does it matter what frequency they use? Well, the NFL ensures that the broadcast from the coach to the quarterback cuts off at the 15-second mark on the play clock. This means that if the defense shifts in alignment after this point, the quarterback and not the coach has to make the decision of whether to adjust the upcoming play. Using a second frequency, though, the Patriots' offensive coordinator would have been able to talk to the quarterback up to the snap of the ball, and even during plays. This would have potentially not only allowed the Patriots' coaching staff to call out presnap adjustments for Brady but also given him an additional set of eyes during plays.

Bryan O'Leary made the case that the Patriots actually did this in his book *Spygate: The Untold Story* and presented the following as evidence. Firstly, immediately after the Spygate scandal erupted onto the national scene, Chris Mortensen reported that the NFL was also investigating a possible Patriots violation regarding the number of frequencies used during the Jets-Patriots game. In the interest of full disclosure, NFL spokesman Greg Aiello later stated the NFL had found no proof of wrongdoing in this matter.

Secondly, just a year before the Spygate story broke, there was another interesting account pertaining to the Patriots' headsets. Allegedly, in 2005, Patriots backup quarterback Doug Flutie picked up Tom Brady's spare helmet during a game and was amazed to overhear a coach telling Brady what the defense was going to do before upcoming plays.

Now, take this with a grain of salt. The information is far from first hand as it supposedly came from a conversation between ESPN analyst John Saunders and Flutie and was shared by Saunders with ESPN contributor Dan Le Batard. There is also some confusion about whether Le Batard talked about the incident during the February 1, 2008, airing of the *Dan Le Batard Show* on 790 AM The Ticket or merely wrote about it in a mailbag column several days later, or perhaps both; and neither a transcript of the radio show or a copy of the mailbag column can be found on the internet today. In *Spygate*, O'Leary states that Flutie heard a Patriots coach continuing to talk to Brady past the 15-second cutoff mark, all the way up to the snap of the ball. O'Leary based this claim on information Le Batard allegedly stated during his radio show. To make matters even more complicated and mysterious, Flutie has refused to discuss the incident, in spite of being asked to address it on numerous occasions.

Lastly, when changes were proposed in the aftermath of Spygate, Goodell proposed periodic league spot checks on coaching booths, communication systems, and headsets. So, while the NFL may have found no proof of wrongdoing regarding the headset accusations against the Patriots, the commissioner and the league certainly appear to also have had concerns, and rightly so. In their pursuit of championships, the Patriots under Bill Belichick have shown a blatant disregard for NFL rules and bylaws, as the next chapter will continue to demonstrate.

17

DEFLATEGATE

The Patriots do not need coaches, they need co-conspirators.[1]—Bryan O'Leary

THE VANISHING FOOTBALLS

On January 15, 2015, just a few days prior to the AFC championship game, the Colts notified NFL officials that they suspected the Patriots routinely underinflated balls. So, when veteran Patriots locker-room attendant Jim McNally brought referee Walt Anderson the balls, Anderson gave them a careful inspection. To the eyes and touch they passed scrutiny, but just to be sure, Anderson also checked the inflation pressure of the footballs. This was nothing atypical, and just part of his customary inspection routine. The footballs were inflated right at the 12.5 psi (pounds per square inch) minimum allowed by the NFL. Satisfied that the balls were in accordance with NFL guidelines, Anderson turned his attention elsewhere.

When the time came for Anderson to take the field, he went to grab the footballs supplied by McNally, but they were gone. Had he misplaced them? Had one of the other officials grabbed them and brought them out onto the field? An official was required to maintain possession of the footballs after inspection until minutes before the game so certainly no one else had taken them. Anderson had never seen anything like this in his 19 years of officiating. Where had they gone?

Stepping onto the field, Anderson was inevitably relieved to find that the balls were already out there. It would have been more than a bit embarrassing to lose half of the balls for the AFC championship game. Whatever had happened could be sorted out later. After all, there was a big game to officiate.

But in the second quarter, after the Colts intercepted a ball, a Colts defender brought the ball back to the sideline where the Indianapolis staff checked the pressure of the football Brady had thrown and discovered it was well below the minimum 12.5 psi. The Colts' staff consequently notified the officiating crew of what it had discovered. Anderson had already checked the balls prior to the game. Why were the Colts so insistent that there was an issue with the balls the Patriots' offense was using?

Still, due to the pregame concerns expressed by the Colts, the Patriots' tainted history, and the magnitude of the game, the accusation could not be taken lightly. The matter was passed up the chain of command to Alberto Riveron, a senior league supervisor for the officiating crews, who had flown out to the game in Foxboro because of the Colts' pregame allegations. Riveron decided the footballs from both teams would be reexamined at halftime.

Under Riveron's supervision, two members of the officiating crew, Clete Blakeman and Dyrol Prioleau, did just that, using two air pressure gauges to double-check each pressure reading. The officials concluded that the four Patriots footballs they checked had dropped to a reading of 11.3 psi on average, well below the required 12.5 psi. One was as low as 10.5. The Colts' balls, on the other hand, were still within the NFL's accepted range. With a game still to play and time running out before the start of the second half, the officials reinflated the Patriots' balls and then went about their business as usual. The Patriots went on to crush the Colts 45–7.

Immediately after the game, NFL security interviewed locker-room attendant McNally, who admitted to liberating the balls from the officials' locker room and taking them onto the field after Anderson's inspection. Of course, the balls were supposed to be left with the official, but McNally downplayed the offense, assuring the NFL security personnel that he had brought the balls straight out onto the field after departing the officials' locker room.

THE INVESTIGATION

The day after the game, reports were already surfacing about the irregularities, and rumors of a league investigation were circulating. Calls by fans to invalidate the Patriots' win over the Colts soon followed. Was the NFL really going to let the Patriots get away with cheating their way to another Super Bowl title? Likewise, the Patriots organization immediately began denying any wrongdoing.

Wary of making the same mistake he had made during Spygate, NFL commissioner Goodell ordered a thorough investigation, which was officially announced on January 23. Wisely, Goodell assigned an independent investigator to look into the matter, lawyer Theodore Wells Jr. In addition to acquiring the seemingly damning football pressure records and interviewing the officials about the suspicious irregularities, Wells found additional evidence of potential ball tampering.

The investigation uncovered video footage of McNally, holding a bag of footballs, ducking into a bathroom for 90 seconds after departing the officials' locker room. This soon became the suspected location where McNally deflated the footballs after having audaciously snuck them out from under Anderson's nose. Wells also got his hands on some seemingly damning texts exchanged between McNally and Patriots equipment assistant John Jastremski. The ones most relevant to the investigation are provided below and have been edited for strong language. The spelling and grammar errors have been left unedited:

May 9, 2014 [7 months before the game]

McNally: You working
Jastremski: Yup
McNally: Nice dude . . . jimmy needs some kicks . . . lets make a deal . . . come on help the deflator
McNally: Chill buddy im just f***** with you . . . im not going to espn . . . yet

October 17, 2014 [after a game in which Brady complained the balls were overinflated]

McNally: Tom sucks . . . im going make that next ball a f***** balloon

Jastremski: Talked to him last night. He actually brought you up and said you must have a lot of stress trying to get them done . . .
Jastremski: I told him it was. He was right though . . .
Jastremski: I checked some of the balls this morn. . . . The refs f***** us . . . a few of then were at almost 16
Jastremski: They didnt recheck then after they put air in them
McNally: F*** tom . . . 16 is nothing . . . wait till next sunday
Jastremski: Omg! Spaz

October 21, 2014

McNally: Make sure you blow up the ball to look like a rugby ball so tom can get used to it before sunday
Jastremski: Omg

October 23, 2014

Jastremski: Can't wait to give you your needle this week :)
McNally: F*** tom . . . make sure the pump is attached to the needle . . . f***** watermelons coming
Jastremski: So angry
McNally: The only thing deflating sun . . . is his passing rating

October 24, 2014

Jastremski: I have a big needle for u this week
McNally: Better be surrounded by cash and newkicks . . . or its a rugby sunday
McNally: F*** tom
Jastremski: Maybe u will have some nice size 11s in ur locker
McNally: Tom must really be working your balls hard this week

October 25, 2014

Jastremski: Size 11?
Jastremski: 2 or 3X?
McNally: Tom must really be on you
McNally: 11 0r 11 half . . . 2x unless its tight fitting
Jastremski: Nah. Hasn't even mentioned it, figured u should get something since he gives u nothing

January 7, 2015

McNally: Remember to put a couple sweet pig skins ready for tom to sign
Jastremski: U got it kid . . . big autograph day for you
McNally: Nice throw some kicks in and make it real special
Jastremski: It ur lucky. 11?
McNally: 11 or 11 and half kid

These texts seem to strongly suggest McNally was deflating game day footballs in exchange for autographed balls and shoes from Tom Brady. Following up on these texts, investigator Wells confirmed that Brady had indeed supplied McNally with two autographed footballs and signed a jersey for him on January 10. The proof was piling up, but the league also wanted evidence the footballs could not have gone from 12.5 psi to an average of 11.3 psi via natural means, as the Patriots were contending.

The league thus contracted with Exponent, a scientific research company, to determine if it was possible for the New England–supplied footballs to have lost approximately 1 psi because of the game-time conditions—such as rain and the 48-degree starting temperature. To determine this, Exponent personnel meticulously reviewed game footage and mimicked every action the balls went through from the time they were measured before the game until the half. After testing, retesting, and seeking outside expert opinions, Exponent concluded that only unnatural means could have resulted in such a large loss of pressure. Additionally, Exponent conducted its own tests and verified that 12 footballs could indeed be deflated in 90 seconds.

On May 6, 2015, the Wells report was released and concluded that "it was more probable than not" that the footballs had been tampered with and that "it was more probable than not" that Tom Brady knew of what was happening. The Wells report also noted the investigation was hampered by Brady's refusal to provide emails, texts, and phone records relevant to the investigation. Brady had argued he could not provide texts, as he had destroyed his phone as a routine security measure. Anyone else routinely destroy their cell phone?

THE PUNISHMENT

With the Wells report now complete, all that was left was for the NFL to hand out a punishment. Although the Patriots' infraction this time around was rather minor compared to the taping of signals during Spygate, Goodell was not about to let the Patriots off easy again. Spygate had brought an intense amount of scrutiny to the NFL from fans, commentators, teams, and politicians alike and had furthermore caused many to question the integrity of the game. The scandal had been a public relations nightmare for the NFL and had never truly gone away.

To make matters worse, Patriots coach Bill Belichick and New England owner Robert Kraft had seemingly mocked the commissioner and the NFL in the aftermath of Spygate. Belichick never publicly apologized as he had agreed with Goodell to do, and worst of all, Kraft had awarded Belichick a huge, early contract extension and a large raise, just days after the NFL issued its punishment. Kraft claimed to be disappointed with Belichick's actions in public but seemed to be rewarding his coach in private. So, when the Wells report pointed the finger at the Patriots' misdeeds, Goodell was more than ready to punish Deflategate and redress Spygate. He fined the Patriots $1 million, took away their first-round draft pick in 2016 and another fourth-round pick in 2017, and suspended Brady for the first four games of the 2016 season.

THE BLOWBACK

Goodell was hoping the matter would now be put to rest, but just like with Spygate, the controversy surrounding Deflategate continued to simmer. While Goodell's punishment had been stern, many NFL teams and fans were still disgruntled. Although the Patriots had blatantly cheated, they had still been crowned AFC and ultimately Super Bowl champions. Many felt the win versus the Colts should have been overturned and the Patriots should never have been allowed to play in the ensuing Super Bowl. Once again, the Patriots had cheated, been caught, and managed to collect another Super Bowl trophy. How many times was the league going to allow this to happen?

Patriots fans were in a dither as well and began poking holes in the Wells report. They challenged Exponent's credentials, claiming that the company routinely provided research for car, oil, and insurance companies facing massive lawsuits and testified with its bent findings on behalf of its clients in court. Long before Deflategate, some believed the company routinely manipulated its research to say whatever clients wanted in exchange for sizable sums. There were also questions about the two gauges the officials had used to check the pressure readings. Their measurements for each football differed by as much as 0.3 to 0.45 psi. Were these things even accurate?

The Patriots' leadership was also unhappy with the results of the Wells report, and the punishment the team had received, but no one was angrier than Brady, who felt he had been unjustly punished and had seen his legacy unfairly tainted. He therefore filed an appeal with the NFL and sat down with Goodell for a 10-hour meeting. The talk failed to sway Goodell, and on July 28 the NFL confirmed Brady's four-game suspension.

Brady was livid and requested that the U.S. Court of Appeals for the Second Circuit of New York hear his case. The court agreed and set a March 3, 2016, date. Kraft was equally incensed by this point and said, "I was wrong to put my faith in the league."[2]

Before the appeal could be heard, news broke that seemed to support Brady's and the Patriots' claim of innocence. John Leonard, who teaches a measurement and instrumentation course at the Massachusetts Institute of Technology—arguably not an unbiased institution in light of its geographical location—conducted his own experiment to see if properly inflated footballs could indeed lose air pressure as quickly as the Patriots had claimed. He replicated the game day conditions that the footballs had experienced and concluded that the decrease in air pressure experienced during the game was consistent with the ideal gas law. By November 2015, his video summary was available for viewing on YouTube. Soon scientists around the nation were replicating his experiment and confirming his results.

When faced with this new scientific data, Goodell and the NFL did nothing. In fact, it would have been very difficult for Goodell to do otherwise. NFL owners had previously told him that if he did not properly punish the Patriots for Deflategate, there would be ramifications. Goodell had no desire to find out exactly what that meant. To make matters worse for Goodell, the Patriots had won the Deflategate game against the Colts and then gone on to win the following game, the 2015 Super Bowl. The public outcry to punish the Patriots in the wake of assumed cheating during yet another Super Bowl run was tremendous. Furthermore, while it may have been possible for the footballs to have lost as much pressure as the Patriots and Leonard claimed, no one could really explain how natural conditions had caused the Colts' balls to drop by an average of only 0.45 psi, while the Patriots' balls had lost an average of 1.02 psi.

With Goodell and the NFL believing they were in the right and moreover unable to drop the matter over fear of public and team-owner perceptions, and with Brady equally determined to clear his name and reverse the four-game ban, the controversy and news coverage dragged on like a bad soap opera. Finally, on April 25, 2016, the entire matter began to wind down when the U.S. Court of Appeals upheld the NFL's suspension of Brady. Judge Denny Chin even stated there was "compelling, if not overwhelming" evidence of tampering. Still Brady fought on, and the same court heard his case again, with the same result. Only after being repeatedly rebuffed and with a sense that nothing he did would make any difference did the Patriots' quarterback finally give up, stating he would not pursue an appeal with the U.S. Supreme Court—insert eye-roll emoji here.

A CONCLUSION

The NFL had finally won. The recalcitrant Patriots railed against the severity of the punishment, but most fans and league insiders felt it was more than justified as a make-up call for the light handling of the Spygate scandal. More importantly to the league, the overall perception was that Goodell had handled the matter well and punished the Patriots appropriately. Not everyone was appeased, but at least the vast majority of NFL fans had been placated. Of course, the Patriots had obtained another championship out of all this, but that was almost a foregone conclusion by now. The Patriots had already won four rings under Belichick. What was one more?

Only one question was left to be answered and the incident could be put to rest. How much did deflating the footballs actually help Tom

Brady? Former NFL quarterback Mark Brunell stated, "There's a huge advantage to having a deflated football," and experts tended to agree.[3] They pointed out that deflating the balls made them easier to throw, grip, and catch, and anyone who has ever played backyard football knows this to be true. Just think how much farther you can chuck a small, easily grasped football than a large, slippery, rock-hard pigskin and how much easier the smaller and softer balls are to catch. During rainy games, the added grip of a smaller ball is even more beneficial, as it reduces the chances of the ball slipping out of the hand when thrown.

The league, though, was unwilling to ascribe any advantage whatsoever to the alleged Deflategate actions. NFL executive Troy Vincent wrote, "It is impossible to determine whether this activity had an effect on the outcome of games or what that effect was. . . . There are many factors which affect the outcome of a game. It is an inherently speculative exercise to try to assign specific weight to any one factor."[4]

Impossible? The NFL simply could have taken a set of properly inflated footballs and another of deflated footballs, tested how accurately and how far each set of balls could be thrown, and then calculated the difference between the two sets. That would have been a fair indicator of how much the deflated footballs helped Tom Brady. The truth is, the NFL simply did not want to know the answer because if the deflated footballs helped—and certainly they did—all of the Patriots' wins while using this scheme could have been called into question. Once again, just like it had done for Spygate, the NFL downplayed the benefits of the Patriots' cheating, as if New England did this just for the joy of paying fines and losing draft picks. The league was once again doing everything in its power to portray NFL games as being played on a level playing field, even when clearly this was not always the case.

EPILOGUE

The truth is, football games, like battles and even wars, can be won or lost with effective spies or well-placed traitors.[1]—Tim Green

Collecting on opponents does not in and of itself win games. It is a force multiplier rather than a panacea. Even knowing exactly what an opponent will do every play of a game will not result in a far inferior team beating its superior. Vince Lombardi's Packers team, which was extremely predictable but whose running game dominated the opposition, is a prime example of this. However, games involving fairly equal teams can easily be won or lost through an advantage gained through spying. Referencing the 1958 NFL championship game that the Colts narrowly won over the Giants, Baltimore coach Weeb Ewbank said, "The difference between winning and losing in a match of top-notch football teams is small, even in apparently lopsided games. When two powerful teams get together and play up to the peak of their ability, it's almost impossible to say what tiny factor made the difference in the narrow margin of victory and defeat."[2] Spying is one of those potential factors, as Ewbank well knew. He had his assistant coach Bob Shaw spy on the Giants prior to "the greatest game ever played."

Besides gaining intelligence, an additional benefit of collection is the time and effort opponents are forced to spend attempting to counter collection efforts. For example during, but even more so after, the Spygate scandal, teams facing coach Bill Belichick's Patriots took numerous precautions to deter and defeat real and imagined dangers.

This was of tremendous benefit to the Patriots. While teams needed to be preparing for one of the great quarterbacks of all time in Tom Brady, and one of the great coaches of all time in Bill Belichick, teams instead wasted precious time and energy focusing on preventing signals from being stolen, play sheets from being pilfered, and listening devices from being planted. A week is a very short amount of time to prepare for an opponent, and distractions create major headaches for opposing coaches.

While collecting information on opponents is clearly advantageous, few teams in the NFL take the activity as seriously as they should, as can be seen by the scarcity of trained intelligence personnel used by teams. While some have employed professionally trained intelligence collectors, such as Ron Wolf with Al Davis's Raiders, these appear to be the exception and not the rule. Most teams still rely on scouts and coaches to gather information on opponents and prospects. The few trained intelligence collectors who work in the NFL typically specialize in protecting information, by virtue of their positions as heads of security rather than as information collectors. Teams that have dedicated intelligence collectors have a distinct advantage over the rest of the league.

As for the evolution of collection, techniques have changed dramatically over the history of the league and will surely continue to evolve. Rule changes and countermeasures have weakened or eradicated some forms of collection but have created opportunities for new techniques to take their place. This trend will continue as the NFL blitzes into the future. Technology will also play a crucial role in changing the way espionage is conducted in the league. Collection has and will continue to become more and more technology driven. A week before the 2020 Super Bowl, OurMine hacked numerous team Twitter accounts in order to demonstrate that they were vulnerable to more malicious hacks. If a group of alleged teen hackers can do this, rival teams can as well. This was demonstrated all too clearly in Major League Baseball when Saint Louis Cardinals analyst Chris Correa was sentenced to 46 months in prison for hacking into the webmail system of the Houston Astros on 48 occasions, beginning in January 2012, to view Astros scouting databases. Undoubtedly, NFL teams will follow suit and attempt to hack into digital playbooks, and drones will be used to spy on the practices of opposing teams, if these methods are not already being utilized.

In regard to the NFL's viability, what the battles with the AFL and AAFC clearly demonstrate is that while the league will continue to face other challengers, the NFL will be extremely difficult to dethrone. Just like siblings bicker among themselves and then rally together when one of their own is threatened by an outsider, NFL teams that squabble and argue in peacetime will band together when challengers arise. While the NFL will inevitably fall from grace at some point, competing leagues will be much more likely to be integrated into the NFL than to supplant it.

As for the Patriots, the NFL's efforts to curtail their illicit collection activities and cheating have completely failed. This point is perhaps best illustrated by the Patriots once again being caught with their hand in the cookie jar in Week 14 of the 2019 season. At a Browns-Bengals game, Bengals security spotted Patriots videographers apparently recording the Bengals' sideline and confiscated the footage.

In a press statement, the Patriots quickly admitted to accidentally committing a minor, unintentional infraction:

> For the past year, the New England Patriots team has produced a series of behind-the-scenes features on various departments within the organization. The seven previous "Do Your Job" episodes are archived on patriots.com. On Sunday, Dec. 8, the content team sent a three-person video crew to the Bengals-Browns game at FirstEnergy Stadium in order to capture one part of a longer feature on the Patriots scouting department, in this case a Patriots pro personnel scout while he was working in the press box.
>
> While we sought and were granted credentialed access from the Cleveland Browns for the video crew, our failure to inform the Bengals and the League was an unintended oversight. In addition to filming the scout, the production crew—without specific knowledge of League rules—inappropriately filmed the field from the press box. The sole purpose of the filming was to provide an illustration of an advance scout at work on the road. There was no intention of using the footage for any other purpose. We understand and acknowledge that our video crew, which included independent contractors who shot the video, unknowingly violated league policy by filming the field and sideline from the press box. When questioned, the crew immediately turned over all footage to the league and cooperated fully.

> The production crew is independent of our football operation. While aware that one of the scouts was being profiled for a "Do Your Job" episode, our football staff had no other involvement whatsoever in the planning, filming or creative decisions made during the production of these features.
>
> We accept full responsibility for the actions of our production crew at the Browns-Bengals game.

This explanation sounded great, but it left a very big question unanswered. Why were there approximately eight minutes of film without a single Patriots employee in the shot? Eight minutes of nothing but the Bengals' sideline and the playing field.[3] When asked this question by Bengals security right after being caught, the Patriots' video crew explained, "We were trying to get some field perspective. That's my bad." Eight minutes is a lot of perspective.

This was all too familiar and eerily reminiscent of Spygate. The cover story sounded like another fabrication former Patriots video coordinator Jimmy Dee had trained his videographers to concoct during the Spygate era. All of this clearly pointed to the likelihood that the Patriots' coaching staff was in on the plot.

As for what the Patriots were after, most likely they were targeting the Bengals' package signals and attempting to match the groups of players that were recorded running on and off the field to their corresponding signals.

To look into the incident, the league sent a team of investigators to New England and conducted interviews, retrieved emails, and even reviewed text messages. Apparently the investigation failed to uncover any more meaningful evidence, because the punishment certainly did not reflect it. The Patriots' organization was fined a paltry $1.1 million and lost a third-round pick in 2021, and Patriots television was banned from filming games in 2021. The Patriots received nothing more than a slap on the wrist, again.[4]

Just as some pretty big questions were left hanging after Spygate, the latest scandal involving the Bengals raised the question: Had the Patriots ever stopped taping opponents' sidelines after having been caught in 2007, or had this been going on ever since?

The NFL had now come full circle since Spygate. All indications pointed to the Patriots having once again engaged in prohibited collection, the league's punishment was once again too weak to deter them from doing this in the future, the league once again passed up another opportunity to conduct a comprehensive investigation of the Patriots' entire spying program, and once again, just months prior to being caught, the Patriots had captured another Super Bowl victory. Above all, the latest incident clearly shows that the Patriots plan to continue their illicit collection techniques into the future and that the team is perfectly happy to trade draft picks and fines for Super Bowl titles—not a bad deal for the Patriots and their fans.

If the league truly wishes to provide a fair playing field, and it should, the NFL must hand out harsher punishments to New England. Take away all of the Patriots' draft choices for a year, or strip their titles for periods they are known to have engaged in illicit activities. If this is too harsh, perhaps the league could simply ban the Patriots from the playoffs for future infractions. There is already historical precedent for this. The first NFL commissioner, Joseph Carr, suspended the Pottsville Maroons in 1925 due to improprieties, thus denying them a league championship.

The problem with this is that taking away championships or banning the Patriots from chasing titles is the last thing the league wants to do because it calls into question the integrity of the game. Issuing such punishments is tantamount to admitting that the Patriots' illicit collection efforts grant them a significant, unfair advantage. The league has never admitted to this for any of the Patriots' scandals and has always downplayed the importance of these stratagems. Frankly, though, the league needs to start emphasizing the integrity of the game over maintaining the perception of integrity.

Furthermore, the league needs to take advantage of the Patriots when they are caught breaking rules and launch a thorough investigation into the entirety of their collection efforts, because if the Patriots are cheating in one area, they are likely cheating elsewhere as well. Kevin Murray, the president of a firm specializing in counterespionage, said this about spying in the NFL: "If it's successful, you'll never know. If it's done correctly, you may see the results of it, but you'd never know it occurred. If you take the failed attempts you see, you can figure that's just the tip of the iceberg."[5] "The tip of the iceberg" is precisely as far as the NFL has shown a willingness to go in investigating the Patriots under the Bill Belichick regime. I point this out not in the spirit of bashing Belichick, the Patriots, the NFL, or the game of football, but in the hopes that highlighting the problem will bring about meaningful change.

Having said that, I will admit I gained a newfound respect and fondness for the villainous Al Davis while researching this book. He was arguably the only coach in the history of the NFL on par with Belichick when it came to being scrupulously unscrupulous. Nonetheless, I found his stories entertaining and his desire to win at all costs somehow endearing and relatable. Perhaps in time, once wounds have healed and emotions have calmed, Belichick will be regarded in a similar light, as a villain as necessary to the entertainment aspect of the NFL as Darth Vader is to the Star Wars story—a character who brought excitement and intrigue to football. Conceivably, his contributions will be appreciated more fully by future generations.

As a parting thought, I would like to point out that the Al Davises and Bill Belichicks of the NFL are people like you and me, with basically the same needs, hopes, dreams, and desires. Are they villains? Maybe. Do they engage in disreputable spying tactics to help their teams win? Certainly. Yet what drives them even more than winning is their desire to stick around a game they love for as long as possible. This requires a tremendous amount of work and luck. Some say the acronym "NFL" stands for "Not for Long," and for good reason.

Everyone's time in the NFL is limited. The careers of players are frighteningly short. Anything over five years is a good run. Age and injury catch up to even the best players, and usually much sooner than expected. Even legendary coaches get fired; just ask Paul Brown, who led the Cleveland Browns to four AAFC and three NFL championships. No one is safe. Just like with players, a coach's career can end at any time and entirely unexpectedly. Knowing their time is fleeting, coaches hold on tenaciously to the sport and job they love and do anything in their power to keep it.

This is simply the same passion that pushes us to continue to play whatever sports we love well past our prime, perhaps well past what common sense dictates. More than anything, this passion to keep doing what we love is what spying in the NFL is all about.

NOTES

PREFACE

1. Michael Austin, "Winning Isn't Everything," *Psychology Today*, July 12, 2010, https://www.psychologytoday.com/blog/ethics-everyone/201007/winning-isnt-everything.
2. Tom Schad, "Could the NFL Draft Be Hacked? Virtual Draft Poses New Cybersecurity Challenges," *USA Today*, April 21, 2020, https://www.usatoday.com/story/sports/nfl/draft/2020/04/21/nfl-draft-2020-hacked-security-breach-virtual-teams/5163797002.

1. COLLECTION DURING PRACTICES

1. Pete Dougherty, "The NFL's Original Spy vs. Spy: Packers-Bears," *Packers News*, September 12, 2015, http://www.packersnews.com/story/sports/nfl/packers/dougherty/2015/09/12/nfls-original-spy-vs-spy/72103086.
2. William Gildea and Kenneth Turan, *The Future Is Now: George Allen, Pro Football's Most Controversial Coach* (Boston: Houghton Mifflin, 1972), 194–95.
3. Lee Grosscup, "Spying in Pro Football," *Sport*, August 1967, http://archive.li/JUDqE.
4. Gary D'Amato and Cliff Christl, *Mudbaths & Bloodbaths: The Inside Story of the Bears-Packers Rivalry* (Madison, WI: Prairie Oak, 1997), 209–10.
5. Josh Katzowitz, *Sid Gillman: Father of the Passing Game* (Covington, KY: Clerisy, 2012), 16.
6. Jeff Miller, *Going Long* (New York: McGraw-Hill, 2003), 85.

7. Peter Richmond, *Badasses: The Legend of Snake, Food, Dr. Death, and John Madden's Oakland Raiders* (New York: HarperCollins, 2010), 44.

8. Dan Pompei, "How the NFL Cheats: Spy Games," Bleacher Report, September 30, 2016, http://bleacherreport.com/articles/2657226-how-the-nfl-cheats-spy-games.

9. Dick Schafrath, *Heart of a Mule* (Cleveland, OH: Gray, 2006), 88–90.

10. Gildea and Turan, *Future Is Now*, 198.

11. Pompei, "How the NFL Cheats."

12. Mike Shanahan with Adam Schefter, *Think Like a Champion* (New York: HarperBusiness, 1999), 210–11.

13. David Maraniss, *When Pride Still Mattered* (New York: Simon & Schuster, 1999), 245.

14. D'Amato and Christl, *Mudbaths & Bloodbaths*, 190.

15. Jeremy Bergman, "Steelers Erect Tarp to Prevent against 'Drones,'" NFL.com, August 23, 2018, https://www.nfl.com/news/steelers-erect-tarp-to-prevent-against-drones-0ap3000000950289.

16. Jeff Davis, *Papa Bear: The Life and Legacy of George Halas* (New York: McGraw-Hill, 2005), 18.

17. Snehith Vemuri, "Peyton Manning: Ex-Broncos Player Explains How Peyton Manning Held Practice in the Woods to Prevent Patriots Spying," Sports Rush, August 18, 2020, https://thesportsrush.com/nfl-news-ex-broncos-player-explains-how-peyton-manning-held-practice-in-the-woods-to-prevent-patriots-spying.

18. Don Pierson, "Spy-Conscious Gibbs Scrambles the Redskins' Practice Signal," *Chicago Tribune*, January 27, 1988, http://articles.chicagotribune.com/1988-01-27/sports/8803250845_1_skins-owner-redskins-quarterback-joe-theismann-redskins-lease.

19. Paul Brown with Jack Clary, *PB: The Paul Brown Story* (New York: Atheneum, 1979), 223–24.

2. LOCKER-ROOM COLLECTION AND SEARCHING FOR PAPERWORK

1. Joe Patoski, *The Dallas Cowboys* (New York: Back Bay Books, 2012), 62.

2. Hank Stram with Lou Sahadi, *They're Playing My Game* (Chicago: Triumph Books, 1986), 157–59.

3. Dan Pompei, "How the NFL Cheats: Spy Games," Bleacher Report, September 30, 2016. http://bleacherreport.com/articles/2657226-how-the-nfl-cheats-spy-games.

4. Scott Allen, "Redskins Fan Finds Released Player's Workbooks in Dumpster, Team Isn't Concerned," *Washington Post*, September 1, 2016, https://www.washingtonpost.com/news/dc-sports-bog/wp/2016/09/01/redskins-fan-finds-released-players-workbooks-in-dumpster-team-isnt-concerned/?utm_term=.930787691cbd.

5. David Fleming, "Don't Touch My Playbook," ESPN.com, January 18, 2008, http://sports.espn.go.com/espn/page2/story?page=fleming/080117.

6. Joshua Robinson, "NFL's Worst Sin: Losing a Playbook," *Wall Street Journal*, August 24, 2012, https://www.wsj.com/articles/SB10000872396390443584045776098621933055\18.

7. Fleming, "Don't Touch My Playbook."

8. Mike Klis, "D. J. Williams Deletes Post of Defensive Formations; But Issue Adds to Woes," *Denver Post*, June 9, 2012, http://www.denverpost.com/broncos/ci_20818370/broncos-dj-williams-makes-play-public-twitter.

9. Fleming, "Don't Touch My Playbook."

10. Gary D'Amato and Cliff Christl, *Mudbaths & Bloodbaths: The Inside Story of the Bears-Packers Rivalry* (Madison, WI: Prairie Oak, 1997), 37–38.

3. LISTENING DEVICES

1. Michael David Smith, "Peyton Manning Feared Patriots Bugging Visitor's Locker Room," *ProFootballTalk* (blog), NBC Sports, August 20, 2015, http://profootballtalk.nbcsports.com/2015/08/20/peyton-manning-feared-patriots-bugging-visitors-locker-room.

2. Greg Bishop, "Paranoia Strikes Deep, into Your Headset It Will Creep," *New York Times*, November 13, 2007, http://www.nytimes.com/2007/11/13/sports/football/13paranoid.html?_r=0.

3. Frank Luksa, "NFL Spy Stories Once Had Comedic Touch," ESPN.com, September 13, 2007, http://sports.espn.go.com/nfl/columns/story?columnist=luksa_frank&id=3017278.

4. Mark Ribowsky, *Slick: The Silver & Black Life of Al Davis* (New York: Macmillan, 1991), 157.

5. Mike Florio, "Saints Call Report of Loomis Espionage '1000 Percent False,'" *ProFootballTalk* (blog), NBC Sports, April 23, 2012, http://profootballtalk.nbcsports.com/2012/04/23/saints-call-espn-report-of-loomis-espionage-1000-percent-false.

6. Mike Freeman, *Bowden: How Bobby Bowden Forged a Football Dynasty* (New York: HarperCollins, 2009), 9–10.

7. Dan Daly, "Cheating: An NFL Tradition for 95 Years," *Pro Football Daly* (blog), January 24, 2015, http://profootballdaly.com/the-nfls-long-glorious-tradition-of-cheating.

8. Jimmy Traina, "Peyton Manning Brings the Heat in Week 2, Accuses Patriots of Bugging Locker Room: TRAINA Thoughts," *Sports Illustrated*, September 21, 2021, https://www.si.com/extra-mustard/2021/09/21/peyton-manning-says-patriots-bugged-locker-room.

9. Ian Henson, "Mike Shanahan on Spygate and Cheating," *Mile High Report*, September 11, 2015, http://www.milehighreport.com/2015/9/11/9296053/mike-shanahan-on-spygate-and-cheating-patriots.

10. Daryl Ruiter, "NFL Investigating Alleged Gameday Texting to Coaches by Browns Front Office Personnel," CBS Cleveland, January 9, 2015, http://cleveland.cbslocal.com/2015/01/09/nfl-investigating-alleged-gameday-texting-to-coaches-by-browns-staff.

11. Seth Walder and Justin Tasch, "Jets Deny Report They Asked NFL to Check for Listening Devices in Patriots Visiting Locker Room," *New York Daily News*, October 31, 2015, https://www.nydailynews.com/sports/football/jets/jets-wanted-locker-room-searched-pats-game-boomer-article-1.2417540.

4. MISCELLANEOUS GAME-TIME COLLECTION

1. Mark Ribowsky, *Slick: The Silver & Black Life of Al Davis* (New York: Macmillan, 1991), 150.

2. John Branch, "Headsets Signal Play-Calling Advantage," *Gazette*, 2002, http://servv89pn0aj.sn.sourcedns.com/~gbpprorg/nfl/headsets.txt (article deleted).

3. Katie Linendoll, "Are NFL Teams Hacking Helmet Headsets?" ESPN.com, October 4, 2012, http://espn.go.com/blog/playbook/tech/post/_/id/2573/robert-griffin-iii-helmet.

4. Linendoll, "Are NFL Teams Hacking?"

5. Linendoll, "Are NFL Teams Hacking?"

6. Melissa Isaacson, "Illegal? Unethical? Or Strategy? For Some, Stealing Signs Is Just Part of the Game. Videotaping, However, Seems to Cross the Line," *Chicago Tribune*, September 16, 2007, http://articles.chicagotribune.com/2007-09-16/news/0709150335_1_matt-estrella-signals-stealing/2.

7. Rick Reilly, "The Silent Treatment," *Sports Illustrated*, January 14, 2002, http://www.si.com/vault/2002/01/14/316765/the-silent-treatment.

8. Scott Sheaffer, "The Truth about Spygate: Punishing Success and Promoting Parity," Bleacher Report, June 14, 2009, http://bleacherreport.com/

articles/199345-the-truth-about-spygate-punishing-success-and-promoting-parity.

9. Jeff Davis, *Papa Bear: The Life and Legacy of George Halas* (New York: McGraw-Hill, 2005), 369.

10. Mark Ribowsky, *The Last Cowboy: A Life of Tom Landry* (New York: Liveright, 2014), 125.

11. Brendan Prunty, "Tom Brady, Eli Manning Differ on Them, but Wristbands Are Now a Common Tool for NFL Quarterbacks," *New Jersey Star-Ledger*, February 3, 2012, http://www.nj.com/giants/index.ssf/2012/02/tom_brady_eli_manning_may_diff.html.

12. Lee Grosscup, "Spying in Pro Football," *Sport*, August 1967, http://archive.li/JUDqE.

13. William Gildea and Kenneth Turan, *The Future Is Now: George Allen, Pro Football's Most Controversial Coach* (Boston: Houghton Mifflin, 1972), 111.

5. ELICITATION

1. Gordon Forbes, *Dick Vermeil: Whistle in His Mouth, Heart on His Sleeve* (Chicago: Triumph Books, 2009), xviii.

2. Michael David Smith, "Bill Belichick Reflects on His Interview with Al Davis," *ProFootballTalk* (blog), NBC Sports, October 1, 2011, http://profootballtalk.nbcsports.com/2011/10/01/bill-belichick-reflects-on-his-interview-with-al-davis.

3. Michael Holley, *Belichick and Brady* (New York: Hachette Books, 2016), 57.

4. Joe Namath, "Fond Farewells: Al Davis Oakland Raiders Owner, 82," *Time*, December 14, 2011,http://content.time.com/time/specials/packages/article/0,28804,2101745_2102136_2102213,00.html.

5. Andrew Joseph, "Ty Law Explained Peyton Manning's Old Scheme to Uncover Game Secrets from Pro Bowl Players," *USA Today Sports*, April 2, 2020, https://ftw.usatoday.com/2020/04/peyton-manning-ty-law-pro-bowl-story-mai-tai-drinks-secrets.

6. Lee Grosscup, "Spying in Pro Football," *Sport*, August 1967, http://archive.li/JUDqE.

7. Jeff Miller, *Going Long* (New York: McGraw-Hill, 2003), 43.

8. David Maraniss, *When Pride Still Mattered* (New York: Simon & Schuster, 1999), 314.

9. Associated Press, "Harbaughs Are Strictly Business," ESPN.com, January 22, 2013, http://www.espn.com/nfl/playoffs/2012/story/_/id/8868301/2013-

nfl-playoffs-jim-john-harbaugh-only-texting-super-bowl-san-francisco-49ers-baltimore-ravens.

10. Gary D'Amato and Cliff Christl, *Mudbaths & Bloodbaths: The Inside Story of the Bears-Packers Rivalry* (Madison, WI: Prairie Oak, 1997), 38–39.

11. D'Amato and Christl, *Mudbaths & Bloodbaths*, 38–39.

6. INSIDER INFORMATION

1. Frank Litsky, "Pro Football; Farewell to Ewbank: Vignettes of a True Coach and Friend," *New York Times*, November 19, 1998, http://www.nytimes.com/1998/11/19/sports/pro-football-farewell-to-ewbank-vignettes-of-a-true-coach-and-friend.html.

2. Paul Brown with Jack Clary, *PB: The Paul Brown Story* (New York: Atheneum, 1979), 234.

3. Bill Parcells and Nunyo Demasio, *Parcells: A Football Life* (New York: Crown Archetype, 2014), 479.

4. Joe Patoski, *The Dallas Cowboys* (New York: Back Bay Books, 2012), 57.

5. Gary D'Amato and Cliff Christl, *Mudbaths & Bloodbaths: The Inside Story of the Bears-Packers Rivalry* (Madison, WI: Prairie Oak, 1997), 190.

7. ADVANCE SCOUTING

1. Hank Stram with Lou Sahadi, *They're Playing My Game* (Chicago: Triumph Books, 1986), 47.

2. Anonymous NFL staff member, telephone conversation with author, September 20, 2017.

3. Josh Katzowitz, *Sid Gillman: Father of the Passing Game* (Covington, KY: Clerisy, 2012), 75–76.

4. Katzowitz, *Sid Gillman*, 165.

5. Paul Zimmerman, *The Last Season of Weeb Ewbank* (New York: Farrar, Straus and Giroux, 1974), 220.

6. David Fleming, "No More Questions," ESPN.com, October 4, 2016, http://www.espn.com/espn/feature/story/_/id/17703210/new-england-patriots-coach-bill-belichick-greatest-enigma-sports.

7. Brian Costello, "Peyton's Film Studying Is Stuff of Legend," *New York Post*, January 30, 2014, http://nypost.com/2014/01/30/peyton-mannings-film-study-obsession-is-stuff-of-legend.

8. David Maraniss, *When Pride Still Mattered* (New York: Simon & Schuster, 1999), 392–95.
9. George Allen, *How to Scout Football* (Mansfield Centre, CT: Martino, 2009), 25.
10. Mike Shanahan with Adam Schefter, *Think Like a Champion* (New York: HarperBusiness, 1999), 27–28.
11. Dave Wyman, "The Importance of Film Study," 710 ESPN Seattle, September 30, 2011, https://sports.mynorthwest.com/6210/the-importance-of-film-study.
12. Katzowitz, *Sid Gillman*, 20.
13. Thomas George, "The ABC's of X's and O's: The Art of Play-Calling in the N.F.L.," *New York Times*, December 15, 1996, http://www.nytimes.com/1996/12/15/sports/the-abc-s-of-x-s-and-o-s-the-art-of-play-calling-in-the-nfl.html.
14. Jon Gruden with Vic Carucci, *Do You Love Football?! Winning with Heart, Passion & Not Much Sleep* (New York: HarperCollins, 2003), 129–30.

8. DEBRIEFS

1. Mike Shanahan with Adam Schefter, *Think Like a Champion* (New York: HarperBusiness, 1999), 103.
2. Mark Craig and Kent Youngblood, "Vikings Turn to Espionage," *Minnesota Star Tribune*, October 17, 2012, http://www.startribune.com/sports/vikings/174680161.html?refer=y.
3. David Fleming, "Facing a Former Team Doug Evans Provided Carolina with Inside Information on Green Bay," *Sports Illustrated*, October 5, 1998, http://www.si.com/vault/1998/10/05/249844/facing-a-former-team-doug-evans-provided-carolina-with-inside-information-on-green-bay.
4. Tim Green, *The Dark Side of the Game: My Life in the NFL* (New York: Warner Books, 1996), 253.
5. Kevin Patra, "Rams' Eric Weddle Won't Share Inside Info on Rams," NFL.com, November 20, 2019, https://www.nfl.com/news/rams-eric-weddle-won-t-share-inside-info-on-ravens-0ap3000001079083.
6. Kevin Acee, "San Diego Chargers Know Seahawks Have a Spy," *San Diego Union-Tribune*, September 23, 2010, http://www.sandiegouniontribune.com/sdut-chargers-know-seahawks-have-spy-2010sep23-story.html.
7. Dan Pompei, "How the NFL Cheats: Spy Games," Bleacher Report, September 30, 2016. http://bleacherreport.com/articles/2657226-how-the-nfl-cheats-spy-games.
8. Patra, "Weddle Won't Share."

9. SIGNALS COLLECTION

1. NFL.com, "Spying in the NFL," NFL.com, September 12, 2007, http://www.nfl.com/videos/new-england-patriots/09000d5d8024b648/Spying-in-the-NFL (article deleted).

2. Gary Myers, "Following Bitter Breakup with Al Davis and Raiders, Mike Shanahan Gets a Measure of Revenge with Steve Young and 49ers," *New York Daily News*, November 13, 2012, http://www.nydailynews.com/sports/football/shanahan-revenge-davis-young-article-1.1201352.

3. Raiders.com staff, "From 'Purple Walrus' to 'James Harden,' Derek Carr Jokes about In-Game Audibles Going Viral," Raiders.com, November 23, 2020, https://www.raiders.com/news/from-purple-walrus-to-james-harden-derek-carr-jokes-about-in-game-audibles-going.

4. David Harris, *The Genius: How Bill Walsh Reinvented Football and Created an NFL Dynasty* (New York: Random House, 2008), 337.

5. Bob Glauber, "Spying Nothing New in the NFL," *Saint Catharines Standard*, September 14, 2007, http://www.stcatharinesstandard.ca/2007/09/14/spying-nothing-new-in-the-nfl (article deleted).

6. Mike Sando, "What's Legal, What's Illegal in NFL Spy Game," ESPN.com, September 13, 2007, http://sports.espn.go.com/nfl/columns/story?columnist=sando_mike&id=3017542.

7. Ross Tucker, "Cheaters Never Win: The Risk of Breaking Rules Not Worth Reward," CNN Sports Illustrated, May 16, 2008, http://sportsillustrated.cnn.com/2008/writers/ross_tucker/05/15/rules/index.html#ixzz2DOnbKT6x(site discontinued).

8. "Gary D'Amato and Cliff Christl, *Mudbaths & Bloodbaths: The Inside Story of the Bears-Packers Rivalry* (Madison, WI: Prairie Oak, 1997), 146–47.

9. Josh Katzowitz, "Players, Coaches 'Totally Against' On-Field Mics Picking Up QB Signals," CBS Sports, September 7, 2014, http://www.cbssports.com/nfl/news/players-coaches-totally-against-on-field-mics-picking-up-qb-signals.

10. Doug Pederson with Dan Pompei, *Fearless: How an Underdog Becomes a Champion* (New York: Hachette Books, 2018), 205.

11. Pederson with Pompei, *Fearless*, 212.

12. Michael Lewis, "What Keeps Bill Parcells Awake at Night," *New York Times*, October 29, 2006, http://www.nytimes.com/2006/10/29/sports/playmagazine/1029play_parcells.html.

13. Tim Green, *The Dark Side of the Game: My Life in the NFL* (New York: Warner Books, 1996), 253.

14. Greg Bishop, "Fear and Loathing," *Sports Illustrated*, September 14, 2015, http://www.si.com/vault/2016/02/11/fear-and-loathing.

10. OPEN-SOURCE AND MEDIA COLLECTION

1. Rick Reilly, “Commitment to Honesty,” ESPN.com, October 14, 2011, http://www.espn.com/espn/story/_/id/7098616/rick-reilly-reflects-al-davis-commitment-honesty.
2. Tim Booth, “Seahawks Hope They Didn’t Spill Too Many Secrets to 49ers,” *Seattle Post-Intelligencer*, September 14, 2017, http://www.seattlepi.com/sports/article/Seahawks-hope-they-didn-t-spill-too-many-secrets-12198583.php (article deleted).
3. Paul Zimmerman, *The Last Season of Weeb Ewbank* (New York: Farrar, Straus and Giroux, 1974), 180.
4. Michael Lewis, “What Keeps Bill Parcells Awake at Night,” *New York Times*, October 29, 2006, http://www.nytimes.com/2006/10/29/sports/playmagazine/1029play_parcells.html.
5. Michael MacCambridge, *Chuck Noll: His Life Work* (Pittsburgh, PA: Pittsburgh Press, 2016), 253–54.
6. William Gildea and Kenneth Turan, *The Future Is Now: George Allen, Pro Football’s Most Controversial Coach* (Boston: Houghton Mifflin, 1972), 198.
7. Lewis, “What Keeps Parcells Awake.”

11. DRAFT PROSPECTS

1. Mandy Antoniacci, “28 of the Greatest Quotes from NFL Legends,” *Inc.*, September 8, 2016, https://www.inc.com/mandy-antoniacci/28-of-the-greatest-quotes-from-nfl-legends.html.
2. Anonymous NFL staff member, telephone conversation with author, September 20, 2017.
3. Albert Breer, “NFL Draft Process Requires Teams to Truly Know Prospects,” NFL.com, February 19, 2014, http://www.nfl.com/news/story/0ap2000000326374/article/nfl-draft-process-requires-teams-to-truly-know-prospects.
4. Pete Williams, *The Draft: A Year Inside the NFL’s Search for Talent* (New York: St. Martin’s Griffin, 2006), 216.
5. Ben Volin, “NFL Teams Go Extra Yard to Vet Prospects before Draft,” *Boston Globe*, April 26, 2015, https://www.bostonglobe.com/sports/2015/04/25/nfl-teams-homework-including-spying-draft-prospects/I5EIHKwSQBvl6fvwQNVkyL/story.html.
6. Williams, *Draft*, 59.

7. Michael MacCambridge, *Chuck Noll: His Life Work* (Pittsburgh, PA: Pittsburgh Press, 2016), 316.
8. Williams, *Draft*, 23.

12. OPPONENTS' DRAFT TARGETS

1. Jeff Legwold, "Denver Broncos tried to 'hide our interest' in Patrick Surtain II before NFL draft, GM George Paton says," ESPN.com, April 30, 2021, https://www.espn.com/nfl/story/_/id/31367147/denver-broncos-tried-hide-our-interest-patrick-surtain-ii-nfl-draft-gm-george-paton-says.
2. Bill Parcells and Nunyo Demasio, *Parcells: A Football Life* (New York: Crown Archetype, 2014), 386.
3. Pete Williams, *The Draft: A Year inside the NFL's Search for Talent* (New York: St. Martin's Griffin, 2006), 286.
4. Michael Holley, *War Room: The Legacy of Bill Belichick and the Art of Building the Perfect Team* (New York: HarperCollins, 2011), 220.
5. Holley, *War Room*, 231.
6. Nick Shook, "Buffalo Bills Fire General Manager Doug Whaley," NFL.com, April 30, 2017, http://www.nfl.com/news/story/0ap3000000805316/article/buffalo-bills-fire-general-manager-doug-whaley.
7. Mark Ribowsky, *Slick: The Silver & Black Life of Al Davis* (New York: Macmillan, 1991), 254.
8. Connor Orr, "The History of Scouting," NFL.com, March 18, 2015, https://www.nfl.com/news/sidelines/the-history-of-scouting.

13. PRO SCOUTING

1. William Gildea and Kenneth Turan, *The Future Is Now: George Allen, Pro Football's Most Controversial Coach* (Boston: Houghton Mifflin, 1972), 231.
2. Matt Yoder, "The Best (Worst) of Roddy White on Twitter," *Awful Announcing* (blog), September 23, 2013, https://awfulannouncing.com/2013/the-best-worst-of-roddy-white-on-twitter.html.
3. "Roddy White Apologizes for Insensitive Adrian Peterson Tweet," Fox Sports, September 12, 2014, http://www.foxsports.com/nfl/story/roddy-white-apologizes-for-insensitive-adrian-peterson-tweet-091214.

4. Edwin Shrake, "Thunder out of Oakland," *Sports Illustrated*, November 15, 1965, https://vault.si.com/vault/1965/11/15/thunder-out-of-oakland.
5. Mike Shanahan with Adam Schefter, *Think Like a Champion* (New York: HarperBusiness, 1999), 166–67.
6. Danny Kelly, "The Unheralded Work of Pro NFL Scouts," Ringer, August 24, 2017, https://www.theringer.com/nfl/2017/8/24/16195480/life-of-pro-scouts.
7. Kelly, "Unheralded Work."
8. Kelly, "Unheralded Work."
9. Kelly, "Unheralded Work."

14. THE AFL AND NFL FIGHT OVER PLAYERS

1. Mark Ribowsky, *Slick: The Silver & Black Life of Al Davis* (New York: Macmillan, 1991), 72.
2. Jeff Miller, *Going Long* (New York: McGraw-Hill, 2003), 11–12.
3. Joe Patoski, *The Dallas Cowboys* (New York: Back Bay Books, 2012), 321.
4. Ken Rappoport, *The Little League That Could* (Lanham, MD: Taylor Trade, 2010), 120–21.
5. Murray Olderman, *Just Win, Baby* (Chicago: Triumph Books, 2012), 93–94.
6. Rappoport, *Little League That Could*, 26.
7. Patoski, *Dallas Cowboys*, 34.
8. Jarrett Bell, "From Upstart to Big Time, How the AFL Changed the NFL," *USA Today*, June 30, 2009, http://usatoday30.usatoday.com/sports/football/nfl/2009-06-14-sw-afl-cover_N.htm.
9. Ribowsky, *Slick*, 150–51.
10. Ribowsky, *Slick*, 148–50.
11. Bell, "From Upstart to Big Time."
12. Olderman, *Just Win, Baby*, 87–88.
13. Olderman, *Just Win, Baby*, 11.

15. SPYGATE

1. Bryan O'Leary, *Spygate: The Untold Story* (Dallas, TX: KLR, 2012), 157.

2. Don Van Natta Jr. and Seth Wickersham, "Spygate to Deflategate: Inside What Split the NFL and Patriots Apart," ESPN.com, September 7, 2015, http://www.espn.com/espn/otl/story/_/id/13533995/split-nfl-new-england-patriots-apart.

3. O'Leary, *Spygate*, 91.

4. "O'Leary, *Spygate*, 98.

5. O'Leary, *Spygate*, 26.

6. Russ Goldman, "Spygate: The Most 'Overblown' Story of the Decade," PatsFans.com, January 10, 2011, http://www.patsfans.com/articles/patriots/3508/SpyGate—The-Most-Overblown-Story-of-the-Decade.html.

7. Van Natta and Wickersham, "What Split the NFL and Patriots."

8. O'Leary, *Spygate*, 124.

9. O'Leary, *Spygate*, 110.

10. Van Natta and Wickersham, "What Split the NFL and Patriots."

11. CBS New York, "Spagnuolo Convinced Patriots Knew Eagles' Defensive Signals in Super Bowl," CBS New York, January 30, 2018, http://newyork.cbslocal.com/2018/01/30/steve-spagnuolo-patriots-stole-signs.

12. Pete Dougherty, "The NFL's Original Spy vs. Spy: Packers-Bears," *Packers News*, September 12, 2015, http://www.packersnews.com/story/sports/nfl/packers/dougherty/2015/09/12/nfls-original-spy-vs-spy/72103086.

13. Van Natta and Wickersham, "What Split the NFL and Patriots."

14. Alan Robinson, "Former Head Coach Cowher: Steelers Tried Stealing Signals, Too," *Trib Live*, January 15, 2014, http://triblive.com/sports/steelers/5423839-74/cowher-patriots-game.

15. Mike Shanahan with Adam Schefter, *Think Like a Champion* (New York: HarperBusiness, 1999), 153–54.

16. THE SKELETONS IN THE CLOSET

1. Tim Green, *The Dark Side of the Game: My Life in the NFL* (New York: Warner Books, 1996), 100.

2. John Tomase, "Pats Employee Filmed Rams," BostonHerald.com, February 2, 2008, http://www.bostonherald.com/sports/football/patriots/view.bg?articleid=1070762&srvc=home&position=0.7.

3. ESPN.com, "Timeline of Events and Disclosures during Spygate Era," ESPN.com, May 12,2008, http://www.espn.com/nfl/news/story?id=3392047.

4. Sporting News, "Marshall Faulk Still Blames 'Spygate' for Super Bowl Loss to Patriots," MassLive, January 30, 2013, http://www.masslive.com/patriots/index.ssf/2013/01/marshall_faulk_still_blames_sp.html.

5. Don Van Natta Jr. and Seth Wickersham, "Spygate to Deflategate: Inside What Split the NFL and Patriots Apart," ESPN.com, September 7, 2015, http://www.espn.com/espn/otl/story/_/id/13533995/split-nfl-new-england-patriots-apart.

6. Mike Florio, "Dansby Suspects Foul Play from 2008 Game in New England," *ProFootballTalk* (blog), NBC Sports, May 14, 2015, https://profootballtalk.nbcsports.com/2015/05/14/dansby-suspects-foul-play-from-2008-game-in-new-england.

17. DEFLATEGATE

1. Bryan O'Leary, *Spygate: The Untold Story* (Dallas, TX: KLR, 2012), 146.

2. ESPN.com, "Deflategate Timeline: After 544 Days, Tom Brady Gives In," ESPN.com, September 3, 2015, http://www.espn.com/blog/new-england-patriots/post/_/id/4782561/timeline-of-events-for-deflategate-tom-brady.

3. Tony Manfred, "Why Using Deflated Footballs Gave the Patriots a Huge Advantage," *Business Insider*, January 21, 2015, https://www.businessinsider.com/advantage-of-deflated-footballs-2015-1.

4. Michael David Smith, "NFL Statement on Deflategate Discipline," *ProFootballTalk* (blog), NBC Sports, May 11, 2015, https://profootballtalk.nbcsports.com/2015/05/11/nfl-statement-on-deflategate-discipline/#:~:text=For%20the%20violation%20of%20the%20playing%20rules%20and,Patriots%20are%20fined%20%241%20million%20and%20will%20.

EPILOGUE

1. Tim Green, *The Dark Side of the Game: My Life in the NFL* (New York: Warner Books, 1996), 251.

2. Weeb Ewbank as told to Neil Roiter, *Goal to Go: The Greatest Football Games I Have Coached* (New York: Hawthorn Books, 1972), 37.

3. TMZ, "New England Patriots Spygate II Video Released and Its Bad for the Pats," TMZ, December 15, 2019, https://www.tmz.com/2019/12/15/patriots-spygate-video-released-new-england-bengals.

4. Ryan Dunleavy, "Patriots Fined, Docked Draft Pick in Spygate II Punishment," *New York Post*, June 28, 2020, https://nypost.com/2020/06/28/patriots-fined-by-nfl-docked-draft-pick-in-spygate-ii-punishment.

5. Mike Freeman, "I Spied with My Own Eyes Some Cheer Worthy of a Sneer," CBS Sports, September 17, 2007, http://www.cbssports.com/columns/story/10357197 (article deleted).

BIBLIOGRAPHY

Acee, Kevin. "San Diego Chargers Know Seahawks Have a Spy." *San Diego Union-Tribune*, September 23, 2010. http://www.sandiegouniontribune.com/sdut-chargers-know-seahawks-have-spy-2010sep23-story.html.

Action News Philadelphia. "Listen: Eagle QB Nick Foles Called the 'Philly Special' Plays in Super Bowl." 6abc, WPVI-TV. February 6, 2018. https://6abc.com/action-news-sports-super-bowl-52-lii-philadelphia-eagles/3034139.

Allen, George. *How to Scout Football.* Mansfield Centre, CT: Martino, 2009.

Allen, Scott. "Redskins Fan Finds Released Player's Workbooks in Dumpster, Team Isn't Concerned." *Washington Post*, September 1, 2016. https://www.washingtonpost.com/news/dc-sports-bog/wp/2016/09/01/redskins-fan-finds-released-players-workbooks-in-dumpster-team-isnt-concerned/?utm_term=.930787691cbd.

Anderson, Dave. "Sports of the Times; Was or Wasn't There a Spy Up on High?" *New York Times*, October 12, 1998. http://www.nytimes.com/1998/10/12/sports/sports-of-the-times-was-or-wasn-t-there-a-spy-up-on-high.html.

Antoniacci, Mandy. "28 of the Greatest Quotes from NFL Legends." *Inc.*, September 8, 2016. https://www.inc.com/mandy-antoniacci/28-of-the-greatest-quotes-from-nfl-legends.html.

Associated Press. "Harbaughs Are Strictly Business." ESPN.com. January 22, 2013. http://www.espn.com/nfl/playoffs/2012/story/_/id/8868301/2013-nfl-playoffs-jim-john-harbaugh-only-texting-super-bowl-san-francisco-49ers-baltimore-ravens.

Augustine, Bernie. "Texans Defensive End J. J. Watt Says He Picked Up on Miami Dolphins' Snap Count by Watching HBO's 'Hard Knocks.'" *New York Daily News*, September 12, 2012. http://www.nydailynews.com/sports/football/texans-defensive-watt-picked-miami-dolphins-snap-count-watching-hbo-hard-knocks-article-1.1157838.

Austin, Michael. "Winning Isn't Everything." *Psychology Today*, July 12, 2010. https://www.psychologytoday.com/blog/ethics-everyone/201007/winning-isnt-everything.

Axisa, Mike. "We Now Know the Extent of Cardinals Hack and the Unprecedented Penalties from MLB." CBS Sports. January 30, 2017. https://www.cbssports.com/mlb/news/we-now-know-extent-of-cardinals-hack-and-the-unprecedented-penalties-from-mlb.

Babb, Kent. "Arrowhead Anxiety: Turnover off the Field Causes Concern." *Kansas City Star*, January 14, 2012. http://www.kansascity.com/news/special-reports/article300461/Arrowhead-anxiety-Turnover-off-the-field-causes-concern.html.

Bamberger, Michael. "Big Brother Is Watching If You're an NFL Draft Prospect, the League's Investigators Have Their Eyes on Your Every Move." *Sports Illustrated*, April 15, 1996. https://www.si.com/vault/1996/04/15/211911/big-brother-is-watching-if-youre-an-nfl-draft-prospect-the-leagues-investigators-have-their-eyes-on-your-every-move.

Belichick, Steve. *Football Scouting Methods*. New York: Ronald, 1962.

Bell, Jarrett. "From Upstart to Big Time, How the AFL Changed the NFL." *USA Today*, June 30, 2009. http://usatoday30.usatoday.com/sports/football/nfl/2009-06-14-sw-afl-cover_N.htm.

Benoit, Andy. "What's Wrong with Cam Newton?" *Sports Illustrated*, December 19, 2016. http://mmqb.si.com/mmqb/2016/12/19/nfl-week-15-cam-newton-struggles-carolina-panthers-offensive-line-receivers-kelvin-benjamin#.

Bergman, Jeremy. "Steelers Erect Tarp to Prevent against 'Drones,'" NFL.com. August 23, 2018. https://www.nfl.com/news/steelers-erect-tarp-to-prevent-against-drones-0ap3000000950289.

Bird, Hayden. "Separating Fact from Fiction on 'Spygate' and Super Bowl XXXVI." Boston.com. January 30, 2019. https://www.boston.com/sports/new-england-patriots/2019/01/30/spygate-rams-walkthrough-patriots-super-bowl.

Bishop, Greg. "Fear and Loathing." *Sports Illustrated*, September 14, 2015. http://www.si.com/vault/2016/02/11/fear-and-loathing.

———. "Former Videographer Details Patriots' Spying." *New York Times*, May 16, 2008. http://www.nytimes.com/2008/05/16/sports/football/16nfl.html.

———. "Paranoia Strikes Deep, into Your Headset It Will Creep." *New York Times*, November 13, 2007. http://www.nytimes.com/2007/11/13/sports/football/13paranoid.html?_r=0.

Bishop, Greg, Michael Rosenberg, and Thayer Evans. "Suspicions of Bill Belichick's Patriots Regime Persist among Opponents." *Sports Illustrated*, September 8, 2015. https://www.si.com/nfl/2015/09/08/patriots-cheating-suspicions-bill-belichick-tom-brady.

Booth, Tim. "Seahawks Hope They Didn't Spill Too Many Secrets to 49ers." *Seattle Post-Intelligencer*, September 14, 2017. http://www.seattlepi.com/sports/article/Seahawks-hope-they-didn-t-spill-too-many-secrets-12198583.php (article deleted).

Bowden, Mark. *The Best Game Ever*. New York: Grove, 2009.

———. "Sacks, Lies and Videotape." *New York Times*, May 18, 2008. https://www.nytimes.com/2008/05/18/opinion/18bowden.html.

Branch, Eric. "49ers Wary of Espionage in Youngstown." *SFGate*, September 26, 2012. http://www.sfgate.com/49ers/article/49ers-wary-of-espionage-in-Youngstown-3897617.php.

Branch, John. "The Deflategate Scientists Unlock Their Lab." *New York Times*, September 21, 2016. https://www.nytimes.com/2016/09/25/sports/football/deflategate-new-england-patriots-nfl-science.html.

———. "Headsets Signal Play-Calling Advantage." *Gazette*, 2002. http://servv89pn0aj.sn.sourcedns.com/~gbpprorg/nfl/headsets.txt (article deleted).

———. "In the N.F.L., It's Not Cheating until You Start Videotaping." *New York Times*, February 17, 2008. http://www.nytimes.com/2008/02/17/sports/football/17nfl.html.

Breer, Albert. "NFL Draft Process Requires Teams to Truly Know Prospects." NFL.com. February 19, 2014. http://www.nfl.com/news/story/0ap2000000326374/article/nfl-draft-process-requires-teams-to-truly-know-prospects.

Brees, Drew, with Chris Fabry. *Coming Back Stronger: Unleashing the Hidden Power of Adversity*. Carol Stream, IL: Tyndale House, 2010.

Brown, Daniel, and Mercury News. "NFL Espionage Tricks Typically Lean toward the Subtle." *Mercury News*, September 19, 2007. http://www.mercurynews.com/2007/09/19/nfl-espionage-tricks-typically-lean-toward-the-subtle.

Brown, Paul, with Jack Clary. *PB: The Paul Brown Story*. New York: Atheneum, 1979.

Butler, Alex. "Spygate II: Drone Potentially Filmed Atlanta Falcons' Super Bowl Practice." UPI. February 9, 2017. http://www.upi.com/Sports_News/NFL/2017/02/09/Spygate-II-Drone-potentially-filmed-Atlanta-Falcons-Super-Bowl-practice/8601486524928.

Byrne, Kerry. "52 Years Ago Today: 'The Best Game Ever.'" Football Nation. December 28, 2010. http://www.footballnation.net/content/52-years-ago-today-the-best-game-ever/7700.

Carucci, Vic. "An Edge through Espionage? More Common Than You Think." NFL.com. September 22, 2010. http://www.nfl.com/news/story/09000d5d81ac208d/article/an-edge-through-espionage-more-common-than-you-think.

CBS New York. "Listen: Boomer Was Told the Jets Asked NFL to Sweep Pats' Locker Room For Bugs." CBS New York. October 30, 2015. https://newyork.cbslocal.com/2015/10/30/jets-patriots-listening-devices-nfl.

———. "Spagnuolo Convinced Patriots Knew Eagles' Defensive Signals in Super Bowl." CBS New York. January 30, 2018. http://newyork.cbslocal.com/2018/01/30/steve-spagnuolo-patriots-stole-signs.

Chadiha, Jeffri. "Draft Is Ultimate Character Study." ESPN.com. March 26, 2013. http://www.espn.com/nfl/draft2013/story/_/id/9092615/nfl-draft-ultimate-character-study.

———. "Legal Spying—Not Videotaping—Widespread in NFL." ESPN.com. September 13, 2007. http://sports.espn.go.com/nfl/columns/story?columnist=chadiha_jeffri&id=3017423.

Chauvin, Christy. "Spy for the NFL—Become a Pro Scout." *WhoDatDish* (blog). June 17, 2013. https://whodatdish.com/2013/06/17/spy-for-the-nfl-become-a-pro-scout.

Cohen, Rich. *Monsters: The 1985 Chicago Bears and the Wild Heart of Football*. New York: Farrar, Straus and Giroux, 2013.

Cole, Jason. "Ancient Antics." Yahoo!Sports. September 13, 2007. http://sports.yahoo.com/nfl/news?slug=jc-historynflcheating.

Coleman, Madeline. "Report: NFLPA Investigating Complaint about Security Cameras in New York Jets Locker Room." *Sports Illustrated*, November 7, 2020. https://www.si.com/nfl/2020/11/07/nflpa-investigating-jets-locker-room-cameras.

Costello, Brian. "Peyton's Film Studying Is Stuff of Legend." *New York Post*, January 30, 2014. http://nypost.com/2014/01/30/peyton-mannings-film-study-obsession-is-stuff-of-legend.

Coughlin, Tom, with Brian Curtis. *A Team to Believe In: Our Journey to the Super Bowl Championship*. New York: Ballantine Books, 2008.

Craig, Mark, and Kent Youngblood. "Vikings Turn to Espionage." *Minnesota Star Tribune*, October 17, 2012. http://www.startribune.com/sports/vikings/174680161.html?refer=y.

Daly, Dan. "Cheating: An NFL Tradition for 95 Years." *Pro Football Daly* (blog). January 24, 2015. http://profootballdaly.com/the-nfls-long-glorious-tradition-of-cheating.

D'Amato, Gary, and Cliff Christl. *Mudbaths & Bloodbaths: The Inside Story of the Bears-Packers Rivalry*. Madison, WI: Prairie Oak, 1997.

DaSilva, Cameron. "The Cowboys' New Practice Facility Looks Like a Mini-NFL Stadium." Fox Sports. November 15, 2016. https://www.foxsports.com/nfl/story/the-cowboys-new-practice-facility-looks-like-a-mini-nfl-stadium-081916.

Davis, Jeff. *Papa Bear: The Life and Legacy of George Halas*. New York: McGraw-Hill, 2005.

Dawidoff, Nicholas. *Collision Low Crossers*. New York: Little, Brown, 2013.

DeArdo, Bryan. "Hines Ward Still Thinks Patriots Cheated in Past Title Games." *Steel City Insider* (blog). CBS Pittsburgh. January 31, 2019. https://247sports.com/nfl/pittsburgh-steelers/Article/Hines-Ward-still-thinks-Patriots-cheated-in-past-title-games-128539218.

———. "Sean McDermott Escorts Bill Belichick's Son off the Field During Pregame Warmups for Patriots-Bills Game." CBS Sports. September 30, 2019. https://www.cbssports.com/nfl/news/sean-mcdermott-escorts-bill-belichicks-son-off-the-field-during-pregame-warmups-for-patriots-bills-game.

Dougherty, Pete. "The NFL's Original Spy vs. Spy: Packers-Bears." *Packers News*, September 12, 2015. http://www.packersnews.com/story/sports/nfl/packers/dougherty/2015/09/12/nfls-original-spy-vs-spy/72103086.

———. "There's No Breaking Kelly's Code." *Packers News*, November 13, 2014. http://www.packersnews.com/story/sports/nfl/packers/dougherty/2014/11/13/theres-no-breaking-kellys-code/19008349.

Dunleavy, Ryan. "Patriots Fined, Docked Draft Pick in Spygate II Punishment." *New York Post*, June 28, 2020. https://nypost.com/2020/06/28/patriots-fined-by-nfl-docked-draft-pick-in-spygate-ii-punishment.

Eisenberg, John. *The League: How Five Rivals Created the NFL and Launched a Sports Empire*. New York: Basic Books, 2018.

ESPN.com. "Deflategate Timeline: After 544 Days, Tom Brady Gives In." ESPN.com. September 3, 2015. http://www.espn.com/blog/new-england-patriots/post/_/id/4782561/timeline-of-events-for-deflategate-tom-brady.

———. "If You Want to Talk Cheating, Talk about George Allen." ESPN.com. January 25, 2015. http://www.espn980.com/2015/01/25/if-you-want-to-talk-cheating-talk-about-george-allen (site discontinued).

———. "Specter Criticizes NFL, Wants Independent Spygate Investigation." ESPN.com. May 15, 2008. http://www.espn.com/nfl/news/story?id=3395829.

———. "Timeline of Events and Disclosures during Spygate Era." ESPN.com. May 12, 2008. http://www.espn.com/nfl/news/story?id=3392047.

Ewbank, Weeb, Jack Buck, and Bob Broeg. *Football Greats*. St. Louis, MO: Bethany, 1977.

Ewbank, Weeb, as told to Neil Roiter. *Goal to Go: The Greatest Football Games I Have Coached.* New York: Hawthorn Books, 1972.

Faas, Ryan. "Why Most NFL Teams Are Ditching Their Playbooks for iPads." Cult of Mac. September 5, 2012. https://www.cultofmac.com/188847/why-most-nfl-teams-are-ditching-their-playbooks-for-ipads-feature.

Fish, Mike. "Specter: Goodell's Spygate Explanations Don't Pass Scrutiny." ESPN.com. February 15, 2008. http://www.espn.com/nfl/news/story?id=3246788.

Fleming, David. "Don't Touch My Playbook." ESPN.com. January 18, 2008. http://sports.espn.go.com/espn/page2/story?page=fleming/080117.

———. "Facing a Former Team Doug Evans Provided Carolina with Inside Information on Green Bay." *Sports Illustrated*, October 5, 1998. http://www.si.com/vault/1998/10/05/249844/facing-a-former-team-doug-evans-provided-carolina-with-inside-information-on-green-bay.

———. "No More Questions." ESPN.com. October 4, 2016. http://www.espn.com/espn/feature/story/_/id/17703210/new-england-patriots-coach-bill-belichick-greatest-enigma-sports.

Florio, Mike. "Dansby Suspects Foul Play from 2008 Game in New England." *ProFootballTalk* (blog). NBC Sports. May 14, 2015. https://profootballtalk.nbcsports.com/2015/05/14/dansby-suspects-foul-play-from-2008-game-in-new-england.

———. "Saints Call Report of Loomis Espionage '1000 Percent False.'" *ProFootballTalk* (blog). NBC Sports. April 23, 2012. http://profootballtalk.nbcsports.com/2012/04/23/saints-call-espn-report-of-loomis-espionage-1000-percent-false.

Forbes, Gordon. *Dick Vermeil: Whistle in His Mouth, Heart on His Sleeve.* Chicago: Triumph Books, 2009.

Fox Sports. "Roddy White Apologizes for Insensitive Adrian Peterson Tweet." FoxSports.com. September 12, 2014. http://www.foxsports.com/nfl/story/roddy-white-apologizes-for-insensitive-adrian-peterson-tweet-091214.

Freeman, Mike. *Bowden: How Bobby Bowden Forged a Football Dynasty* (New York: HarperCollins, 2009.

———. "I Spied with My Own Eyes Some Cheer Worthy of a Sneer." CBS Sports. September 17, 2007. http://www.cbssports.com/columns/story/10357197 (article deleted).

Gabriel, Greg. "The Evolution of Scouting." National Football Post. June 22, 2014. http://www.nationalfootballpost.com/the-evolution-of-scouting.

Gaydos, Ryan. "Dallas Cowboys Practice Gets Rooftop Onlooker and Fans Accuse New England Patriots of Spying." Fox News. November 21, 2019. https://www.foxnews.com/sports/cowboys-practice-rooftop-patriots-game.

George, Thomas. "The ABC's of X's and O's: The Art of Play-Calling in the N.F.L." *New York Times*, December 15, 1996. http://www.nytimes.com/1996/12/15/sports/the-abc-s-of-x-s-and-o-s-the-art-of-play-calling-in-the-nfl.html.

Gildea, William, and Kenneth Turan. *The Future Is Now: George Allen, Pro Football's Most Controversial Coach*. Boston: Houghton Mifflin, 1972.

Glauber, Bob. "Spying Nothing New in the NFL." *Saint Catharines Standard*, September 14, 2007. http://www.stcatharinesstandard.ca/2007/09/14/spying-nothing-new-in-the-nfl (article deleted).

Goldberg, Dave. "Spying Nothing New in NFL." *Tucson Citizen*, September 14, 2007. http://tucsoncitizen.com/morgue/2007/09/14/63059-spying-nothing-new-in-nfl (article deleted).

Goldberg, Debbie. "Cheerleaders Say Visiting Players Spied on Them." *Washington Post*, January 24, 2002. https://www.washingtonpost.com/archive/politics/2002/01/24/cheer

leaders-say-visiting-players-spied-on-them/2d5a9ca9-83fb-4223-b936-998c24a90da2/?utm_term=.da19957d5bcf.

Goldman, Russ. "Spygate: The Most 'Overblown' Story of the Decade." PatsFans.com. January 10, 2011. http://www.patsfans.com/articles/patriots/3508/SpyGate—The-Most-Overblown-Story-of-the-Decade.html.

Gonzalez, Antonio. "NFL Headsets Going Digital in New Technology Wave." *Times Leader*. August 14, 2012. https://www.timesleader.com/archive/42897/stories-nfl-headsets-going-digital-in-new-technology-wave191346.

Gosselin, Rick. "Who Was the Best Player Ever to Come out of the USFL?" Talk of Fame Network. September 9, 2015. https://www.si.com/nfl/talkoffame/nfl/who-was-the-best-player-ever-to-come-out-of-the-usfl.

Gowton, Brandon Lee. "One Eagles Player Spilled the Beans on Which Quarterback Will Be Starting against the Falcons." Bleeding Green Nation. September 2, 2018. https://www.bleedinggreennation.com/2018/9/2/17813306/eagles-vs-falcons-nick-foles-carson-wentz-starting-quarterback-jordan-hicks-reveal-philadelphia-nfl.

Gramling, Gary. "Zoom Bombs, Bad Passwords, and a Big Target: Why the NFL Draft Season Is Ripe to Be Hacked." *Sports Illustrated*, April 16, 2020. https://www.si.com/nfl/2020/04/16/why-nfl-draft-season-is-ripe-for-hacking-how-it-could-happen.

Green, Jeremy. "Advance Scouting Makes Spying Unnecessary." ESPN.com. September 14, 2007. http://sports.espn.go.com/nfl/columns/story?columnist=green_jeremy&id=3051500.

Green, Tim. *The Dark Side of the Game: My Life in the NFL*. New York: Warner Books, 1996.

Greenberg, Andy. "A One-Minute Attack Let Hackers Spoof Hotel Master Keys." Wired.com. April 25, 2018. https://www.wired.com/story/one-minute-attack-let-hackers-spoof-hotel-master-keys.

Grosscup, Lee. "Spying in Pro Football." *Sport*, August 1967. http://archive.li/JUDqE.

Gruden, Jon, with Vic Carucci. *Do You Love Football?! Winning with Heart, Passion & Not Much Sleep*. New York: HarperCollins, 2003.

Halberstam, David. *The Education of a Coach*. New York: Hyperion, 2003.

Harris, David. *The Genius: How Bill Walsh Reinvented Football and Created an NFL Dynasty*. New York: Random House, 2008.

Heath, Jon. "Broncos Will Have Just 3 Training Camp Practices Closed to the Public." *USA Today*, July 12, 2019. https://broncoswire.usatoday.com/2019/07/12/denver-broncos-news-only-three-training-camp-practices-closed-to-public.

Heavy.com. "Ernie Adams: 5 Fast Facts You Need to Know." Heavy.com. September 8, 2015. https://heavy.com/sports/2015/09/ernie-adams-nfl-new-england-patriots-spygate-deflategate-outside-the-lines-espn-bill-belichick-football.

Henson, Ian. "Mike Shanahan on Spygate and Cheating." *Mile High Report*, September 11, 2015. http://www.milehighreport.com/2015/9/11/9296053/mike-shanahan-on-spygate-and-cheating-patriots.

Holley, Michael. *Belichick and Brady*. New York: Hachette Books, 2016.

———. *War Room: The Legacy of Bill Belichick and the Art of Building the Perfect Team*. New York: HarperCollins, 2011.

Isaacson, Melissa. "Illegal? Unethical? Or Strategy? For Some, Stealing Signs Is Just Part of the Game. Videotaping, However, Seems to Cross the Line." *Chicago Tribune*, September 16, 2007. http://articles.chicagotribune.com/2007-09-16/news/0709150335_1_matt-estrella-signals-stealing/2.

Jensen, Chad. "NFL Insider Sheds Conflicting Light in Broncos' WR Priorities in the Draft." FanNation. April 7, 2020. https://www.si.com/nfl/broncos/news/denver-broncos-wide-receiver-priorities-exposed-by-nfl-insider.

Johnson, Jimmy, as told to Ed Hinton. *Turning the Thing Around*. New York: Hyperion, 1993.

Joseph, Andrew. "Ty Law Explained Peyton Manning's Old Scheme to Uncover Game Secrets from Pro Bowl Players." *USA Today Sports*, April 2, 2020. https://ftw.usatoday.com/2020/04/peyton-manning-ty-law-pro-bowl-story-mai-tai-drinks-secrets.

Jubera, Drew. "How Donald Trump Destroyed a Football League." *Esquire*, January 13, 2016. http://www.esquire.com/news-politics/a41135/donald-trump-usfl.

Katzowitz, Josh. "Players, Coaches 'Totally Against' On-Field Mics Picking Up QB Signals." CBS Sports. September 7, 2014. http://www.cbssports.com/nfl/news/players-coaches-totally-against-on-field-mics-picking-up-qb-signals.

———. *Sid Gillman: Father of the Passing Game*. Covington, KY: Clerisy, 2012.

Kelly, Danny. "The Unheralded Work of Pro NFL Scouts." Ringer. August 24, 2017. https://www.theringer.com/nfl/2017/8/24/16195480/life-of-pro-scouts.

Klis, Mike. "D. J. Williams Deletes Post of Defensive Formations; But Issue Adds to Woes." *Denver Post*, June 9, 2012. http://www.denverpost.com/broncos/ci_20818370/broncos-dj-williams-makes-play-public-twitter.

Krieger, Dave. "Krieger: NFL Quick to Silence Tale of the Tape." *Denver Post*, November 27, 2010. http://www.denverpost.com/2010/11/27/krieger-nfl-quick-to-silence-tale-of-the-tape.

Levy, Marv. *Where Else Would You Rather Be?* New York: Sports Publishing, 2012.

Lewis, Michael. "What Keeps Bill Parcells Awake at Night." *New York Times*, October 29, 2006. http://www.nytimes.com/2006/10/29/sports/playmagazine/1029play_parcells.html.

Lillibridge, Marc. "A Former Player's Perspective on Film Study and Preparing for an NFL Game." Bleacher Report. November 30, 2012. http://bleacherreport.com/articles/1427449-a-former-players-perspective-on-film-study-and-preparing-for-a-nfl-game#.

Linendoll, Katie. "Are NFL Teams Hacking Helmet Headsets?" ESPN.com. October 4, 2012. http://espn.go.com/blog/playbook/tech/post/_/id/2573/robert-griffin-iii-helmet.

Litsky, Frank. "Pro Football; Farewell to Ewbank: Vignettes of a True Coach and Friend." *New York Times*, November 19, 1998. http://www.nytimes.com/1998/11/19/sports/pro-football-farewell-to-ewbank-vignettes-of-a-true-coach-and-friend.html.

Luksa, Frank. "NFL Spy Stories Once Had Comedic Touch." ESPN.com. September 13, 2007. http://sports.espn.go.com/nfl/columns/story?columnist=luksa_frank&id=3017278.

MacCambridge, Michael. *Chuck Noll: His Life Work*. Pittsburgh, PA: Pittsburgh Press, 2016.

Magee, Jerry. "Videogate Just Latest Chapter in Long History of NFL Spying." *San Diego Union-Tribune*, September 13, 2007. http://www.utsandiego.com/sports/chargers/20070913-9999-1s13nflcol.html.

Manfred, Tony. "Why Using Deflated Footballs Gave the Patriots a Huge Advantage." *Business Insider*, January 21, 2015. https://www.businessinsider.com/advantage-of-deflated-footballs-2015-1.

Maraniss, David. *When Pride Still Mattered*. New York: Simon & Schuster, 1999.

Maule, Tex. "Would You Buy a Used Playbook from This Man?" *Sports Illustrated*, July 24, 1972. http://www.si.com/vault/1972/07/24/612577/would-you-buy-a-used-playbook-from-this-man.

McKenna, Henry. "The Timeline for Spygate 2.0: Patriots-Bengals." *Patriots Wire* (blog). *USA Today*, December 16, 2019. https://patriotswire.usatoday.com/gallery/patriots-bengals-timeline-spygate-2-0-videotaping.

Mell, Randall, and Craig Barnes. "Spy vs. Spy: Football Coaches Work to Put a Blanket on the Undercover Operations of Others." *SunSentinel*, October 6, 1996. http://articles.sun-sentinel.com/1996-10-06/sports/9610070178_1_tennessee-tech-northern-arizona-spy (article moved or deleted).

Menzer, Joe. "Scouts Honor: The Importance of Background Checks." Panthers.com. November 27, 2015. https://www.panthers.com/news/scouts-honor-the-importance-of-background-checks-16386448.

Miller, Jeff. *Going Long*. New York: McGraw-Hill, 2003.

Miller, Mike. "Jack Vainisi: The Drafting Genius behind the Packers Dynasty." Madison.com. April 23, 2009. http://host.madison.com/sports/jack-vainisi-the-drafting-genius-behind-the-packers-dynasty/article_3965e117-959a-524a-8e98-8de214462d21.html.

Mitchell, Kirk. "Signs of Trouble for Kenny McKinley: Debts and a Gun." *Denver Post*, December 1, 2010. https://www.denverpost.com/2010/12/01/signs-of-trouble-for-kenny-mckinley-debts-and-a-gun.

Moldea, Dan. *Interference: How Organized Crime Influences Professional Football*. New York: William Morrow, 1989.

Monaghan, Shane. "AFL vs. NFL: The Battle for Jim Grabowski, 50 Years Later." Medill Reports Chicago. April 27, 2016. https://news.medill.northwestern.edu/chicago/afl-vs-nfl-the-battle-for-jim-grabowski-50-years-later.

Moore, Jack. "The St. Louis Cardinals Have Hacked Their Way into Sports Spying History." Vice.com. June 21, 2015. https://sports.vice.com/en_us/article/d7bm4a/the-st-louis-cardinals-have-hacked-their-way-into-sports-spying-history.

Mortensen, Chris. "Sources: Goodell Determines Pats Broke Rules by Taping Jets' Signals." ESPN.com. September 11, 2007. https://www.espn.com/nfl/news/story?id=3014677.

Myers, Gary. *Coaching Confidential: Inside the Fraternity of NFL Coaches*. New York: Crown Archetype, 2012.

———. "Following Bitter Breakup with Al Davis and Raiders, Mike Shanahan Gets a Measure of Revenge with Steve Young and 49ers." *New York Daily News*, November 13, 2012. http://www.nydailynews.com/sports/football/shanahan-revenge-davis-young-article-1.1201352.

Namath, Joe. "Fond Farewells: Al Davis Oakland Raiders Owner, 82." *Time*, December 14, 2011. http://content.time.com/time/specials/packages/article/0,28804,2101745_2102136_2102213,00.html.

Newton, David. "Eugene Robinson, Arrested before Last Falcons Super Bowl, Won't Let 'One Mistake' Define Him." ESPN.com. January 26, 2017. https://www.espn.com/blog/atlanta-falcons/post/_/id/25416/ex-falcon-eugene-robinson-wont-let-one-super-bowl-mistake-define-him.

New York Daily News. "Report: Patriots Taped Giants in 2006." February 22, 2008. http://www.nydailynews.com/sports/football/giants/report-patriots-taped-giants-2006-article-1.308455.

New York Times. "Specter's Floor Statement on New England Patriots Videotaping." May 14, 2008. https://www.nytimes.com/2008/05/14/sports/football/14specterstatement.html.

NFL.com. "Spying in the NFL." NFL.com. September 12, 2007. http://www.nfl.com/videos/new-england-patriots/09000d5d8024b648/Spying-in-the-NFL (article deleted).

Nocera, Joe. "True Scandal of Deflategate Lies in the N.F.L.'s Behavior." *New York Times*, January 22, 2016. https://www.nytimes.com/2016/01/23/sports/football/nfl-ignores-ball-deflation-science-at-new-england-patriots-expense.html.

Ochoa, R. J. "Look: Losing Cowboys Playbook Comes at a Heavy Price." *Inside the Star* (blog). May 31, 2017. https://insidethestar.com/look-losing-cowboys-playbook-comes-heavy-price.

Olderman, Murray. *Just Win, Baby*. Chicago: Triumph Books, 2012.

O'Leary, Bryan. *Spygate: The Untold Story*. Dallas, TX: KLR, 2012.

O'Leary, Daniel. "Richard Sherman Says Seahawks Had Peyton Manning's Signals Figured Out in Super Bowl XLVIII: Report." *New York Daily News*, February 4, 2014. http://www.nydailynews.com/sports/football/seahawks-sherman-knew-denver-hand-signals-super-bowl-article-1.1602485.

Orr, Connor. "The History of Scouting." NFL.com. March 18, 2015. https://www.nfl.com/news/sidelines/the-history-of-scouting.

Paige, Woody. "The Hills Have Eyes, & Cameras." *Denver Post*, March 1, 2008. http://www.denverpost.com/sports/ci_8423219.

Parcells, Bill, and Nunyo Demasio. *Parcells: A Football Life*. New York: Crown Archetype, 2014.

Parker, Garrett. "The Ten Biggest Scandals in NFL History." MoneyInc.com. Accessed August 19, 2021. https://moneyinc.com/nfl-scandals.

Patoski, Joe. *The Dallas Cowboys*. New York: Back Bay Books, 2012.

Patra, Kevin. "Rams' Eric Weddle Won't Share Inside Info on Rams." NFL.com. November 20, 2019. https://www.nfl.com/news/rams-eric-weddle-won-t-share-inside-info-on-ravens-0ap3000001079083.

Payton, Sean, and Ellis Henican. *Home Team*. New York: New American Library, 2010.

Pederson, Doug, with Dan Pompei. *Fearless: How an Underdog Becomes a Champion.* New York: Hachette Books, 2018.

Phillips, Wade, with Vic Carucci. *Son of Bum.* New York: Diversion Books, 2017.

Pierson, Don. "Spy-Conscious Gibbs Scrambles the Redskins' Practice Signal." *Chicago Tribune*, January 27, 1988. http://articles.chicagotribune.com/1988-01-27/sports/8803250845_1_skins-owner-redskins-quarterback-joe-theismann-redskins-lease.

Pompei, Dan. "How the NFL Cheats: Spy Games." Bleacher Report. September 30, 2016. http://bleacherreport.com/articles/2657226-how-the-nfl-cheats-spy-games.

———. "Inside the NFL's Secret World of Injuries." Bleacher Report. December 14, 2017. https://bleacherreport.com/articles/2749101-inside-the-nfls-secret-world-of-injuries.

Prunty, Brendan. "Tom Brady, Eli Manning Differ on Them, but Wristbands Are Now a Common Tool for NFL Quarterbacks." *New Jersey Star-Ledger*, February 3, 2012. http://www.nj.com/giants/index.ssf/2012/02/tom_brady_eli_manning_may_diff.html.

Pulkkinen, Levi. "Reggie Rogers, Ex UW Star, Sentenced to Prison for DUI, Hit and Run." *Seattle Post-Intelligencer*, June 24, 2009. http://www.seattlepi.com/local/article/Reggie-Rogers-ex-UW-star-sentenced-to-prison-1304753.php.

Raiders.com staff. "From 'Purple Walrus' to 'James Harden,' Derek Carr Jokes about In-Game Audibles Going Viral." Raiders.com. November 23, 2020. https://www.raiders.com/news/from-purple-walrus-to-james-harden-derek-carr-jokes-about-in-game-audibles-going.

Rappoport, Ken. *The Little League That Could.* Lanham, MD: Taylor Trade, 2010.

Reeves, Dan, with Dick Connor. *An Autobiography.* Chicago: Bonus Books, 1998.

Regan, Brett. "Patriots under NFL Investigation for Allegedly Spying on Bengals." FanBuzz. December 10, 2019. https://fanbuzz.com/nfl/patriots-cheating-bengals.

Reilly, Rick. "Commitment to Honesty." ESPN.com. October 14, 2011. http://www.espn.com/espn/story/_/id/7098616/rick-reilly-reflects-al-davis-commitment-honesty.

———. "The Silent Treatment." *Sports Illustrated*, January 14, 2002. http://www.si.com/vault/2002/01/14/316765/the-silent-treatment.

Reiss, Mike. "Patriots' Coach Replies on Taping Allegations." *New York Times*, November 8, 2008. http://www.nytimes.com/2008/02/18/sports/18iht-PATS.1.10135407.html.

Ribowsky, Mark. *The Last Cowboy: A Life of Tom Landry.* New York: Liveright, 2014.

———. *Slick: The Silver & Black Life of Al Davis.* New York: Macmillan, 1991.

Richmond, Peter. *Badasses: The Legend of Snake, Food, Dr. Death, and John Madden's Oakland Raiders.* New York: HarperCollins, 2010.

Robinson, Alan. "Former Head Coach Cowher: Steelers Tried Stealing Signals, Too." *Trib Live.* January 15, 2014. http://triblive.com/sports/steelers/5423839-74/cowher-patriots-game.

Robinson, Joshua. "NFL's Worst Sin: Losing a Playbook." *Wall Street Journal*, August 24, 2012. https://www.wsj.com/articles/SB10000872396390444358404577609862193305518.

Ruiter, Daryl. "NFL Investigating Alleged Gameday Texting to Coaches by Browns Front Office Personnel." CBS Cleveland. January 9, 2015. http://cleveland.cbslocal.com/2015/01/09/nfl-investigating-alleged-gameday-texting-to-coaches-by-browns-staff.

Sando, Mike. "Last 15 Seconds Should Be Quiet Time." ESPN.com. September 25, 2007. http://www.espn.com/nfl/columns/story?columnist=sando_mike&id=3035449.

———. "What's Legal, What's Illegal in NFL Spy Game." ESPN.com. September 13, 2007. http://sports.espn.go.com/nfl/columns/story?columnist=sando_mike&id=3017542.

Schad, Tom. "Could the NFL Draft Be Hacked? Virtual Draft Poses New Cybersecurity Challenges." *USA Today*, April 21, 2020. https://www.usatoday.com/story/sports/nfl/draft/2020/04/21/nfl-draft-2020-hacked-security-breach-virtual-teams/5163797002.

Schafrath, Dick. *Heart of a Mule.* Cleveland, OH: Gray, 2006.

Shanahan, Mike, with Adam Schefter. *Think Like a Champion.* New York: HarperBusiness, 1999.

Sheaffer, Scott. "The Truth about Spygate: Punishing Success and Promoting Parity." Bleacher Report. June 14, 2009. http://bleacherreport.com/articles/199345-the-truth-about-spygate-punishing-success-and-promoting-parity.

Shook, Nick. "Buffalo Bills Fire General Manager Doug Whaley." NFL.com. April 30, 2017. http://www.nfl.com/news/story/0ap3000000805316/article/buffalo-bills-fire-general-manager-doug-whaley.

Shula, Don, with Lou Sahadi. *The Winning Edge*. New York: E. P. Dutton, 1973.

Silverstein, Tom. "Aaron Rodgers Uses Sign Language to Run No-Huddle." *Milwaukee Journal Sentinel*, September 3, 2014. http://archive.jsonline.com/sports/packers/aaron-rodgers-uses-sign-language-to-run-no-huddle-b99343840z1-273881291.html.

Smith, Michael David. "At Least Five Teams Have Suspected Patriots of Headset Tampering." *ProFootballTalk* (blog). NBC Sports. September 11, 2015. https://profootballtalk.nbcsports.com/2015/09/11/at-least-five-teams-have-suspected-patriots-of-headset-tampering.

———. "Bill Belichick Reflects on His Interview with Al Davis." *ProFootballTalk* (blog). NBC Sports. October 1, 2011. http://profootballtalk.nbcsports.com/2011/10/01/bill-belichick-reflects-on-his-interview-with-al-davis.

———. "Leonard Fournette Tweets, Then Deletes, That He'll Play on Sunday." *ProFootballTalk* (blog). NBC Sports. September 29, 2018. https://profootballtalk.nbcsports.com/2018/09/29/leonard-fournette-tweets-then-deletes-that-hell-play-on-Sunday.

———. "NFL Statement on Deflategate Discipline." *ProFootballTalk* (blog). NBC Sports. May 11, 2015. https://profootballtalk.nbcsports.com/2015/05/11/nfl-statement-on-deflategate-discipline/#:~:text=For%20the%20violation%20of%20the%20playing%20rules%20and,Patriots%20are%20fined%20%241%20million%20and%20will%20.

———. "Peyton Manning Feared Patriots Bugging Visitor's Locker Room." *ProFootballTalk* (blog). NBC Sports. August 20, 2015. http://profootballtalk.nbcsports.com/2015/08/20/peyton-manning-feared-patriots-bugging-visitors-locker-room.

———. "Rob Johnson: Gregg Williams Told Me He Had a Training Camp Spy." *ProFootballTalk* (blog). NBC Sports. October 11, 2015. http://profootballtalk.nbcsports.com/2015/10/11/rob-johnson-gregg-williams-told-me-he-had-a-training-camp-spy.

———. "Steve Scarnecchia's First Offense Was Involvement with Patriots." *ProFootballTalk* (blog). NBC Sports. November 27, 2010. http://profootballtalk.nbcsports.com/2010/11/27/steve-scarnecchias-first-offense-was-involvement-with-patriots.

———. "Tony Dungy on Stealing Signals: It's Been Done Legally for Years." *ProFootballTalk* (blog). NBC Sports. February 8, 2017. http://profootballtalk.nbcsports.com/2017/02/08/tony-dungy-on-stealing-signals-its-been-done-legally-for-years.

Sporting News. "Marshall Faulk Still Blames 'Spygate' for Super Bowl Loss to Patriots." MassLive. January 30, 2013. http://www.masslive.com/patriots/index.ssf/2013/01/marshall_faulk_still_blames_sp.html.

SportsDay staff, *Dallas Morning News*. "Troy Aikman: Jimmy Johnson Filmed Signals as Head Coach of the Dallas Cowboys." *Dallas Morning News*, September 11, 2015. http://sportsday.dallasnews.com/dallas-cowboys/cowboysheadlines/2015/09/11/troy-aikman-jimmy-johnson-filmed-signals-head-coach-dallas-cowboys.

Steadman, John. "1958 Colts Had Better Team—and a Big Edge." *Baltimore Evening Sun*, December 25, 1988. https://www.latimes.com/archives/la-xpm-1988-12-25-sp-1373-story.html.

Stotts, Stewart. *Curly Lambeau: Building the Green Bay Packers*. Madison: Wisconsin Historical Society, 2007.

Stram, Hank. with Lou Sahadi. *They're Playing My Game*. Chicago: Triumph Books, 1986.

Switzer, Barry, with Bud Shrake. *Bootlegger's Boy*. New York: William Morrow, 1990.

TMZ. "New England Patriots Spygate II Video Released and Its Bad for the Pats." TMZ. December 15, 2019. https://www.tmz.com/2019/12/15/patriots-spygate-video-released-new-england-bengals.

Traina, Jimmy. "Peyton Manning Brings the Heat in Week 2, Accuses Patriots of Bugging Locker Room: TRAINA Thoughts." *Sports Illustrated*, September 21, 2021. https://www.si.com/extra-mustard/2021/09/21/peyton-manning-says-patriots-bugged-locker-room.

Tucker, Ross. "Cheaters Never Win: The Risk of Breaking Rules Not Worth Reward." CNN Sports Illustrated. May 16, 2008. http://sportsillustrated.cnn.com/2008/writers/ross_tucker/05/15/rules/index.html#ixzz2DOnbKT6x (site discontinued).

Underwood, John. "Mile-High Hopes in High Old Denver." *Sports Illustrated*, October 22, 1962. https://www.si.com/vault/1962/10/22/592306/milehigh-hopes-in-high-old-denver.

Uthman, Daniel. "NFL Teams Often Turn to Tactics Such as Spying and Counter-spying to Learn about—and Keep Up with—Their Opponents." *Oregonian*, 2006. http://www.apsportseditors.org/contest-winners/best-writing-of-2006 (site discontinued).

Van Natta, Don, Jr., and Seth Wickersham. "Spygate to Deflategate: Inside What Split the NFL and Patriots Apart." ESPN.com. September 7, 2015. http://www.espn.com/espn/otl/story/_/id/13533995/split-nfl-new-england-patriots-apart.

Vemuri, Snehith. "Peyton Manning: Ex-Broncos Player Explains How Peyton Manning Held Practice in the Woods to Prevent Patriots Spying." Sports Rush. August 18, 2020. https://thesportsrush.com/nfl-news-ex-broncos-player-explains-how-peyton-manning-held-practice-in-the-woods-to-prevent-patriots-spying.

Volin, Ben. "NFL Teams Go Extra Yard to Vet Prospects before Draft." *Boston Globe*, April 26, 2015. https://www.bostonglobe.com/sports/2015/04/25/nfl-teams-homework-including-spying-draft-prospects/I5EIHKwSQBvl6fvwQNVkyL/story.html.

Walder, Seth, and Justin Tasch. "Jets Deny Report They Asked NFL to Check for Listening Devices in Patriots Visiting Locker Room." *New York Daily News*, October 31, 2015. https://www.nydailynews.com/sports/football/jets/jets-wanted-locker-room-searched-pats-game-boomer-article-1.2417540.

Walker, James. "Social Scouting: How NFL Teams Track Prospects Online." ESPN.com. April 22, 2017. http://www.espn.com/nfl/story/_/id/19205874/inside-how-nfl-teams-monitor-social-media-accounts-prospects.

Warren, Matt. "Carolina Panthers Change Offensive Calls to Avoid Buffalo Bills Espionage." *Buffalo Rumblings* (blog). SB Nation. September 16, 2017. https://www.buffalorumblings.com/2017/9/16/16319464/carolina-panthers-change-offensive-calls-to-avoid-buffalo-bills-espionage-joe-webb-kaelin-slay.

Wells, Theodore V., Jr., Brad S. Karp, and Lorin L. Reisner. *Investigative Report concerning Footballs Used during the AFC Championship Game on January 18, 2015.* Paul, Weiss, Rifkind, Wharton & Garrison LLP. May 6, 2015. http://online.wsj.com/public/resources/documents/Deflategate.pdf.

Wickersham, Seth. "The Far Sideline." ESPN.com. December 12, 2014. http://www.espn.com/espn/feature/story/_/id/12014699/scot-mccloughan-nfl-best-talent-scout-self-employed-living-farm.

Williams, Pete. *The Draft: A Year inside the NFL's Search for Talent*. New York: St. Martin's Griffin, 2006.

Wyman, Dave. "The Importance of Film Study." 710 ESPN Seattle. September 30, 2011. https://sports.mynorthwest.com/6210/the-importance-of-film-study.

Yoder, Matt. "The Best (Worst) of Roddy White on Twitter." *Awful Announcing* (blog). September 23, 2013. https://awfulannouncing.com/2013/the-best-worst-of-roddy-white-on-twitter.html.

Zimmerman, Paul. "Al to World: Get out of Our Way." *Sports Illustrated*, September 5, 1984. https://www.si.com/vault/1984/09/05/633945/al-to-world-get-out-of-our-way.

———. *The Last Season of Weeb Ewbank.* New York: Farrar, Straus and Giroux, 1974.

Zimniuch, Frank. *Crooked: A History of Cheating in Sports*. Plymouth, UK: Taylor Trade, 2009.

INDEX

ABOUT THE AUTHOR

Kevin Bryant is an army veteran with more than 20 years of experience safeguarding and gathering information for the Department of Defense, including 13 years as a special agent during which he conducted national security investigations and instructed federal agents in training. Kevin graduated from the University of California Santa Cruz (UCSC) with a BA in history, and graduated with top honors from American Military University with an MA in intelligence studies and an MS in sports management. During his senior year of high school, he was selected to the East-West Ambassadors National Select soccer team, composed of elite high school players from across the United States, and in college he played NCAA soccer for UCSC.

CPSIA information can be obtained
at www.ICGtesting.com
Printed in the USA
BVHW030740130422
634122BV00001B/1